D1596869

By the same author

*'The Scientific Movement' and Victorian Literature*
(Harvester Press/St. Martin's Press, 1982)

*Science and Religion in the Nineteenth Century* (edited by)
(Cambridge University Press, 1984)

# WOMAN TO WOMAN

## Female Friendship in Victorian Fiction

# TESS COSSLETT

*Lecturer in English Literature*
*University of Lancaster*

**HUMANITIES PRESS INTERNATIONAL, INC.**
Atlantic Highlands, NJ

First published in 1988 in the United States of America by
Humanities Press International, Inc.,
Atlantic Highlands, NJ 07716

© Tess Cosslett, 1988

**Library of Congress Cataloging-in-Publication Data**

Cosslett, Tess
    Woman to woman : female friendship in Victorian fiction / Tess
Cosslett.
        p.    cm.
    Includes index.
    ISBN 0-391-03591-6 : $45.00
    1. English fiction—19th century—History and criticism.
2. English fiction—Women authors—History and criticism. 3. Women
in literature. 4. Friendship in literature. 5. Women and
literature—Great Britain—History—19th century. I. Title.
PR878.W6C67 1988
823'.8'09352042—dc19                                               88-8856
                                                                      CIP

Printed in Great Britain

For my female friends

What should we think of a community of slaves, who betrayed each other's interest? of a little band of shipwrecked mariners upon a friendless shore, who were false to each other? of the inhabitants of a defenceless nation, who would not unite together in earnestness and good faith against a common enemy?

Mrs Sarah Ellis, *The Daughters of England*, 1845

... for a minute the two women clasped each other as if they had been in a shipwreck.

George Eliot, *Middlemarch*, 1872

... female friendship – in general so scorned and scoffed at – may be the invisible means of strengthening in virtue, comforting in sorrow, and, without once interfering with any nearer or dearer tie, may heighten inexpressibly the happiness and well-doing of each.

Grace Aguilar, *Women's Friendship: A Story of Domestic Life*, 1850

# Contents

# Introduction

The representation of friendships between women is often of special significance in the works of women writers, involving as it does issues of female solidarity and female self-definition. It was Virginia Woolf, in *A Room of One's Own*, who first drew attention to the importance of female friendship as a subject for women writers – though she sees it as a *new* subject, hitherto unexplored:

> 'Chloe liked Olivia', I read. And then it struck me how immense a change was there. Chloe liked Olivia perhaps for the first time in literature.... And I tried to remember any case in the course of my reading where two women are represented as friends.

In the past, Woolf goes on to say, women were more often presented as rivals, because they were seen solely 'in their relation to men'.[1] It has, however, been pointed out that female friendship was by no means unexplored fictional territory when Woolf 'discovered' it: as Annis Pratt says, 'Chloe had been liking Olivia for several centuries before Virginia Woolf noticed it.'[2] Female friendships in eighteenth-century novels have been ably analysed by Janet Todd, in *Women's Friendship in Literature*,[3] but there has been relatively little study of the topic in Victorian literature.[4] Elizabeth Abel, in a study of friendships between women characters in contemporary fiction, suggests a possible reason for this lack of interest: 'The conventions of nineteenth-century fiction tended to fit the portrayal of female friendship into the narrative progression toward the marriage of the heroine(s), limiting the potential scope and depth of the female relationship. . .'

1

Reading this remark in the context of the article as a whole, it is clear that fictional 'conventions' are something negative as far as Abel is concerned: they get in the way of a truthful in-depth exploration of the reality of female friendships. For instance, she complains that some recent books and films give a 'misleading' portrayal of female friendships, which is produced by 'primarily narrative and thematic considerations'. By contrast, she is going to explore 'Serious novels that focus on the actual friendships of women.'[5] Abel's approach here seems to me to be mistaken (and representative of much feminist criticism),[6] in assuming that fiction can and does simply represent 'actuality', and in assuming that 'narrative considerations' are obstacles to this task. Fiction, I would say, actually *consists* in narrative devices and conventions, and these reflect, embody or even create *not* 'reality' or 'experience', but ideology. As Rachael Blau DuPlessis puts it:

> ... literature as a human institution is, baldly, organised by many ideological scripts. Any literary convention – plots, narrative sequences, characters in bit parts – as an instrument that claims to depict experience, also interprets it.... narrative structures and subjects are like working apparatuses of ideology, factories for the 'natural' and 'fantastic' meanings by which we live. Here are produced and disseminated the assumptions, the conflicts, the patterns that create fictional boundaries for experience.[7]

A simple example of this would be the Victorian (and of course earlier) convention that novels end with the marriage of the heroine. This does not reflect the fact that most women got married – there was a large and growing proportion of single women; nor that the writers were married; nor that the writers personally believed that marriage was a good thing – rather it reflects the social assumption that marriage was the only desirable goal for a woman. Reversals, or revisions, of this expected ending still carry ideological implications – for instance, that a woman cannot have a career and be married. In reversing or revising the convention, narrative techniques and devices are still being used. A less simple example of what I mean would be the convention in many nineteenth-century novels that the heroine is motherless.[8] Clearly this does not tell us that there were no mother-daughter relationships in the nineteenth century, rather it represents an ideological polarity for women of family/autonomy: on the one hand, the safe female world in which, by definition, nothing happens, and a woman's identity replicates her mother's; on the other, the dangerous world of the unprotected female, who has to find her own identity, about which stories can be written. I would see similar kinds of ideological implication in the conventions that structure the ways female friendship is portrayed in Victorian literature.

It is, then, precisely the relationship of female friendship to the structure of the conventional marriage-plot that interests me. While the containment of female friendship within such a structure suggests a devaluing of female–female bonds as opposed to female–male ones, if we look at the placing and function of these friendships in the narrative, a different implication emerges. Again and again, female friendship figures crucially at important turning-points of the narrative in the works of women writers such as Charlotte Brontë, George Eliot and Elizabeth Barrett Browning. The importance of the idea of female friendship can be measured by its crucial role in the narrative, rather than by the whole book being 'about' a female friendship. The coming together of two women is often essential to the resolution of the plot, figuring as a necessary stage in the heroine's maturation and readiness for the marriage that conventionally closes the action. At these turning-points transforming interchanges occur in which potential rivals discover solidarity, or women who seemed to be static representations of conventionally opposite types merge and exchange identities, altering all the structural relationships in the narrative.

What is especially interesting about these interchanges is that they nearly always operate to assimilate one or both of the women into marriage. This is contrary to what a feminist might expect or hope to find – but very rarely is a female friendship set up as a substitute for or in competition with a male–female relationship, and I think we must beware of trying to read Victorian representations of female friendship in this way. They are not anticipatory images of modern feminist solidarity or lesbian consciousness: though, as I shall show, a more conservative model of solidarity is involved. The assimilation to marriage can work through the plot: a very common device here is for two women who are *potential* rivals to discover or declare solidarity, and to arrange between themselves which of them is to have the man – sometimes there is a scene in which each in turn offers him selflessly to the other, or, more simply, the 'rival' gives him back to his rightful owner. Here we have an interesting

deviation from Woolf's picture of women in literature as necessarily
enemies, because they are rivals. The convention that women are
enemies, because they are in competition for men, is counteracted
here by the contradictory convention that women are self-sacrificing
angels; and women writers *use* this convention to build a position of
power for their female characters. Instead of the two rivals being
passive victims of the man's choice, they actively decide the matter
between themselves – though in the guise of self-renunciation. The
focus is not on the man's problems of choice, but on the interaction
between the women.

So this is one common way in which the female friends assimilate
each other to marriage, by resolving plot complications. Another
way, involving symbolic structure rather than plot structure, is by
the friends taking on some of each other's qualities, so as to make
one or both of them more suitable for marriage, or more ready to
accept marriage. Here, the friendship seems to operate as a partial
merging of identities between the two women. In nearly every case,
the important friendships are between women of different types –
angels and monsters, Madonnas and Magdalens, etc. – who
represent the different possibilities of female identity and role
allowed by society. But the merging and exchange of qualities
between these types blur their distinctions and challenge their
rigidity. Partly, a point is being made about female solidarity;
partly, a process of *negotiation* about acceptable female identities is
going on. This is one of my central ideas: that is, that the female
friendship is the place where the woman writer[9] can negotiate with
and between the dominant images of female identity. Often it is a
matter of the powerful, independent heroine being made more
acceptable by taking on some of the self-sacrificing qualities of her
angelic friend, or the sexual vulnerability of her fallen friend, or by
converting her heartless superficial friend by her superior moral
influence. We can see this process of negotiation and assimilation
negatively – the independent heroine being assimilated to the status
quo – or more positively – the heroine assimilating to herself the
acceptable traits of womanhood, in the same way as many Victorian
women reformers made use of the ideology of 'woman's sphere', and
her superior moral influence, to create a position of power for
themselves.[10]

I am assuming here that women writers did have a certain
freedom to negotiate within ideology – that their plot-devices and

symbolic structures could combine and merge contradictory elements from dominant ideologies. There are special reasons why the representation of female friendship might be an area of problematic negotiations for the woman writer in particular. To understand them, we must look at the significance of female friendship in the conservative and influential ideology of 'women's sphere'. In Deborah Goreham's book *The Victorian Girl and the Feminine Ideal*, she examines many conduct books, advice books for mothers, and moral tales for girls, all based in this ideology, and remarks that

> Friendships between girls, like so many other aspects of a girl's life, were meant to foster femininity. Whereas friendships between boys and young men were seen as developing 'manliness', group loyalty, and the ability to fight battles in the public arena, girls' friendships were seen as important because they would encourage the development of a personality capable of intimacy and the mutual sharing, with other girls and women, of a domestic environment.[11]

Similarly, Martha Vicinus, in *Independent Women*, comments that schoolgirl friendships 'taught girls intimacy and socialised them into the world of women. Indeed, Victorians found them an important means of reinforcing a girl's identity with her mother at a time when she would ordinarily be breaking away from her.'[12] Female friendship leads towards, not away from, traditional female roles.

This conclusion is confirmed if we look at the writings of Mrs Sarah Ellis, arch-proponent of the idea of 'women's sphere'. Mrs Ellis held that women were intellectually inferior to men, but morally superior: their sphere was the home, where they could exercise moral influence on their men. She was very keen on the idea of female solidarity – women together could support and admonish each other, keeping each other in line, but also helping each other to bear the hardships of women's position, and increasing their collective force for good in the world. In *The Daughters of England* she imagines

> A circle of young female friends, who love and trust each other, who mutually agree to support the weak in their little community, to confirm the irresolute, to reclaim the erring, to soothe the irritable, and to solace the distressed; what a realisation does this picture present of the brightest dreams of imagination, when we think what women might be to her own sex, and to the community at large.[13]

For Mrs Ellis, female friendship helps to keep women in their place, but also transforms that place into a strong female community.

Thus friendship between women serves a powerful function in the ideology of 'women's sphere', and it is therefore not surprising that fictional female friendship always seems to lead to assimilation in traditional womanly roles. But Victorian women writers, by the very act of being writers, were moving *away* from the traditional female role, into the 'male' sphere. This position would somehow have to be reconciled with, or found a place within, the dominant ideology of 'women's sphere'.[14] We must not see this ideology as merely an oppressive force that prevented these writers from being 'themselves': in Mrs Ellis herself we have an example of a woman writer turning what seems to be an anti-female ideology into a new source of power within dominant ideologies[15] – her views and assumptions could therefore appear very *attractive* to women seeking a position of power. We could thus expect complex and ambivalent negotiations to be going on around the area of female friendship in the work of women writers: female friendship is the point where the female community asserts its claims and its values, where specifically 'female' qualities are nurtured, where the exceptional woman meets up with the 'common lot of womanhood'.[16] These negotiations are most obvious in relationships between independent, unconventional heroines and angelic conventional friends, where the unconventional heroine is to some degree *overawed* by the goodness of her angelic friend, and wants to be like her; while on the other hand, wanting to assert her difference and her superiority. In other novels, the unconventional heroine turns out to be *more* wifely and *more* motherly than the woman who *seemed* the perfect womanly type, who has to be rescued and restored to her wifely role by the sympathy and friendly guidance of the heroine. We could see here a negotiation going on involving the woman writer's sense of her own exceptionality as a woman, and her attempt to reconcile it with her ideological bonds to concepts of traditional womanhood and the community of 'ordinary' women. Interestingly, in some of the later 'New Woman' novels and stories, the writers' desire to present a strong, independent heroine in fact leads them *away* from presentations of female friendship, despite lip-service being paid to the ideal of female solidarity. Female friendship is something that threatens to pull the New Woman back into the world of traditional womanhood.

Of course, even more important than female friendship in reproducing the values of this traditional women's world was the mother–daughter bond: Vicinus sees schoolgirl friendships as *substituting* for this relationship. But I have already commented on the relative absence of mothers in Victorian fiction, and in many cases their role is taken over by female friends,[17] who have less restrictive power. Frequently, pairs of female friends alternate mother and child roles in their relationship. This model invests the friendships with all the unquestionable moral value of the mother–daughter bond, and also allows for extremes of emotional intensity and physical closeness. This permissible physicality in particular differentiates relationships between women from relationships between women and men. Are these then lesbian relationships? It seems to me that this question is impossible to answer. Clearly, it is the effect of convention and propriety, not sexual preference, that the depiction of physical closeness between mother and daughter, or two women acting those roles, is acceptable, and between men and women it is not. A lesbian writer may have found a loophole here to express her feelings, but there is no way to tell if this was the case. Moreover, if we define lesbianism as a preference for relationships with women as an alternative to those with men, these friendships do not qualify, as they operate to assimilate the women into heterosexual relationships.[18] The novel in which the female friendship is presented as an alternative to male–female relationships,[19] and where it operates to lead the women *away* from marriage, is Charlotte Brontë's *Shirley*. Here, interestingly, the model for the relationship is not mother–daughter, but man–woman – it begins as a 'courtship' of the 'feminine' Caroline by the 'masculine' Shirley. But *this* relationship is hardly presented as physical at all:[20] physical intensity is reserved for Caroline's relationship with her real mother, Mrs Pryor. If, on the other hand, we define lesbianism much more widely, as part of a 'continuum' including mother–daughter relationships,[21] all these female friendships can be seen as lesbian – but here the definition seems so broad as not to be of much use. In any case, it is open to a lesbian critic to read all these instances of female friendship as lesbian, for her own purposes – but this is not one of my purposes here. I am interested in how Victorian women writers used the representation of female friendship to negotiate within contemporary ideologies, and 'lesbian' was not a concept available to them.

The emotional intimacy and sympathetic identification that goes
on between fictional friends is not just there because mothers are
absent: it was seen as an important and valuable characteristic of
female friendships in any case. As Goreham says, 'Girls' friendships,
it was believed, should foster the feminine qualities of empathy and
expressiveness, and should develop a capacity for sustained
intimacy.'[22] Mrs Ellis also sees female friendship as helping to
initiate a woman into an exclusively female sensitivity and
emotionalism:

> In the circle of her private friends, as well as from her own heart, she
> learns what constitutes the happiness and the misery of woman, what is
> her weakness and what her need, what her bane and what her blessing.
> She learns to comprehend the deep mystery of that electric chain of
> feeling which ever vibrates through the heart of woman, and which man,
> with all his philosophy, can never understand.[23]

Through female friendship, the 'female' speciality in the emotional
life is passed on; and intimacy together with identification
encourages the reproduction of accepted 'female' identity. Not only
are these ideals reflected in scenes of sympathetic mutuality between
women in fiction, but, as I have suggested, on the symbolic level we
find mergings and exchanges of identity going on between seemingly
opposite types of friend. The pattern of the friendship is set up as a
debate on the possible female identities a woman can take up; the
merging of these identities represents a complex process of
negotiation about acceptable female identity. Here, identification
does not lead to simple reproduction of a static feminine ideal; it is
made use of to stretch the limits of that ideal, and to include more
diverse possibilities within it. These possibilites of identification and
transformation do not appear to be available to male characters, in
works by women or men: male alter-egos are either eliminated, or
pursue their victims to destruction.[24]

It would be easy to read these various characteristics of fictional
female friendship – emotional intimacy, mother–daughter patterns,
merging identities – as evidence of specifically female psychological
traits, and explain them by reference to psychological theory. When
I began this project, I was very impressed by the relevance of the
theory of female identity put forward by Nancy Chodorow in her
book *The Reproduction of Mothering*.[25] Chodorow's ideas have
been used by other critics investigating female friendship in

literature,[26] and seemed to offer a useful model, which conveniently distinguishes between the qualities of female friendships and male friendships, female identity and male identity. Put simply, her theory is that because primary parenting is always done by women, not men, the identities of male and female children are formed differently. Boys form their identity by *differentiating* themselves from the mother: they find it easier to think of themselves as separate people acting in the world. For girls, however, the process is more problematic, and they never really completely separate from their mothers. Their identity is more fluid, they are more open to emotional contact, and less able to act as separate people in the world. In Chodorow's model, when they are grown up, both women and men long to re-experience the closeness of their bond to the mother: but while men can get this sort of emotional closeness and nurturing from women, women cannot get it from men, as men have formed their identities by closing off this part of their natures. Women, therefore, turn to their relationships with *children* to re-experience the maternal bond, and this is why women are still the primary parents – the system is psychologically self-perpetuating. Instead of turning to children, however, women may also turn to other women – this is where female friendship comes in, as Chodorow says:

> Women try to fulfill their need to be loved, try to complete the relational triangle, and try to re-experience the sense of dual unity they had with their mother, which the heterosexual relationship tends to fulfill for men. . . . One way that women fulfill these needs is through the creation and maintenance of important personal relations with other women. . . . Given the triangular situation and emotional asymmetry of her own parenting, a woman's relation to a man *requires* on the level of psychic structure a third person, since it was originally established in a triangle.[27]

This relational model seemed especially helpful to me if I was going to investigate a fiction that included female friendships within a narrative structured on a male–female romance: it provides a 'triangular' model that does not set the two women up as hostile rivals for the man. Chodorow also provides suggestions as to how female friendships are different from male ones: female friendship will involve more merging of identity and sympathetic emotional closeness, like the mother–child relation – and this of course fits in with what I have discovered about the relationships between female

friends in the literature I have read. Chodorow also seemed to
explain why these female friendships always operate to assimilate
the women to marriage. Female friendships, in so far as they imitate
a woman's relationship to her mother, or to her child, operate to
draw her back into the female world of fluid identity and
'mothering', and away from the self-assertion and independence of
the 'male' world. I soon, however, began to have reservations about
the usefulness of a psychological theory like Chodorow's. It seemed
to be unacceptably ahistorical and essentialist in its concept of
'female identity'.[28] To apply it to literature meant that I had to
ignore the roles played by literary convention and ideology, and
assume an untenable model of fiction as a simple reflection of
women's experience. I was led to be especially suspicious of
Chodorow when I found her *descriptions* of women's friendships
could be read as *prescriptions* in Victorian conduct books: to quote
Goreham again, with a different emphasis:

> Girls' friendships, *it was believed, should* foster the feminine qualities of
> empathy and expressiveness, and *should* develop a capacity for sustained
> intimacy.... Friendships between girls, like so many other aspects of a
> girl's life, *were meant* to foster femininity. Whereas friendships between
> boys and young men were seen as developing 'manliness', group loyalty,
> and the ability to fight battles in the public arena, girls' friendships *were
> seen* as important because they *would encourage* the development of a
> personality capable of intimacy and the mutual sharing, with other girls
> and women, of a domestic environment. (my italics)[29]

So here, what Chodorow presents as inevitable psychological
characteristics of women, are being presented as part of a
programme of socialisation, based on ideological assumptions as to
what women and men are and should be like. Chodorow thus
appears as merely the latest manifestation of this Victorian ideology
of women's friendship and women's 'nature'.

Psychological theories also could not explain the gap between the
way female friendships are portrayed in fiction, and what we can
find out about them from biography and social history. The social
historian Carroll Smith-Rosenberg, drawing her evidence mainly
from letters, has shown how long-standing, continuous, loving
relationships with other women were central to many nineteenth-
century women's lives.[30] But very rarely are women's fictions
structured around such relationships, as opposed to the male-female
romance structure.[31] As Janice Swanson puts it,

When female friendships appear, they are like islands in a tossed sea of relations between rivals. These islands are generally comprised of no more than moments when women, suddenly aware of the forces which separate them, come to a deep sharing of that recognition. . . . Seldom do we have the chance to observe women in a sustained relationship which nurtures them, revolving around interests other than a heterosexual attachment.[32]

Here, I think, the important point is what is considered as suitable material for a *narrative* as opposed to a letter: what counts as an event in a story. The world of women's friendships seems to be perceived as something *static*, outside the action that makes a story. In narrative, men are thought to be needed to create tensions and initiate significant action. (These narrative conventions are of course not neutral: they carry ideological implications about the ways men's and women's lives are defined and valued.) The eighteenth-century epistolary novel allows the best of both worlds, with the women's friendship centrally important through their exchange of letters, while it is at the same time outside the male-centred action which they narrate to each other. In Victorian novels, women's friendships are present only in momentary 'islands', though, as I have suggested, they play an important part through their placing in the narrative and their effect on its structure. Often they are differentiated not only from male–female and male–male relations, but also, as Swanson suggests, from other relations between women in the narrative, which form a pattern of inter-female rivalry, betrayal and oppression.[33] By contrast, the women's friendship stands out as uniquely precious, an 'island' of peace and understanding. It often takes place in some world beyond normal social relations – in Nature, in Italy, or at a moment of crisis when normal relations are broken down or broken through. This means the friendship is immensely important, but also safely insulated from the world of everyday events. A political point is being made about the necessity for female solidarity, but at the same time any revolutionary implications for society as a whole are being firmly contained. In 'New Woman' fiction, this kind of containment has a different effect, serving to emphasise New Woman's isolation and heroic individualism in a hostile society.

In my first three chapters, I analyse and compare a number of narratives (poems as well as novels) in which the female friendship is

thus contained within a male–female romance structure, where it
operates to assimilate the women to conventional roles, and to bring
about the male–female resolution (this need not be marriage – in
*The Mill on the Floss* it means Maggie's death in the arms of her
brother; in *Villette*, Lucy's unconsummated union with M. Paul).
Some kind of female–female resolution always seems to be necessary
before the male–female resolution can happen: problems of female
identity and allegiance must be sorted out first. In each chapter, I
have concentrated on relatively few texts, so that the specific details
of the interaction between the friends in each narrative can be
followed. In order to bring out recurring patterns and devices, I have
arranged my material in these chapters thematically, according to
the types of women who are friends, rather than by author. I am
interested in how these types are constructed, and then merged and
changed, through their friendship. Often, the different types each
have their own conventional type of plot – for instance, the fallen
woman conventionally acts out a tragedy of retribution and death,
while the 'angel' woman acts out a conventional comedic marriage
plot. Through women's friendship, these different types of plot
become entwined and altered – the women intrude into each other's
stories, and exchange plots, or act out each other's wishes. A crucial
intersection of plots of course occurs at the point where two women
discover they are rivals for the same man – this is where we often
find scenes of solidarity and mutual renunciation, as the women
settle between themselves who is to have him. In all these
interchanges, negotiations are going on to construct an acceptable
and yet powerful form of female identity.

The model for these friendships is nearly always the maternal one
– the friends act as mother-substitutes to each other, providing
physical and emotional sustenance, moral influence and example,
and social initiation into the world of adult womanhood and
marriage. The friendships often spring from an intense 'mother-
want'[34] on both sides – not just because actual mothers are absent,
but because they are inefficient, or because other women have acted
as betrayers and oppressors. As I have suggested, the friendships can
often be distinguished from other relationships between and among
the sexes in the narratives, giving the effect of 'islands' of security.
Sometimes, overt proclamations of female solidarity are made, by
narrator or characters. I am interested in what kind of solidarity is
envisaged, and on what it is based; and also whether it is in harmony

with the meanings implied by the narrative and symbolic structures. A solidarity *against* men, or *against* patriarchal institutions is never promoted: rather, it is a solidarity against those, men or women, who break the ostensible rules of patriarchy – male seducers, female flirts or hypocritical moralisers. Fallen women can be included in this solidarity, in that they are rescued and protected; other women can be helped to resist temptation.

Many of these patterns and conventions are broken by Charlotte Brontë's novel *Shirley*, to which I devote Chapter 4. Here, the female friendship disrupts and breaks out of the male–female romance structure in which it is nominally enclosed. Structurally, the narrative falls apart: a more sustained treatment of female friendship breaks up the conventional pattern, and yet there are many indications that such a female friendship *cannot* be fully developed in terms of current conventions of representation. The conventional pattern is reimposed at the end, but in a forced and awkward manner. Caroline and Shirley's friendship does not operate to assimilate the women to marriage, and their typology does not conform to convention. Their friendship is presented as an alternative to male–female romance, and it leads them into a separate female world from where they make subversive criticisms of the world that is run by men. What is especially interesting about *Shirley* is the way that changes in the ideological function of the friendship are accompanied by disruption of the narrative structure: we can see here how indissolubly structure and meaning are intertwined. Nor is it a simple matter of convention obstructing what Charlotte Brontë really wanted to say – the construction of the women's friendship makes use of other, incongruous, conventions drawn from Romantic nature poetry and Gothic romance.

In my final chapter, I look at some 'New Woman' novels and stories from the end of the century. Here, I was expecting to find the developments begun in *Shirley* to be further realised: female friendship would become even more central, perhaps evolving its own narrative structure to replace the male–female romance; female solidarity against the patriarchy would become a more overt idea, structuring the plot accordingly. But this is not at all what I found: instead, there seemed to be two main patterns. In some of these stories, the patterns I analyse in Chapters 1–3 recur: female friendship is contained within a male–female romance structure, and operates to assimilate women to traditional womanly roles. The friendship is again a site of negotiations about acceptable female identity – the only difference is that more radical positions are evolved through this process. 'New Woman' was being presented as essentially no threat to traditional institutions – in fact, even as their upholder. This would correspond with the way 'Independent Women' made use of existing ideologies of womanhood to bring about their reforms in women's social and educational position, creating new opportunities in the name of old pieties.[35] In other New Woman stories, proclamations *about* female solidarity are counteracted and undermined by narratives that show solidarity between women either as impossible, or as increasing women's weakness and leading to defeat, not strength. Solidarity is still defined as leading to assimilation in traditional womanly roles, so it can only weaken a New Woman intent on finding other roles for women. Moreover, the New Woman writers make use of an ideology of *individualism* to create their heroines, rather than an ideology of female solidarity. Independence and freedom are their goals, and these must be defined against an oppressive society – there is no place here for a supportive female community. In this type of story, friends of opposite types do not merge to form acceptable identities – instead, they split apart and diverge in narratives of separation and defeat. Marriage as an ending is replaced by death or isolation, not by a relationship between women.

In all these narratives, the representation of female friendship is a crucial point where concepts of female identity – of what it is, or should be, to be a woman – are revealed. The intersections of convention and ideology, structure and meaning, can be investigated at this point, leading to a clearer understanding of how women's texts can be read in a feminist context. The ideological negotiations that are going on in the texts here can only increase our respect for the power women have always had to transform their constraints.

I would like to acknowledge the help and advice of the English Literature Department Nineteenth Century Seminar, the Women's Research Seminar (both at Lancaster University), and the Northern Feminist Network Seminar, all of whom listened to drafts of parts of this book. The Women Writers Course at Lancaster first gave me the idea for this book, and I would like to thank Alison Easton (my co-teacher) and the students for enthusiasm and ideas. Many thanks to my husband, Greg Myers, for help and encouragement, use of the word-processor, and keeping Alice occupied. Thanks also to Janice Mitchell for looking after Alice, and to Lancaster University for two terms' sabbatical leave. Paula Day, Sara Morris and Alison Easton also provided support and help with my less conscious problems about the project, as well as invaluable female friendship.

# Chapter One

# Angels and Monsters

The ways in which friendship between women can operate to assimilate them to conventional 'womanly' roles are seen at their clearest in relationships between rebellious, unconventional heroines and 'angelic' women who conform to conventional ideals of womanhood. The 'angelic' friend is not merely there for contrast, or for the unconventional woman to define herself against: instead, the heroine is powerfully drawn towards the ideal her friend represents, an ideal which she attempts to emulate or vicariously share. A complex process of negotiation about acceptable female identities is going on. We can read into this process the woman writer's problems about her own unconventionality – her need to be unconventional and yet to conform to acceptable standards of 'womanliness', and also her need to reconcile her difference from other women with her unconscious identity or conscious solidarity with them. These tensions are dramatised as the two women take on each other's identities and intrude into each other's plots at significant turning points in the narrative.

I want to look first at a poem by Christina Rossetti, 'The Lowest Room',[1] that shows the two types and their interaction at its simplest: here, the rebellious woman is simply crushed by her identification with her angelic sister. Then I will trace this type of relationship in more detail in two novels, *The Mill on the Floss* and *Villette*, where there are more complex, two-way identifications going on between the two women. In both novels, the women are rivals for the same man, the conventional romantic hero; and the heroine's resignation of him to her rival marks her departure from the conventional love-plot, which is handed over to the 'angel' for completion. This suggests a final *separation* between the two types: but in both novels too the angel-woman exerts a powerful fascination on the heroine, that modifies her behaviour in more conventional directions, or reflects her inner wishes. In addition, in both novels it is suggested that inside or behind the angel's conventional role there lurks a 'real' Lucy Deane, a 'real' Paulina Home, with whom the heroine has a sustaining female bond.

Rossetti's 'The Lowest Room' begins with two sisters sitting together: the younger, prettier one is contentedly doing her embroidery; the elder, the speaker of the poem, is full of discontent. She has been reading Homer, and she longs for the excitement, violence, and direct expression of deep feeling of those heroic 'golden days':

> 'He stirs my sluggish pulse like wine,
>   He melts me like the winds of spice,
> Strong as strong Ajax' red right hand,
>   And grand like Juno's eyes...

> 'Then men were men of might and right,
>   Sheer might, at least, and weighty swords:
> Then men in open blood and fire
>   Bore witness to their words...

> 'Calm in the utmost stress of doom,
>   Devout towards adverse powers above,
> They hated with intenser hate
>   And loved with fuller love.'

There is a distinct hint here of a sexual thrill provided by reading Homer – '"He stirs my sluggish pulse like wine/He melts me like the winds of spice"' – and this is confirmed when she cries, '"Oh better then be slave or wife/Than fritter here blank life away".' Though at first it is the heroic actions of the men that she envies, even as a woman in such a society she would participate in its more intense and passionate way of life. Even the women at their weaving are more creative, and closer to heroic action and mythic power, than is her sister at her embroidery:

> 'The princess laboured at her loom,
>   Mistress and handmaiden alike;

Beneath their needles grew the field
    With warriors armed to strike.

'Or, look again, dim Dian's face
    Gleamed perfect through the attendant night;
Were such not better then those holes
    Amid that waste of white?'

Here, I am assuming the 'holes' in the 'waste of white' describe the broderie anglaise her sister is sewing – a meaningless repeated pattern with no story to it. There is a neat reversal of black and white here – Dian's face, the moon, gleaming whitely through the black night, as opposed to the black holes in the white embroidery. The whiteness of the moon is mythic presence, not the absence of the 'holes'; the surrounding black of the night is 'attendant', in relationship, to the presiding moon, as opposed to the meaningless white 'waste', which, in the next verse, is linked to the meaningless, trivial life of the sisters: 'A shame it is, our aimless life'. The white embroidery could also signify marriage, or preparation for marriage, as opposed to the powerful singleness represented by Diana.

The younger sister, however, is unimpressed by her sister's complaints and longings. She sits placidly sewing – 'She laughed a feminine low laugh/Yet did not stay her dexterous hand' – and she is quite contented with her lot: 'To me our days seem pleasant days/Our home a haven of pure content.' She rebukes her sister's praise for Achilles, insisting that his actions are merely *animal*, not fully human. Her perspective is explicitly Christian:

'Homer, though greater than his gods,
    With rough-hewn virtues was suffised
And rough-hewn men: but what are such
    To us who learn of Christ?

The gentle and humble Christian qualities of the younger sister are also stressed: 'For mild she was, of few soft words/Most gentle, easy to be led.' The elder sister accepts the rebuke, and her sister's superiority:

I elder sister by six years;
    Not half so glad, or wise, or good:
Her words rebuked my secret self
    And shamed me where I stood.

Here we learn that the poem's speaker has erred not only in her
pagan longings, but in an envy of her more successful, integrated
sister: 'She never guessed her words reproved/A silent envy nursed
within.' For the younger sister's conventional Christian acceptance
and resignation is made easy to her by her innate conformity to the
conventional image of the feminine. First, her looks are right:

> Her tresses showed a richer mass
>> Her eyes looked softer than my own
> Her figure had a statelier height
>> Her voice a tenderer tone.

The elder sister is involved in books, which offer a dream-like escape
from her lot, and, as we have seen, also fuel her discontent; the
younger sister conventionally gathers flowers, displaying an
irrational feminine 'intuition', that assimilates her to the natural
world, the conventional images of 'rose' and 'peach':

> I chose a book to read and dream:
>> Yet half the while with furtive eyes
> Marked how she made her choice of flowers
>> Intuitively wise
>
> And ranged them with instinctive taste
>> Which all my books had failed to teach;
> Fresh rose herself, and daintier
>> Than blossom of the peach.

Naturally, this sister has a suitor – at this point she hears his step,
and stops her work and blushes. The only previous point where she
has 'faltered', when 'her needle erred' briefly, was while listening to
her sister's Homeric fantasy, when the thought of some harm
coming to her 'lord' had struck her: '"But just suppose the
horse,/Suppose the rider fell?"' Her feelings are directed entirely to
her suitor – she is not troubled by the self-searchings and
comparisons of female lots that engross her sister. Her destiny is
simple: in the last section of the poem, we move forward twenty
years, and find she is now 'a stately wife', and has a daughter
'golden-curled' like herself, 'Fair image of her own fair youth'; and
she herself seems hardly to have changed at all. The elder sister
meanwhile has resigned herself to her contrasting lot:

> to live alone
> In mine own world of interests,
> Much felt, but little shown.

She has learnt to take the second place to her sister, to be patient, 'year after tedious year'. Having accepted her sister as a standard, her single life can only appear tedious and empty, without the rich mythic significance of 'Dian's face'.

These two sisters represent a powerful and enduring relationship of types in Victorian literature. The elder, unconventional and discontented, is associated with a past world of myth and heroism. She escapes from present social realities by reading books, and has an intense inner life. Though full of frustrated passion, she is physically unattractive and unacceptable as a conventional marriage partner. Her desires are 'natural' in the way wild animals are natural. The younger sister is conventionally attractive, very blonde, and skilled at feminine accomplishments such as embroidery and flower-arranging. Her conventional Christian goodness and piety is instinctive – it does not imply an intense inner life. She is socially acceptable and accepting: she has no problem in fitting the conventional role of wife and mother. She is 'natural' in the way plants are natural, but she does not change or grow: her daughter is a replica of herself, and she does not age. The rebellious sister also does not grow – but with her we feel a potential for change that is stifled and held down by her acceptance of her sister's wisdom.

Variations on these two contrasting types appear often in Victorian literature. For instance, we might think of the 'mannish', active, ugly, dark Marian Halcombe and the passive, blonde, 'feminine' Laura Fairlie in Wilkie Collins' *The Woman in White*. But here the contrast is mainly seen from the point of view of the man, Walter Hartwright, who has a comradely relationship with Marian, and a romantic relationship with Laura. Marian's sexual potential is also only seen by another man, Count Fosco, in whose exotic imagination she attains her full heroic status. But Collins is not interested in what the contrast means to the women themselves, in the ways they might compare and relate their roles, influence or exchange them. This is what interests women writers. What is most striking in Rossetti's poem is the way the speaker is so aware of the limitations of her role, and the acceptability and power of her sister's, which is yet unattainable for her. The sister functions as an image of the conventional woman's role, which threatens and rebukes the unconventional woman, who is unable to be like this, who does not want to be like this, and yet who envies the woman who can be like this. So here, the elder sister is won over by the younger sister, she is overawed by her beauty and her piety. The conventional ideal has such a hold on her mind that she cannot break free of it, and her longings for another kind of life are suppressed as sinful.

The relationship between the sisters is, thus, seen as *hierarchical*: the elder learns to accept that she is 'second' not 'first'. Relations between conventional and unconventional women often involve this kind of contrast, comparison and evaluation, as the unconventional woman's identity is defined and valued against the socially acceptable feminine ideal. The hierarchy is often, however, a shifting one, as now one woman and now the other is seen as superior. Even in Rossetti's poem, at the end, a different set of values is suggested, which may reverse the 'first' and 'last' of this world:

> Yea, sometimes still I lift my heart,
>   To the Archangel's trumpet-burst,
> When all deep secrets shall be shown
>   And many last be first.

The marriage of the younger sister does place this female relationship within the conventional narrative progression towards marriage; but the poem concentrates on the sisters' relationship (obviously this is structurally easier in a short poem than a long novel); the husband does not appear as a character. In this it is similar to *Goblin Market*, where we learn at the end of the poem that the sisters both married. 'The Lowest Room' is unusual, however, in that the story is told from the perspective of the unmarried sister, who is outside the conventional 'story'. In this, it reminds me of Lucy Snowe's perspective on Paulina's 'story' in *Villette*. Rossetti's poem is also interesting in that most of it is taken up with an alternative 'story', the Homeric fantasy, told by the elder sister, though at the end this is suppressed in favour of the younger sister's conventional marriage story. Similarly, in *The Mill on the Floss*, Maggie's more heroic story of struggle, renunciation and rescue breaks into and temporarily disrupts Lucy's conventional romance with Stephen. The difference is, of course, that in Eliot's novel the unconventional heroine's aspirations do not remain on the level of fantasy (though this may be questionable in relation to Maggie's rescue of Tom), but *are* allowed to disrupt the conventional narrative structure. In the novels I shall be looking at, the two women often seem to belong to two different types of story, and their meetings signal interchanges of different types of narrative. For instance, Lucy Snowe's renewed friendship with Paulina coincides with, and perhaps permits, Paulina's taking over Dr John and the conventional romantic plot from Lucy, both disappointing her and freeing her for her unconventional relationship with M. Paul. And in *The Mill on the Floss*, Maggie and Lucy's friendship in the penultimate book of the novel allows Maggie's irruption into Lucy's plot, her temporary take-over of Stephen.

The poem by Rossetti provides a very useful model for us to begin to understand the friendship of Maggie and Lucy. Eliot was certainly aware of this kind of fictional pairing: in *Silly Novels by Lady Novelists* (1856) she ridicules the opening of a novel called *The Enigma*: 'The spirited young lady, with raven hair, says, "All life is an inextricable confusion;" and the meek young lady, with auburn hair, looks at the picture of the Madonna which she is copying, – and – "*There* seemed the solution of that mighty enigma."'[2] The Rossetti poem, also written in 1856, begins similarly with the discontented sister saying,

> 'Oh what is life, that we should live?
>   Or what is death, that we must die?
> A bursting bubble is our life:
>   I also, what am I?'

The contrasting hair colours of the two women are also stressed by Rossetti – the elder going grey, the younger with a 'golden head'. Eliot, of course, also gives us the dark Maggie and the fair Lucy, but she comments self-reflexively, through Maggie, on the conventionality of this division: Maggie returns Philip his copy of Mme de Staël's *Corinne*:

> 'I didn't finish the book', said Maggie. 'As soon as I came to the blond-haired young lady reading in the park, I shut it up and determined to read no further. I foresaw that that light complexioned girl would win away all the love from Corinne and make her miserable. I'm determined to read no more books where the blond-haired women carry

away all the happiness. I should begin to have a prejudice against them –
I want to avenge Rebecca and Flora Mac-Ivor, and Minna and all the
rest of the dark unhappy ones.' (pp. 432–3)[3]

The references to *Corinne* remind us of another, earlier source of
these contrasting types: Corinne, dark, Italian, passionate, artistic,
loses her lover to her blond, conventional, passive, English half-
sister.[4] Maggie's words make us expect Eliot is about to reverse this
plot, as Philip predicts:

> 'Well, perhaps you will avenge the dark woman in your own person: –
> carry away all the love from your cousin Lucy. She is sure to have some
> handsome young man of St. Ogg's at her feet now – and you have only
> to shine upon him – your fair little cousin will be quite quenched in your
> beams.' (p. 433)

Of course, this story does come true: Eliot is to insist on the sexual
attractiveness and power of her unconventional heroine. But from
Maggie's point of view there is a difficulty – her friendship with
Lucy and value for her character:

> 'As if I, with my old gowns, and want of all accomplishments, could
> be a rival of dear little Lucy, who knows and does all sorts of charming
> things, and is ten times prettier than I am – even if I were odious and
> base enough to wish to be her rival. Besides, I never go to aunt Deane's
> when anyone is there: it is only because dear Lucy is good and loves me
> that she comes to see me, and will have me go to see her sometimes.' (p.
> 433)

Lucy, with her goodness, prettiness and accomplishments is being
described very much like the younger sister in Rossetti's poem. It is
Maggie's friendship for Lucy, allied with her other ties to the past,
that prevents her from acting out Philip's prediction to its logical
conclusion of marrying Stephen. It is crucially important to her not
to abuse Lucy's trust, and to return Stephen to her; and their final
meeting of reconciliation is essential before Maggie can go on to the
consummation of her reunion with Tom in the flood. *The Mill on
the Floss* does not of course follow the conventional narrative
progression towards marriage: though Philip's prediction suggests a
marriage between Maggie and Stephen, and Lucy plots determinedly
to marry Maggie to Philip, Maggie rejects both these endings.

Nevertheless, the novel does end with a coming-together of the extreme male and female poles, Maggie and Tom, back into a primal unity. This male/female reconciliation can only happen, however, after the female/female reconciliation between Maggie and Lucy.

There is, however, a fundamental contradiction in the presentation of Lucy and Maggie's relationship. On the one hand, Lucy is being used like the younger sister in Rossetti's poem, to embody an image of conventional womanhood, an image that Maggie cannot possibly live up to, that continually reproaches her. In this sense, Maggie's need not to hurt Lucy signifies the hold that conventional values have over her in her decision to give up Stephen and return home: it is a capitulation of the unconventional to the conventional woman, as in 'The Lowest Room'. But, against this interpretation, Eliot creates in the last part of the book the sense of a real and sustaining friendship between the two women, which is deliberately contrasted with the bleak and hostile relationships between women in the rest of society. Against this background, it shines out as something unique and valuable. We can also contrast it with the predominant hostility and rivalry between the men in the book, and the low level of emotional communication between men and women. Eliot insists that there is a 'real' Lucy underneath the conventional image, a Lucy who can appreciate and even envy Maggie's unconventionality, and who has the uncommon quality of love for other women. On this reading, Maggie's reconciliation with Lucy signifies her need to reaffirm values of loyalty and affection between women that are not accounted for by conventional society, which would approve instead the conventional solution of her marriage to Stephen.

Our first introduction to Lucy is through Mrs Tulliver's perception of her as the ideal daughter, the image against which Maggie is measured and found wanting: '". . . an' there's her cousin Lucy's got a row o' curls round her head, an' not a hair out of place. It seems hard as my sister Deane should have that pretty child; I'm sure Lucy takes more after me nor my own child does"' (pp. 60–1). Lucy's appearance is right, and so is her behaviour – Mrs Tulliver contrasts her with her own 'naughty' children, especially Maggie: '"And there's Lucy Deane's such a good child – you may set her on a stool, and there she'll sit for an hour together and never offer to get off – I can't help loving the child as if she was my own, and I'm sure she's more like *my* child than sister Deane's" ' (p. 96). Lucy represents the conventionally acceptable feminine qualities, prettiness, neatness and passivity: the dark, untidy, restless Maggie is unacceptable by these standards. Interestingly, Mrs Tulliver repeats that Lucy seems more like her natural daughter than Maggie does. Mrs Tulliver was also a model girl child who 'never cried when she was a baby on any slighter ground than hunger and pins, and from the cradle upwards had been healthy, fair, plump, and dull-witted, in short, the flower of her family for beauty and amiability' (pp. 61–2). Mrs Tulliver's ideal of mother and daughter as replicas of each other and of socially acceptable feminity recalls the younger sister in Rossetti's poem, with her look-alike daughter. The standard of feminine behaviour is passed on from mother to daughter. Unconventional women like Maggie or the elder sister are excluded from this circular relationship, while it still holds its emotional power over them. Lucy's identification as the 'natural' daughter of Mrs Tulliver means that Maggie's problems with Lucy involve her problems with her mother, and with the feminine values her mother represents. Conversely, her later emotional closeness to Lucy compensates for the closeness her mother is unable to give her at this stage, and, significantly, Maggie is reconciled to her mother just before her final reconciliation with Lucy.

Mrs Tulliver's descriptions of Lucy create her as a static type, whose function is to define Maggie's identity by contrast. But when Lucy herself appears, the relationship between the two girls becomes more complex. Lucy, we find, is not just another placid dull-witted Mrs Tulliver: she has an appreciation of Maggie that Mrs Tulliver lacks, and Maggie has an admiration for Lucy that she never feels for her mother. The narrator also supplies a 'deeper' reading of the contrast between the two girls:

> Certainly the contrast between the cousins was conspicuous and to superficial eyes was very much to the disadvantage of Maggie, though a connoisseur might have seen 'points' in her which had a higher promise for maturity than Lucy's natty completeness: it was like the contrast between a rough, dark, overgrown puppy and a white kitten. (pp. 116–17)

The narrator here revises the meaning of the contrast – Maggie is allowed to be potentially *more* beautiful than Lucy, if judged by more refined standards. The unconventional heroine is not only more intelligent and energetic than the conventional woman, she also wins on the conventional grounds of beauty. Similarly, she is allowed later to 'carry off all the love' from Lucy: she takes over and disrupts the conventional love-story which Lucy and Stephen are enacting. She is not innately ugly and inevitably frustrated like the elder sister in Rossetti's poem; nor is she frustrated by her lover's conventional standards like Corinne; but, once she has been compensated with all the advantages of love and beauty, she does finally frustrate herself, and hand the love-plot back to Lucy. The seeds of this final frustration are evident in her childhood admiration of Lucy: connoisseurs may prefer Maggie's beauty, but *she* wishes to be like Lucy:

> Maggie always looked at Lucy with delight. She was fond of fancying a world where the people never got any larger than children of their own age, and she made the queen of it just like Lucy with a little crown on her head and a little sceptre in her hand ... only the queen was Maggie herself in Lucy's form. (p. 117)[5]

Like the elder sister in Rossetti's poem, Maggie accepts Lucy's conventionally 'feminine' appearance as her own standard. On the other hand, she still wants to be 'queen' herself, rather than accepting, like the elder sister, her position as 'second and not first'. The conflict between these two wishes – to have power and admiration for herself, and yet to be like Lucy – structures not only her dilemma about Stephen at the end of the book, but her continuing problems with her own identity in relation to acceptable female behaviour.

While Maggie longs to look like Lucy, Lucy enjoys the freedom and imagination that Maggie represents for her: Lucy is more than the prettiness and passivity that Mrs Tulliver admires. Timidly, she defies her mother's representation of her wishes on the matter of staying at the Tullivers':

> After various reasons for refusal, Mrs. Deane appealed to Lucy herself.
> 'You wouldn't like to stay behind without mother, should you, Lucy?'
> 'Yes, please, mother,' said Lucy, timidly, blushing very pink all over her little neck. (p. 118)

Lucy, unlike Tom, appreciates Maggie's imaginative ability: when Tom finds a toad,

... Lucy wished Maggie to enjoy the spectacle also, especially as she would doubtless find a name for the toad and say what had been his past history; for Lucy had a delighted semi-belief in Maggie's stories about the live things they came upon ... Tom had a profound contempt for this nonsense of Maggie's ... but Lucy, for the life of her, could not help fancying there was something in it, and at all events thought it was very pretty make-believe. So now the desire to know the history of a very portly toad, added to her habitual affectionateness, made her run back to Maggie and say, 'O, there is such a big, funny toad, Maggie! Do come and see.' (pp. 161–2)

Later in the novel, Lucy herself plots delightedly to bring about a 'fairy-tale' marriage between Maggie and Philip – for her, Maggie seems to represent all the romance that is missing from her conventional life. But she is deceived in thinking Maggie's imaginative qualities are merely 'pretty', or can be managed by her: invited too closely into her life, Maggie nearly destroys her. Similarly, as a child, Lucy enjoys 'the rare treat of doing something naughty', when she goes with Tom to the pond: but this excursion ends in the disaster of Maggie pushing her into the mud.

At this point in the novel, Maggie, Lucy and Tom form a triangle, in which the two women are in rivalry for the man's affection. Tom's choice of Lucy as companion, and his ostracism of Maggie, inflame Maggie's anger against Lucy:

As long as Tom seemed to prefer Lucy to her, Lucy made part of his unkindness. Maggie would have thought a little while ago that she could never be cross with pretty little Lucy, any more than she could be cruel to a little white mouse; but then, Tom had always been quite indifferent to Lucy before, and it had been left to Maggie to pet and make much of her. As it was, she was actually beginning to think that she should like to make Lucy cry, by slapping or pinching her, especially as it might vex Tom, whom it was no use to slap even if she dared, because he didn't mind it. (p. 162)

Though Maggie is reacting as a conventional female rival here, we do see how it is Tom's behaviour that disrupts a normally friendly female relationship: the two girls' usual relationship with each other is not competitive. And part of what Tom has done is to take Lucy away from Maggie, her usual companion and admirer. Moreover, as we have seen, Lucy is not exulting in her victory, but very concerned to include Maggie in her adventure with Tom. Maggie's exclusion by Tom has been brought about by a series of actions that have taken her further and further from the feminine ideal represented by Lucy: first, she has cut off her hair, then she has knocked over Tom's card-house, and finally spilt wine on his clothes. In the card-house scene, Tom has compared her clumsiness unfavourably with Lucy's gentle dexterity. The narrator has also just contrasted the two girls: 'As for Lucy, she was just as pretty and neat as she had been yesterday: no accidents ever happened to her clothes, and she was never uncomfortable in them, so that she looked with wondering pity at Maggie pouting and writhing under the exasperating tucker' (p. 146). This contrast is reminiscent of the sisters in Rossetti's poem, one content and 'comfortable' with her lot, the other restricted and uncomfortable.

Thus Tom's preference for Lucy signals that he too prefers the conventional feminine ideal, against which he judges Maggie, while he is blind to Maggie's real qualities, which are more truly appreciated by Lucy, her female friend. Maggie, driven to an extreme of social rejection, reacts by pushing the oppressive ideal of feminity into the mud, trying to render Lucy as unattractive and unacceptable as herself. But the act of course results not in Maggie's acceptance, but in her complete self-alienation, as she runs away to join the gypsies. Yet the extreme of unconventionality represented by the gypsies turns out not to be what she imagined – they do not provide freedom and power – and, frightened by their strange ways, she only longs the more to go home and be accepted again.

Lucy fades from the story at this point, and reappears in the last two Books as Maggie's friend, hostess and confidante. They are somewhat artificially kept apart: in Maggie's conversation with Philip, we hear of visits to Lucy, but we are not shown them; and Maggie's stay with Lucy, we hear later, has been delayed by Mrs Deane's illness. These devices to keep the two friends apart function to intensify Maggie's loneliness and complete social isolation, so that her female life of enclosure and inwardness can be explored and contrasted with Tom's outward, active life in the world. Here, Eliot is investigating the state we find the elder sister in at the end of Rossetti's poem, living a tedious, unfulfilled life of restriction, immersed in a secret inner world of feeling.

Lucy's reappearance in the sixth Book of the novel is absolutely necessary to bring about Maggie's social and sexual debut. She also functions to dramatise an explicit theme of the value of female friendship, and to continue a questioning of Maggie's female identity, as the two friends are drawn to each other's qualities. Their ambivalent interrelation is central to Maggie's dilemma about Stephen, and their final reconciliation is necessary before the plot can resolve itself. Lucy is reintroduced in Chapter 1 of Book Sixth, conversing with Stephen. The patronising, complacent and superficial nature of Stephen's relationship to her is almost immediately contrasted with the genuineness of her affectionate plans for Maggie. Of course, Lucy is sitting doing her embroidery, while Stephen plays with her scissors, and with her: an idyllic scene, but rather trivial and oversweet. The triviality, however, seems to be more on Stephen's side than on Lucy's: she is aware of, though not alarmed by, the limitations of his attitude:

'Yes, I know you think I am silly.'
'I think you are perfectly charming.'
'And my silliness is part of my charm?'
'I didn't say *that*.'
"But I know you like women to be rather insipid. Philip Wakem betrayed you: he said so one day when you were not here.' (p. 470)

Philip, who has more serious attitudes to women, is also invoked again by Lucy to question Stephen's taste, and possibly the quality of his relationship to Lucy. They are about to sing the duet of Adam and Eve from Haydn's *Creation*: '"Philip burst into one of his invectives against 'The Creation' the other day", said Lucy, seating herself at the piano. "He says it has a sort of sugared complacency and flattering make-believe in it, as if it were written for the birthday fête of a German Grand Duke"' (p. 474). Significantly, the whole chapter is ironically entitled 'A Duet in Paradise'. While their sugary 'duet' goes on, Lucy is also trying to tell Stephen about Maggie's impending visit: 'There is no girl in the world I love so well as my cousin Maggie.' She is full of benevolent intentions for Maggie: 'I want her to come to me now, and have a long, long holiday.'

Even now, her mind, with that instantaneous alternation which makes two currents of feeling or imagination seem simultaneous, is glancing continually from Stephen to the preparations she has only half finished in Maggie's room. Cousin Maggie shall be treated as well as the grandest lady visitor – nay, better, for she shall have Lucy's best prints

and drawings in her bedroom, and the very finest bouquet of spring
flowers on her table. Maggie would enjoy all that – she was so fond of
pretty things! (pp. 476–7)

Lucy is planning to draw Maggie into her own world of luxury and
ladylike leisure – a 'long holiday' from her usual life of privation
and self-reproach.

Lucy's two trains of thought, on Stephen and on Maggie, lead us
on to a very important contrast that the narrator now makes,
between the superficial nature of Stephen's appreciation of Lucy,
and her true rarity, which lies precisely in her love for other women:

> Was not Stephen Guest right in his decided opinion that this slim
> maiden of eighteen was quite the sort of wife a man would not be likely
> to repent of marrying? – a woman who was loving and thoughtful for
> other women, not giving them Judas-kisses with eyes askance on their
> welcome defects, but with real care and vision for their half-hidden pains
> and mortifications, with long ruminating enjoyment of little pleasures
> prepared for them? Perhaps the emphasis of his admiration did not fall
> precisely on this rarest quality in her – perhaps he approved his own
> choice of her chiefly because she did not strike him as a remarkable
> rarity. A man likes his wife to be pretty, but not to a maddening extent.
> A man likes his wife to be accomplished, gentle, affectionate and not
> stupid; and Lucy had all these qualifications. . . . He meant to choose
> Lucy: she was a little darling, and exactly the sort of woman he had
> always most admired. (pp. 477–8)

Here, once again, we have the contrast between Lucy as socially
approved, conventional feminine type, and the 'real' Lucy, who is
unconventional in her love for women in general, instanced by her
particular love for the unconventional Maggie. Lucy's desire to
promote a friendship between Maggie and Stephen, and her
complete lack of jealousy, are continually stressed by the narrator.
For instance, as Stephen gazes in fascination at Maggie, Lucy, 'sweet
child, was only rejoicing that Stephen was proving to Maggie how
clever he was, and that they would certainly be good friends after
all' (p. 490). She determines *not* to tell Maggie that Stephen has said
'She is not my type of woman' (pp. 490–1), and, at the Bazaar, 'she
felt nothing but pleasure in the sight of Maggie's attractiveness' (p.
549). Earlier, the narrator asks, 'Is it an inexplicable thing that a girl
should enjoy her lover's society the more for the presence of a third

person, and be without the slightest spasm of jealousy that the third person had the conversation habitually directed to her?' (pp. 515–16).

The narrator clearly expects the readers to be surprised by such an instance of female friendship. As we saw, she stresses its *rarity*, implying it is a precious quality. The relationships between other women in the book certainly bear this out. The Dodson sisters mainly relate by criticising each other, or competing in the newness of their bonnets (Aunt Pullet) or the oldness of their clothes (Aunt Glegg). They do not rally round to support Mrs Tulliver in her troubles, but to admonish and blame her. In the last Book, we learn more about the female society of St Ogg's, and their attitudes. Unlike Lucy, they resent Maggie's beauty and her success with the men: 'There was something rather bold in Miss Tulliver's direct gaze, and something undefinably coarse in her style of beauty, which placed her, in the opinion of all feminine judges, far below her cousin Miss Deane' (p. 548). The conventional hierarchy of female acceptability is being re-established – but the narrator makes it clear that it is jealousy that lies behind it. Society's later judgement of Maggie's conduct with Stephen is also seen as hypocritical, and the narrator stresses that it is *women* who enforce these judgements: 'Public opinion, in these cases, is always of the feminine gender – not the world, but the world's wife' (p. 619). If Maggie had returned *married* to Stephen, this female 'public opinion' would have condoned her action, and welcomed her into society; as she returns unmarried and without Stephen, she is labelled 'a designing bold girl', whose conduct is 'detestable'. 'The world's wife' makes this judgement 'with that fine instinct which is given her for the preservation of society' (pp. 620–1). Here, the way women judge each other is seen to be dictated by a superficial set of social conventions, which bear no relation to the real moral questions involved, or the true nature of the people who are judged. The men of St Ogg's do not intervene, shrugging their shoulders 'at the mutual hatred of women. It was the general feeling of the masculine mind at St Ogg's that women were not to be interfered with in their treatment of each other' (p. 637). The women act as a sort of moral police, enforcing their own oppression. Their 'mutual hatred' is a product of their social position as women, which means they must compete for men and must preserve their 'reputations' – Maggie is 'shrunk from by every woman who had to take care of her own reputation – and of society' (p. 636). Against this 'mutual hatred' and oppression, Maggie and Lucy's friendship stands out as uniquely valuable and worth preserving.

The intimate and supportive quality of their friendship is best conveyed in a chapter called 'Confidential Moments' (Ch. 3), when Lucy joins Maggie in her bedroom. The narrator again emphasises the unusual nature of this scene, at least as far as the implicitly male reader is concerned: 'If it appears to you at all incredible that young ladies should be led on to talk confidentially in a situation of this kind, I will beg you to remember that human life furnishes many exceptional cases' (p. 495). They begin by discussing Stephen, Maggie asking 'how could I dislike any one that promised to make you happy, you dear thing!' (p. 496), and then Maggie pours out her secret about her relationship with Philip: 'The narrative lasted long, for Maggie had never before known the relief of such an outpouring: she had never before told Lucy anything of her inmost life; and the sweet face bent towards her with sympathetic interest, and the little hand pressing hers, encouraged her to speak on' (p. 497). The only other such self-revelatory outpouring allowed to Maggie in the book is perhaps with Dr Kenn – but that is a very different kind of confessional relationship, compared to the sympathetic mutuality of the two women here. This bedroom scene forms a symmetrical contrast with an earlier scene, in the girls' childhood, when they were taken into Aunt Pullet's bedroom with Mrs Tulliver, to participate in the feminine mysteries of the Bonnet. The comic triviality of the two older women's interaction over the Bonnet contrasts with the seriousness and intensity of Maggie and Lucy's confidences.

In counterpoint to their sympathetic intimacy, the two friends are also still being evaluated as contrasting types. When we first see them together again, Maggie is called 'that dark lady', and she begins by 'holding up one of Lucy's long curls, that the sun might shine through it' (p. 479). As they discuss Stephen, Lucy inadvertently reveals a fear of sexual relations with him: ' "I would rather not be engaged: – when people are engaged, they begin to think of being married soon . . . and I should like everything to go on for a long while just as it is. Sometimes I am quite frightened lest Stephen should say that he has spoken to papa" ' (p. 479). This attitude contrasts strongly with the sexual urgency of Maggie's later relationship with Stephen. It is the 'dark lady' who is the passionate one, and whose desires break up the conventional love story of her fair cousin. But, as before, both women are attracted to and even take on some of the qualities of the other. Lucy, as ever, is attracted to Maggie's unconventional 'romantic' qualities, though without fully understanding in what they consist; Maggie is drawn towards Lucy's social world of beauty and luxury. It is Lucy who brings about Maggie's appearance as an attractive and socially desirable young lady, both by literally dressing her up, and by transferring some of her own qualities of attractiveness and social status to Maggie.

In thus assisting Maggie's 'coming out', Lucy is taking on the role of mother, as described by Susan Peck Macdonald:

> The particular kind of mothering abstractly required by these adolescent heroines is made clear within the social context of the novels. The heroine's task is to survive the perils of 'coming out'. She must move out of the private (perhaps even tomboyish) world of her family into the social world where she will take her place as a woman – ready to marry and to mother in her turn. Her mother's task, abstractly seen, is to ease the transition from the private and individualistic world of adolescence into the social and therefore somewhat conventionalized world of maturity.

Macdonald remarks on the inadequacy of Maggie's mother to perform this function,[6] but does not notice that Lucy acts as a surrogate here. Maggie sees her as a 'fairy-godmother' (p. 526) – like Cinderella's fairy-godmother, Lucy gives her the opportunity to enter society as a beautiful woman. Before the 'culmination of Maggie's career as an admired member of society in St Ogg's' (p. 547), at the Bazaar, she has been 'taken before Lucy's cheval glass and made to look at the full length of her tall beauty, crowned by the night of her massy hair. Maggie had smiled at herself then, and for the moment had forgotten everything in the sense of her own beauty' (p. 555). Lucy has provided the means to a self-satisfaction that Maggie has never had before. Her admiration and advice, and her social world of beauty and luxury, provide the 'glass' which reflects back Maggie's new, acknowledged beauty. There is a sharp contrast here with Maggie's religious phase, when she deliberately turned her looking-glass to the wall, trying to care nothing for her appearance, and to efface part of her female identity, which Lucy now restores to her.

But Maggie's beauty is still of an unconventional sort, and it is this that Lucy finds attractive, admiring it as something romantically uncanny. '"I can't think what witchery it is in you, Maggie, that makes you look best in shabby clothes; though you really must have a new dress now.... Now, if *I* were to put anything shabby on, I should be quite unnoticeable – I should be a mere rag"' (p. 480). Maggie's beauty is defined here as *natural*, as opposed to Lucy's, which needs artificial assistance from her clothes. The natural is associated with the magic here by the image of witchcraft – both are outside the socially conventional world of Lucy. The image recurs when Maggie tells Lucy about her relationship with Philip, and Lucy says, '"Ah, now I see how it is you know Shakespeare and everything, and have learned so much since you left school – which always seemed to me witchcraft before – part of your general uncanniness"' (pp. 497–8). Lucy's admiration of Maggie's appearance creates a new hierarchy, in which Maggie's beauty has more power than hers. Later, Maggie is being dressed up by Lucy, Aunt Pullet and Mrs Tulliver. Mrs Tulliver comes out with the old evaluation of Maggie's appearance: '"Maggie's arms *are* a pretty shape.... They're like mine used to be; only mine was never so brown: I wish she had *our* family skin."' But Lucy corrects this estimate – she has become a 'connoisseur' of Maggie's beauty: '"Nonsense, Aunty! ... you don't understand these things. A painter would think Maggie's complexion beautiful."' In Lucy's friendship, Maggie is now rightly valued: yet Uncle Pullet has the last word, suggesting a more disturbing quality to Maggie's unconventionality: '"there was a song about the 'Nutbrown Maid' too – I think she was crazy like – crazy Kate – but I can't justly remember"' (p. 493). Earlier, in her conversation with Lucy, Maggie has also suggested that her naturalness is not romantic to her, as she compares herself to '"the poor uneasy white bear I saw at the show. I thought he must have got so stupid with the habit of turning backwards and forwards in that narrow space that he would keep doing it if they set him free"' (p. 481). The animality that attracts others only makes Maggie feel imprisoned in her social lot, and when it is freed it causes chaos. Maggie, introduced into St Ogg's society by Lucy, is very much a white bear in sheep's clothing.

Lucy's attraction to the romance of Maggie's beauty and 'witchcraft' is dangerously naive, not only because Maggie 'bewitches' Stephen, but because being taken for a witch, an unconventional woman, can only result in self-destruction, as Maggie knew as a child, commenting on a picture in the book she is reading: '"That old woman in the water's a witch – they've put her in, to find out whether she's a witch or not, and if she swims she's a witch, and if she's drowned – and killed, you know, – she's innocent, and not a witch, but only a poor silly old woman"' (p. 66). While Lucy delightedly frees Maggie's witch-like qualities, Maggie, at the end of the novel, struggles to prove she is *not* a witch, and to be a good woman like Lucy – but of course she can only prove this goodness by drowning. Lucy and Maggie's first private conversation in Book Sixth ends with Maggie complimenting Lucy on her goodness – '"I wish I were like you"' (p. 481) – as Lucy has just complimented her on her beauty. By the end of the novel, however, the hierarchy of goodness will also have been reversed, and the unconventional woman will be shown to be most good as well as most beautiful.

Lucy, of course, is blind to Maggie's struggles to be good, until it is too late. She, meanwhile, is naively promoting a 'fairy-tale' ending to Maggie's story: after Maggie tells her about her relationship with Philip, she says,

'There is something romantic in it – out of the common way – just what everything that happens to you ought to be. And Philip will adore you like a husband in a fairy tale. O I shall puzzle my small brain to contrive some plot that will bring everybody into the right mind – so that you may marry Philip, when I marry – someone else.' (p. 498)

But, from Maggie's perspective, Lucy's 'romantic' plot is just the conventional narrative progression towards marriage – a convention that cannot contain her story, which is more radically unconventional than Lucy's romantic 'fairy tale'.

Instead, Maggie is borne away in a boat by Stephen, to awake suddenly to the wrong she is doing to Lucy and Philip. In Lucy's case, it is her betrayal of Lucy's trust and friendship that reproaches Maggie, rather than the thought that she has deprived her of Stephen: '"O, what is Lucy feeling now? – She believed in me – she loved me – she was so good to me – think of her"' (p. 602). Before Maggie literally awakens, she has had a significant dream involving Lucy:

She was in a boat on the wide water with Stephen, and in the gathering
darkness something like a star appeared, that grew and grew till they saw
it was the Virgin seated in St Ogg's boat, and it came nearer and nearer
till they saw the Virgin was Lucy and the boatman was Philip – no, not
Philip, but her brother, who rowed past without looking at her . . . (p.
596)

Lucy, Philip and Tom represent the forces that call Maggie back
from Stephen – Lucy and Philip by their goodness and pain, and
Tom by his conventional judgementalism. Lucy has become the
Virgin – not only a figure of possible rescue, but also of reproach in
her extreme goodness and suffering. Later, she appears to Maggie's
imagination as an almost Christ-like image:

Maggie was haunted by a face cruel in its very gentleness: . . . that pale
image became more and more distinct – the picture grew and grew into
more speaking definiteness under the avenging hand of remorse; the soft
hazel eyes in their look of pain, were bent for ever on Maggie and pierced
her the more because she could see no anger in them. (p. 640)

Just as Maggie is haunted and influenced by the *voices* of men[7] –
Tom, Philip, Stephen, Thomas à Kempis – so she is haunted by
Lucy's *image*: the men telling her what to do, and Lucy showing her
what to be. Lucy's preternatural Christian goodness is different only
in degree from the goodness of the younger sister in Rossetti's poem;
it overawes and reproaches Maggie, not just because she has in fact
hurt Lucy, but because she has not lived up to Lucy's standard, her
wish to be like her.

So when Lucy appears for their final reconciliation, there are two
contradictory meanings to the scene: on the one hand, a valuable and
unusual female friendship is reaffirmed; and on the other, the
unconventional woman's slavery to the conventional ideal is
confirmed. In both interpretations, Lucy's arrival sets a seal of
approval on Maggie's action in leaving Stephen – it *does* restore
Lucy to her, and win Lucy's admiration: '"You did what it must
have been very hard to do."' Maggie gains Lucy's forgiveness, and
can give back Stephen to her: '"He wanted to be true to you. He
will come back to you. Forgive him"' (p. 642). As in *Middlemarch*
and *Aurora Leigh*, a scene in which two women affirm their
friendship, and one gives up a man to the other, is necessary before
the final male–female coming together. Instead of the man choosing

between the two female 'rivals', it is the women who arrange between themselves who is to have him. The scene here has a final twist – Lucy's parting words are, '"You are better than I am. I can't ..."' (p. 643). What does she mean? She has clearly forgiven Maggie: the only possible thing she *can't* do, and Maggie can, is perhaps to return Maggie's generosity, and give Stephen back to her again, giving up her own claim. Thus the unconventional woman wins in the goodness and self-sacrifice competition, as she has won in the beauty competition – but at the price of bowing to convention, and effacing her own identity, in order to win approval.

The scene ends as they 'clasped each other in a last embrace' (p. 643) – a premonition of the next chapter, where Tom and Maggie drown clasped together 'in an embrace never to be parted' (p. 655). A unification with both the female and the male is necessary for Maggie's completion. Both embraces are similarly ambiguous: either she embraces the conventional feminine image of Lucy, and the conventional masculine judgements of Tom; or she embraces the unconventional ties of brother and sister and female friends, as opposed to the marriage of conventional narrative. The marriage plot, much delayed, plays itself out for Lucy in the final chapter, when 'years after' Stephen revisits Tom and Maggie's tomb again 'with a sweet face beside him' (p. 656). This is the final justification of Maggie's action – her last gift to Lucy. Nevertheless, this conventional marriage ending can only seem tame in contrast to Maggie's heroic fatal union with Tom, in the same way that Paulina's happy marriage to Dr John in *Villette* seems tame in contrast to Lucy's union with and tragic loss of M. Paul. The resolution of the heroine's plot is differentiated from the conventional marriage of her friend, which is diminished or devalued by the contrast. The male–female bond into which the heroine is assimilated is far from conventional – drowning with her brother, or being set up in a school by her lover, who then gets drowned himself, or, in other novels, marriage to a man who is poor, plain, an outsider, or otherwise socially unacceptable. The necessity to give the heroine's plot a conventional male–female resolution, but at the same time to stress its difference from the resolution of her conventional friend's plot, epitomises the complex process of negotiation that is going on in the fictional friendships between conventional and unconventional women.

\* \* \*

In *Villette*, Lucy Snowe is surrounded by female characters who provide her with possible role-models or self-images: Miss Marchmont, the old maid; Mme Beck, the crafty career woman; Vashti, the passionate actress. Among these are her two female friends, Paulina Home and Ginevra Fanshawe. Both of them represent female roles that are barred to Lucy, by her social position and her physical appearance. Ginevra is the beautiful, self-indulgent flirt and successful husband-hunter; Paulina is the beautiful, angelic child-woman, who makes the conventional romantic marriage. Brontë suggests a necessary connection between these two types: M. Home de Bassompierre is Paulina's father and Ginevra's godfather, and his wife, Paulina's mother, looked exactly like Ginevra, her niece. Ginevra's knowing manipulation of men is perhaps the unacceptable (but more honest) face of Paulina's helpless dependency on father and husband, her unconscious ability to attract male protection. Both are part of a system where marriage provides a woman with her only social identity and means of support. Lucy, outside this system, unable to compete with these women, uses them as comparisons in her discovery of her own female identity. She is both drawn towards them, as people she might like to be, and repelled, as she finds reasons for preferring to be as she is. She has to engage with them, as they represent images of her own failure as a conventional woman; but by the end of the novel she has rejected them both, as she finds her own identity and her own unconventional way of relating to a man who is neither the perfect 'catch' nor the handsome romantic protector. Unlike Maggie in *The Mill on the Floss*, Lucy Snowe is not allowed her own sort of more powerful beauty with which to challenge and defeat her rival angel-woman: the reverse happens. The faint possibilities of a romance with Dr John are snatched from Lucy by the reappearance of Paulina, his natural mate. But Paulina reappears at the moment when Lucy has most clearly seen Dr John's limitations, and his incompatibility with her, in his tame and conventional reactions to Vashti's passionate performance. Paulina and Dr John are allowed to carry off and complete the conventional love-plot, while Lucy discovers more interesting and more satisfactory possibilities in her relationship with M. Paul.

Lucy's relationship with Ginevra and Paulina is not, however, merely this simple rejection of them as desirable models. Her initial attraction towards them is not just an attraction to something she cannot have: they also seem to represent unacknowledged elements in her own character, elements that she later integrates into her own sense of identity. We can contrast Lucy's complex attraction to both women, with her simple rejection of the images of womanhood she is presented with in the picture gallery at Villette. The paintings present the two contrasting and complementary male views of woman's role: the sensuous, fleshy Cleopatra, her body displayed to the male gaze: and the series of insipid 'Anges', virgin, bride, mother, widow (p. 278).[8] Lucy, as single woman, can identify with neither extreme, and rejects both with scorn. We can approximate Ginevra and Paulina to this pairing: Ginevra as the sensual woman, Paulina as the angel. Though Dr John dislikes the Cleopatra, and cries scornfully, '"Compare that mulatto with Ginevra!"' (p. 282), he is deceived about Ginevra's character at this point, and falsely regards her as an 'angel'. He also says of the picture, '"My mother is a better-looking woman"' (p. 282), suggesting his preferences are on the side of the 'angels', which is confirmed by his eventual choice of Paulina. It is Ginevra's ridicule of his mother that alerts him to her true nature. *Her* eventual husband, De Hamal, appreciates the Cleopatra greatly. Both Ginevra and Paulina, however, are clearly much more complex and attractive than the gallery pictures. The paintings represent how women are seen by men – from Lucy's point of view these images are unreal and ludicrous. Ginevra and Paulina are the women who approximate to, or make use of, or are confined within, these male images. Thus we see Ginevra's hearty enjoyment of her ability to manipulate men, or Paulina's extreme care to fit the 'frosty' virgin image the 'fastidious' Dr John wants to have of her (pp. 466–7). Lucy, in her friendships with the two women, sees behind the scenes, as far as the male world is concerned, to these 'inner' aspects of their identities. In Ginevra's frank greed and self-indulgence, and in Paulina's sensitivity and efforts at self-repression, Lucy finds (or projects) elements of herself.

I shall deal with Lucy's relationship with Ginevra more briefly in a different context in Chapter 3 – here, I want to examine Lucy's friendship with the angelic Paulina. From when she first appears in the book as little Polly, Paulina has an uncannily close relationship with Lucy. As a child, she seems to express all Lucy's unexpressed needs and emotions; as an adult, Lucy claims a peculiar kinship with her.[9] Lucy, so often misread by those around her, claims that Paulina alone reads her clearly:

Madame Beck esteemed me learned and blue: Miss Fanshawe, caustic,
ironic, and cynical; Mr. Home, a model teacher, the essence of the sedate
and discreet: somewhat conventional perhaps, too strict, limited and
scrupulous, but still the pink and pattern of governess-correctness; whilst
another person, Professor Paul Emmanuel to wit, never lost an
opportunity of intimating his opinion that mine was a rather fiery and
rash nature – adventurous, indocile, and audacious. I smiled at them all.
If anyone knew me it was little Paulina Mary. (p. 386)

Interestingly, Paulina Mary's view of Lucy's character is *not* given
here: we are left to infer it from their relationship. The implication
is also there that Paulina is Lucy's second self: as Lucy says earlier, 'I
wondered to find my thoughts hers: there are certain things in which
we so rarely meet with our double that it seems a miracle when that
change befalls' (p. 361). In a book in which names are so important,
it cannot be a coincidence that 'Paulina' is the female form of
'Paul', the man who comes to know Lucy best and appreciate her
most. In some way, Paulina must be intended as Lucy's closest
female friend/counterpart, as Paul is her male counterpart. Lucy's
friendship with Paulina is by no means as close and sustaining as the
female friendships in *Jane Eyre* or *Shirley* – but in the context of
*Villette* it does stand out – as Lucy says, 'I liked her. It is not a
declaration I have often made concerning my acquaintance, in the
course of this book; the reader will bear with it for once' (p. 461)
    Polly as a child, unlike Lucy Deane, is not already the model of
approved female behaviour. Though she has a neat, doll-like
appearance, her passionate, agonised dependence on the men in her
life makes her more like Maggie. When she is grown up, we see her
sewing diligently and skilfully, like the younger sister in 'The Lowest
Room'; but as a child, we see what this womanly accomplishment
has cost her:

> ... holding in her hands a shred of a handkerchief, which she was
> professing to hem, and at which she bored perseveringly with a needle,
> that in her fingers seemed almost a skewer, pricking herself ever and
> anon, marking the cambric with a track of minute red dots; occasionally
> starting when the perverse weapon – swerving from her control –
> inflicted a deeper stab than usual; but still silent, diligent, absorbed,
> womanly. (p. 73)

Polly exemplifies the sufferings that are needed to fit oneself to the conventional 'womanly' role – needle, and feelings, must be 'controlled' or they inflict their wounds. The dependence on men that is a necessary part of the role must not be too much displayed, or it will alienate them. Polly provides Lucy with an object lesson in the sufferings of a totally dependent creature: 'One would have thought the child had no mind or life of her own, but must necessarily live, move, and have her being in another: now that her father was taken from her, she nestled to Graham, and seemed to feel by his feelings: to exist in his existence' (p. 83). Graham's careless behaviour can thus make her suffer: she learns to make herself less vulnerable – 'I remarked that never after this rebuff did she seek him, or follow him, or in any way solicit his notice' (p. 85) – but she still masochistically lies at his feet with dog-like devotion when he ignores her.

Lucy, by contrast, presents herself as wise and calm, detached and independent. But there are many signs that Paulina is expressing Lucy's suppressed feelings here[10] – signs that are confirmed in Lucy's behaviour later in the book. For instance, Lucy is 'oppressed' by the excess of feeling in the scene between Paulina and her father:

> ... it was a scene of feeling too brimful, and which, because the cup did not foam up high or furiously overflow, only oppressed one the more. On all occasions of vehement, unrestrained expansion, a sense of disdain or ridicule comes to the weary spectator's relief....
> ... I wished she would utter some hysterical cry, so that I might get relief and be at ease. (p. 71)

Lucy wants the relief of disdain or ridicule – but this indicates how powerfully she sympathises with Paulina's feelings, and how much her usual pose of disdain for Polly and her demonstrations is a refuge from her own capacity for deep feeling. Later, Polly quizzes Lucy about Lucy's feelings for Graham – Lucy admits to liking him ' "a little" ', but insists he is ' "full of faults" '; but significantly she does not answer the question which points most closely to her identity with Polly: ' "Have you no pain just here" (laying her elfish hand on her elfish breast), "when you think *you* shall have to leave Graham; for *your* home is not here?" ' (p. 92). Soon after this, Lucy invites the chill, suffering Polly into her own bed, and soothes and warms her. It has often been noted that her thoughts about Polly here are in fact fears and predictions about her own future life: ' "How will she get through this world, or battle with this life? How will she bear the shocks and repulses, the humiliations and desolations, which books, and my own reason, tell me are prepared for all flesh?"' (p. 93).

Later in the book, we learn that even as a child Lucy had felt attracted to Graham. After her breakdown and 'rebirth' at La Terrasse, she is able to admit this, and remember a scene between her and Polly that she has concealed before:

> ... I whispered to myself –
> 'Ah! that portrait used to hang in the breakfast-room, over the mantel-place: somewhat too high, as I thought. I well remember how I used to mount a music-stool for the purpose of unhooking it, holding it in my hand, and searching into those bonny wells of eyes, whose glance under their hazel lashes seemed like a pencilled laugh; and well I liked to note the colouring of the cheek, and the expression of the mouth.' I hardly believed fancy could improve on the curve of that mouth, or of the chin; even my ignorance knew that both were beautiful, and pondered, perplexed over this doubt: 'How was it that what charmed so much, could at the same time so keenly pain?' Once, by way of test, I took little Missy Home, and, lifting her in my arms, told her to look at the picture.
> 'Do you like it, Polly?' I asked. She never answered, but gazed long, and at last a darkness went trembling through her sensitive eye, as she said, 'Put me down.' So I put her down, saying to myself: 'The child feels it too.' (p. 243)

Here Lucy reveals a hidden kinship with Polly's obsessive admiration of Graham, and her capacity to be hurt by him. The words 'so keenly pain' must refer to her own experience, not to her observation of Polly's, as she then confirms that Polly 'feels it too'. Thus in the first few chapters of the book, Lucy is using Polly to express and observe her own feelings about Graham: she is as potentially vulnerable to the helpless emotional dependence of the conventional woman's role as is Polly. And, after her recovery at La Terrasse, we soon find this overtly expressed, to the reader if not to anyone else, in her feelings for the rediscovered Graham/Dr John. While she had pitied in Polly 'that monomaniac tendency I have ever thought the most unfortunate with which man or woman can be cursed' (p. 69), when she thinks she has lost Dr John's first letter to her, '"Oh! they have taken my letter!" cried the grovelling, groping monomaniac' (p. 326). Her childhood conversations with Polly, in which she urged restraint, and emphasised Graham's faults, while

Polly expressed her helpless need for him, anticipate her own inner debates about Dr John. She alternates between characterising him as a sun-god-like hero, and a vain, complacent egoist; she writes two letters to him, one pouring out her real feelings, which she then destroys, and one cold reply dictated by 'Reason', which she sends. In the first chapters of the book, before Lucy has admitted this inner conflict in herself, it is externalised in the relationship between her and Polly, as well as in Polly's struggles with her own feelings. This is why, although the two children do not show much affection towards each other, it is to Lucy alone that Polly reveals her 'inner self': 'While lavishing her eccentricities regardlessly before me – for whom she professed scarcely the semblance of affection – she never showed my godmother one glimpse of her inner self' (p. 90). This corresponds to Lucy's later feeling that only Polly sees Lucy's real self.

In the final childhood scene, when Lucy embraces and warms Polly in her own bed, we have an image of reconcilement between the two halves of Lucy's personality, which contrasts with the later, violent image of Lucy as both Jael and Sisera, the rational, repressive Jael nailing down the Sisera of her feelings, who nevertheless still turns on the nail. But it is because Lucy is allowing her feelings to stir, because she is owning, rather than distancing them, that this new violence of repression is needed. Lucy's desires are no longer a child to be pitied and comforted, and sometimes ridiculed: they have grown strong and tyrannical.

From this reading of Lucy's friendship with the child Polly, we can see what a hold the image of female emotional dependency on hero-like men has got on Lucy's mind. Paulina does not operate as a monitory image of the angelic woman Lucy should but cannot be, like Lucy Deane does for Maggie. Instead, at this stage, she is a warning image of the pains and costs of conventional female dependency. When we meet Paulina again, however, we find that these pains get their appropriate reward, in male homage and protection, for a woman who can completely fill the angel-woman role. It is for a woman like Lucy, poor, plain and obscure, that the dependent role is really dangerous. It is also an inappropriate role for one who is both forced to be independent, and also has independent and rebellious elements in her own nature. Lucy eventually forges herself a more appropriate identity in her combative and unconventional relationship with M. Paul. Paulina is involved with that other part of Lucy's nature that is attracted to Dr John, the conventional man who cannot see Lucy's true nature, and can only appreciate a woman who can adapt herself convincingly to his ideal of the feminine. Lucy is deeply ambivalent about Dr John: while the 'real' Lucy that he cannot see is sometimes the fiery, passionate Lucy who admires Vashti, and who is seen by M. Paul, Lucy also implies that there is a 'real' Lucy who is just like Paulina, and that Dr John cannot see *her* because she lacks Paulina's social advantages. The situation is further complicated by the fact that Lucy claims that Dr John cannot see the real Paulina *either*, who is only visible to Lucy: he can only see her superficial feminine image, not her underlying strength. I think that what is happening here is that half of Lucy still wants Dr John (or the author wants him for her) – the conventional man, the conventional woman's role, still have a tremendous hold over the excluded unconventional woman's imagination. Lucy thus vicariously obtains Dr John through this identification with Paulina, even while she despairingly bewails his loss, and while in other moods she prefers M. Paul. Thus sometimes Paulina is being claimed as a soul-mate, and sometimes ridiculed by comparison with M. Paul's spaniel; sometimes she is the possessor of all earthly happiness, while Lucy is a wretched outcast, and sometimes Lucy can declare, of her relationship with M. Paul, 'I envied no girl her lover, no bride her bridegroom, no wife her husband; I was content with this my voluntary, self-offering friend' (p. 501).

Lucy's friendship with the grown-up Paulina thus serves both for Lucy to reject Paulina's angel-women role, and for her vicariously to share it. Paulina is presented as a more acceptable, socially advantaged, lucky version of herself.[11] The occasion of her reappearance in the novel is significant. Dr John has disappointed Lucy with his calm, disapproving attitude to the passionate performance – this signals her recognition of the differences between them, of his inadequacy to understand her inner life. At this point the theatre catches fire – the rebellious passion of Vashti spills off the stage and manifests its power and its danger. In the ensuing panic, a young woman who turns out to be Paulina is nearly trampled to death, and is rescued by Dr John: rebellious female passion is obviously dangerous to child-like angel-women. Dr John has found a more appropriate bride than the Lucy who could sympathise with Vashti's violence: the theatre scene can be read as a parting of the ways between Lucy and Dr John, as she finds him inadequate and hands him over to a more insipid woman. But Lucy too is threatened by the fire. Vashti is also a warning to her of the self-destruction caused by female rebellion: Paulina can therefore be seen as a new self-image for Lucy, combining 'fire' and 'ice', with her '"gentle hoar-frost ... surrounding so much pure, fine flame"'.[12]

That Paulina is still functioning as an alter-ego for Lucy is suggested by her uncanny way of appearing in Lucy's bedroom at La Terrasse: 'between the candles, and before the glass, appeared something dressing itself – an airy, fairy thing – small, slight, white – a winter spirit. I declare, for one moment I thought of Graham and his spectral illusions' (p. 357). The reference to the 'spectral illusions' is to the previous 'apparition' of the ghostly nun, who also represents part of Lucy's nature. As a child, Paulina also had this uncanny quality, and seemed to 'haunt' the rooms (p. 69). Paulina has, however, changed since she was a child: she has learnt self-control, to temper and surround her 'flame' with 'frost', so she resembles 'a lamp chastely lucent, guarding from extinction, yet not hiding from worship, a flame vital and vestal' (p. 359). It is the sort of balance Lucy would like to achieve. It is Paulina's self-control that sets her apart from other women, as far as Lucy is concerned, and makes her a valued friend: 'I was not accustomed to find in women or girls any power of self-control, or strength of self-denial.... The little Countess promised an exception' (p. 373). Paulina has learnt well the lessons Lucy had tried to teach her at Bretton – it is no wonder she remembers her time with Lucy there with an affection she hardly showed at the time (though Lucy of course is an unreliable narrator – she may have suppressed or refused to see evidence of Paulina's liking for her). Thus Paulina remembers '"the comfort and protection by which you soothed an acute distress"' (p. 358), and that '"I had an odd content in being with you even when I was a little, troublesome, disobedient girl"' (p. 463). Paulina clearly takes Lucy as her model of self-control:

'... if I liked Dr John till I was fit to die for liking him, that alone could not license me to be otherwise than dumb – dumb as the grave – dumb as you, Lucy Snowe – you know it – and you know you would despise me if I failed in self-control, and whined about some rickety liking that was all on my side.' (p. 463)

Paulina here implies a knowledge of Lucy's own feelings for Dr
John, and her suppression of them. She identifies with Lucy, but
also signals a new departure: Dr John *has* declared his love for her,
Paulina *can* speak of her feelings. Lucy's relationship with Dr John
is about to be re-enacted with a happy outcome, beginning with
Paulina's reception of the precious 'first letter', which she treasures
as obsessively as Lucy treasured her first letter from him. Lucy no
longer gets letters from Dr John, she has buried all the ones she has,
and symbolically given him up; but while Paulina supplants her, as
her alter-ego she also re-enacts the relationship *for* her. In Paulina,
Lucy is provided with the right elements 'to attract and enchain, to
subdue and excite Dr John' (p. 459). These elements include wealth
and social standing: 'Had he seen Paulina with the same youth,
beauty, and grace, but on foot, alone, unguarded, and in simple
attire, a dependent worker', he would not have been so 'vanquished'
(p. 459). Similarly, Lucy wonders if she herself had been more
fortunate, would he have noticed and appreciated her more: 'Had
Lucy been intrinsically the same, but possessing the additional
advantages of wealth and station, would your manner to her, your
value for her, have been quite what they actually were?' (p. 410) All
this implies that Lucy and Paulina could be the same person, under
fortunate and unfortunate aspects – and this is confirmed when Lucy
gives Paulina and Dr John's love her blessing, and recalls her fears
for Paulina as a child:

> 'As a child I feared for you; nothing that has life was ever more
> susceptible than your nature in infancy: under harshness, or neglect,
> neither your outward nor your inward self would have ripened to what
> they now are. Much pain, much fear, much struggle would have troubled
> the very lines of your features, broken their regularity, would have
> harassed your nerves into the fever of habitual irritation: you would have
> lost in health and cheerfulness, in grace and sweetness.' (p. 467)

Surely Lucy is describing herself here, and implying that Paulina
could have turned out like Lucy if she had not had such good luck.
Lucy is implying an intrinsic similarity between herself and Paulina,
and therefore her own intrinsic right to Dr John. If she cannot have
him, he is to be given to the person she could have been under more
favourable circumstances. Her identification with Paulina is
increased by her claiming to see more of Paulina's character than Dr
John himself does, and to find there a strength that makes Paulina

more like Lucy herself, less of the helpless child her father and lover
see:

> In Paulina there was more force, both of feeling and character, than
> most people thought – than Graham himself imagined – than she would
> ever show to those who did not wish to see it. . . . Graham would have
> started had any suggestive spirit whispered of the sinew and stamina
> sustaining that delicate nature; but I, who had known her as a child,
> knew, or guessed, by what a good and strong root her graces held to the
> firm soil of reality. (pp. 399–400)

Here, as when Paulina answers Graham's first letter, we have the
idea that she is playing a part for Graham, being the ice-maiden or
the child-like dependant that he wants her to be. Lucy retains power
over Dr John by knowing by what deceptions he can be pleased, and
by knowing his wife better than he does himself. Lucy, through
Paulina, both participates in and subtly undermines the angel-
woman role.

While Lucy thus becomes thoroughly involved in and identified
with Paulina's 'capture' of Dr John, she is also separating herself
from Paulina, asserting herself in a different identity. She refuses to
become Paulina's companion, maintaining 'I was no bright lady's
shadow' (p. 382); and she refuses to 'share' Paulina's life with
Graham ' " I have my sort of life apart from yours" ' (p. 520). She is
naturally jealous of the lovers, and firmly silences Paulina in her
hurtful praises of Graham's beauty: 'It was best to answer her
strongly at once, and to silence for ever the tender, passionate
confidences which left her lips sweet honey, and sometimes dropped
in my ear – molten lead' (p. 520). She complains about the lovers'
'infatuation of egotism', which 'will have witness of their happiness,
cost that witness what it may' (pp. 520–1). As well as a vicarious
participator in Paulina's happy love for Graham, Lucy is also
Graham's rejected lover. But as well as rejected lover, she is also the
person with her own 'sort of life', and a different and more valuable
kind of love for M. Paul. Her relationship with Paulina contains all
these ambivalences. When Paulina and Graham are dismissed from
the story to their conventionally happy ending, it is a triumph for
Lucy-as-Paulina, it is a defeat for Lucy as spinster by Paulina as
wife, and it is also Lucy as lover of M. Paul dismissing
Lucy/Paulina and the banal conventionality of what she wanted. In
this complex and ambivalent way, Brontë lays to rest the angel-

woman ideal, and her demands on the female identity of her
heroine.

This laying to rest is necessary before Lucy can go on to find love
with M. Paul, a love which is only revealed when she *loses* the
self-control she and Paulina have built up, and storms jealously at
M. Paul. Paulina's ice-maiden act is not the way to attract him. M.
Paul can now be fully recognised as her other alter-ego. Social and
fictional convention are taken care of in the narrative progression to
the marriage of Paulina and Graham: Lucy goes on beyond this
ending to her own sort of fulfilment, and her never-to-be-achieved
marriage with M. Paul.

# Chapter Two

# Madonnas and Magdalens

Friendships between 'pure' and 'fallen' women often display extremes of intensity and commitment in fiction by Victorian women. Far from being irreconcilable opposites, these two types merge and exchange their characteristics. These friendships seem to function to raise and resolve problems about female sexuality – problems which have to be negotiated before the conventional marriage ending can take place. Either an independent heroine comes to recognise her own sexuality through her contact with a 'fallen' woman; or the 'fallen' woman is reclaimed for respectability by her 'pure' sister. The first of these patterns can be found in both George Eliot's *Adam Bede* and Elizabeth Barrett Browning's *Aurora Leigh*, which contain some striking parallels; the second appears in Christina Rossetti's *Goblin Market*. As some of my argument about *Adam Bede* has already been made elsewhere, though in a different context and to a different conclusion,[1] I have decided to devote more space to *Aurora Leigh*, which is also the less well-known text. In my section on *Goblin Market*, while I begin by reading the friendship between Lizzie and Laura as a Madonna/Magdalen relationship, I also suggest another way of reading it, which has important parallels with the female friendships in *Wives and Daughters* and *Shirley*, novels I discuss in later chapters. Finally, I argue that the contradictory structure of Lizzie and Laura's friendship can be explained if it is read in the context of the contemporary conservative ideology of 'women's sphere'. Thus what seems to us a 'radical' assertion of female solidarity within an all-female world, is also a 'reactionary' parable about female repression and confinement. *Aurora Leigh* also appears to offer us an image of a 'radical' sisterly solidarity between Aurora and Marian, outside the world of men; but this too is undercut in various ways, and once again female friendship serves to assimilate women into traditional roles. In each case, however, positions of power are found within those roles, through the processes of negotiation and identity-exchange that have gone on between the women friends.

While I have used the catchwords 'Madonnas' and 'Magdalens' to describe the female pairings in *Aurora Leigh* and *Adam Bede*, it is an important feature of these relationships that it is the fallen woman, the 'Magdalen', who is the mother – her fall being marked by the child she bears. The 'pure' woman is childless and single. Her status as 'Madonna' comes not from maternity, but from her roles as rescuer and as sufferer. In this, she is like the rescuing image of the suffering Lucy that appears to Maggie. But in this case it is she who is the 'heroine,' either in moral terms (Dinah), or because the main focus of the story is on her (Aurora). The heroine is thus the more socially acceptable of the pair: instead of an unconventional heroine defining herself against the accepted ideal of womanhood, these heroines look the other way, towards the socially outcast figure of the Magdalen. Nevertheless, neither of these heroines is conventional in the way Lucy Deane is – they are exceptionally intelligent and independent, and both have refused marriage proposals in order to continue their own work. In this sense, they are as much social 'outsiders' as are the 'fallen' women they befriend. We might see here a natural alliance between the spinster and the Magdalen[2] but, strangely, the spinster is transformed into a married woman by this alliance. Both Aurora and Dinah seem to resolve problems about their own sexuality through their transforming contact with a 'fallen' woman: they are finally enabled to give up their independence and accept marriage. Most explicitly, we see Dinah taking over Hetty's role at the farm, Hetty's lover Adam, and Hetty's sexual 'bloom' as opposed to her own former pallor, and our final view of her is as a mother. The contact with the fallen woman seems to lead to the heroine's assimilation into conventional marriage. Though we could say that Aurora's marriage of equals with the maimed and repentant Romney is not a conventional marriage in the same way that Dinah's is, nevertheless Aurora unsays her earlier high words of female independence, and admits her need of love. In narrative terms, the 'fallen' woman's story had of course conventionally to lead to death. Barrett Browning daringly allows Marian to live, but she frequently speaks of herself as 'dead' since her rape, unable to marry, or to exist in any other role except that of mother. In contrast, the 'pure' woman's story therefore has to carry the conventional romantic plot, ending in marriage.[3] This resolution, however, is not possible until the two women have come together in a transforming interchange.

It was not in itself unusual for pure women to befriend fallen women in Victorian literature. In *Oliver Twist*, for instance, Dickens emphasises Rose Maylie's friendliness and generosity towards the prostitute Nancy, whom she offers to 'save'; and Charles Kingsley, in *Alton Locke*, has Eleanor end up living in a household of reformed prostitutes. In both these cases, as with Aurora Leigh and Marian Erle, class barriers are also broken down. Though as Kate Millett says, 'One of the chief effects of class within patriarchy is to set one woman against another, in the past creating a lively antagonism between whore and matron',[4] the Victorian matron (and, even more, the 'pure' single woman) was ideally supposed to be always ready to save and reform the properly contrite whore. The reform of prostitutes was an expected part of the plans of the religious sisterhoods founded at the time, and Martha Vicinus remarks, 'In a society fascinated with sexuality as a symbol of man's fallen nature, the picture of highly controlled and pure women caring for prostitutes had a peculiar appeal and reassurance.' She also points out, however, that 'throughout the process distance was always kept between the penitents and the sisters. Contamination was avoided by strict regulation and physical separation.'[5] This distance is broken down by Eliot and Barrett Browning, emotionally, physically and psychically, as the two women take on aspects of each other's identities – a closeness which is not part of male portrayals of such friendships. An added reason for intimacy between these fictional women, is of course that each pair are potential rivals for the same man; yet, interestingly, there is no antagonism of the kind Dickens shows between Rosa Dartle and Emily in *David Copperfield*. While Thomas Hardy does offer us a picture of sympathy between 'pure' and 'fallen' rivals, in *The Woodlanders*, the closeness between Felice and Grace is briefly forced on them by circumstances, and their mutual sympathy only fleeting, compared with the permanence of Aurora and Marian's bonds, and the intensity of Dinah and Hetty's.

While the emphasis in Dinah and Hetty's relationship is very much on Dinah 'saving' and reforming the erring Hetty in the accepted way, in *Aurora Leigh* Marian's essential purity is stressed, and the 'rescue' Aurora provides is emotional and financial, not moral. But, more than this, Marian is herself endowed with 'holy' and Madonna-like qualities. Here, Barrett Browning is following the lead of Mrs Gaskell, who, in *Ruth*, had deliberately confused and combined the qualities of Madonna and Magdalen in her 'fallen' heroine.[6] Marian, like Ruth, is a victim in need of help, not a sinner in need of reform; she is, in fact, even more sinless than Ruth, having been raped while drugged, rather than seduced. She is presented as a victim of male sexuality and female betrayal; and this role, I shall argue, is extremely important to her significance to Aurora. Another difference between Barrett Browning's and Eliot's portrayals of the relationship between the 'pure' and the 'fallen' woman, is that in *Aurora Leigh* an explicit point is being made about the value of female solidarity and mutual support. A valuable and reciprocal friendship is created between Aurora and Marian, based on the ideal of sisterhood and a mutual need for mothering. In *Adam Bede*, on the other hand, the ideal of female solidarity is less important: Dinah is drawn to Hetty through her Christian love for a sinner she wants to reclaim. This friendship is also much less reciprocal than Aurora's and Marian's: Hetty is presented as too weak and trivial in character to contribute much to the relationship in terms of mutual support. Hetty does have a transforming effect on Dinah's identity, but this is read on the symbolic level, rather than as a social phenomenon. By contrast, in *Aurora Leigh*, Aurora and Marian's friendship is created both as a social phenomenon and as part of a pattern of imagery of female solidarity. Symbolic action and imagery are used to stress the equality and reciprocity of the relationship. Like Lucy and Maggie's friendship in *The Mill on the Floss*, it shines out as precious against a background of women's betrayal of other women. In *Aurora Leigh*, this overt social message of female solidarity coexists more harmoniously than in *Mill on the Floss* with what the women signify to each other as social and psychological types, and how they affect each other's identities on the symbolic level.

Aurora first meets Marian in London – Aurora's upper-class cousin Romney intends to marry the working-class Marian as a gesture of social equality and solidarity. Aurora meets her, and gives Marian her approval. In a strange way, Marian is standing in for Aurora at this point: Aurora has already refused Romney, because she feels he does not appreciate her vocation as poet, and does not love her. Instead,

> What you love
> Is not a woman, Romney, but a cause:
> You want a helpmate, not a mistress, sir.
> A wife to help your ends, – in her no end. (II 400–3)

In Marian, Romney is getting exactly this: she is totally devoted to him and his schemes, and has never thought to ask whether he loves her. She has made the bargain that Aurora would not, and Aurora is both admiring and critical:

> This perhaps was love –
> To have its hands too full of gifts to give,
> For putting out a hand to take a gift [...]
> With women of my class 'tis otherwise:
> We haggle for the small change of our gold,
> And so much love accord for so much love,
> Rialto prices. Are we therefore wrong?
> If marriage be a contract, look to it then,
> Contracting prices should be equal, just; (IV 176–8, 187–92)[7]

and she goes on to liken Marian's one-sided devotion to an Indian widow throwing herself on the pyre, the only 'advance' being that Marian asks 'to consume entire/For a living husband', not a dead one (IV 199–200). Clearly, Romney's choice of Marian arouses in Aurora all her own conflicts about the selfishness or otherwise of preserving her own independent vocation, about the compatibility of career and love. Romney now appears, and makes it clear he has taken Aurora's words of refusal literally – he wants to marry Marian as a 'helpmate', not because he loves her. Of course, the plot is to show that he needs (and has always needed) a strong poetess like Aurora, not a devoted slave like Marian: but once again, it is not his process of choice that is dramatised, but the interaction between the two women. Marian is to become strong enough to stand alone without Romney, and Aurora is to realise her need for him; and the final understanding is to come about by each woman in turn giving up the man to the other.

Romney's cold-hearted speech about his extremely theoretical reasons for marrying Marian repels Aurora, and she turns instead to kiss Marian, prefiguring their later closeness:

> The man had baffled, chafed me, till I flung
> For refuge to the woman, – as, sometimes,
> Impatient of some crowded room's close smell,
> You throw a window open and lean out
> To breathe a long breath in the dewy night
> And cool your angry forehead. She, at least,
> Was not built up as walls are, brick by brick,
> Each fancy squared, each feeling ranged by line [...] (IV 348–54)

Aurora reacts away from the rational man with his suppressed feelings, to the restorative responsiveness of the woman. The contrast of brick wall and open window is extremely effective. It is only when Romney has been 'feminised' by his blinding, and by Aurora's poetry, at the end of the book, that he can become a fitting partner for her.

In the open window image, Marian is identified with Nature and its refreshing qualities – 'the dewy night'; and throughout she is described in terms of Nature, especially animals:

> like dumb creatures (now
> A rustling bird, and now a wandering deer,
> Or squirrel 'gainst the oak-gloom flashing up
> His sidelong burnished head, in just her way
> Of savage spontaneity), that stir
> Abruptly the green silence of the woods,
> And make it stranger, holier, more profound;
> As Nature's general heart confessed itself
> Of life, and then fell backward on repose. (IV 159–67)

This likeness to small dumb creatures is similar to the way George Eliot describes Hetty Sorrell, as a kitten or a duckling, though in Marian's case without the heartless amorality implied by Eliot's images. The animal imagery suggests Marian's sexuality, and also her vulnerability, as opposed to the more self-possessed, intellectual Aurora. Aurora's attraction to Marian as a manifestation of Nature is of a piece with the importance of Nature in Aurora's life. Nature has always been a sustaining, specifically female, maternal presence for her, to which she was able to escape from the stifling rigidities of her aunt's house. Her contact with Nature there signifies her hold on her own identity, as opposed to the conventional female mould her aunt wants to fit her into. After a period of death-like withdrawal, she reawakens to a sense of self, and we are given a description of her own room, a little 'green' chamber, with an open window 'which let in/The outdoor world with all its greenery' (I 573–4). The image is of course re-echoed in the image of Marian as refreshing open window: Marian is part of the female Nature that sustains Aurora's creativity and sense of self. Aurora's sexuality is displaced into descriptions of Nature – most notably in her homesick descriptions of Italy:[8]

> My multitudinous mountains, sitting in
> The magic circle with the mutual touch
> Electric, panting from their full deep hearts
> Beneath the influent heavens and waiting for
> Communion and commission. (I 622–6)

The English landscape, that helps her to recover herself, does not have this passionate intensity:

> Rather say,
> A sweet familiar nature, stealing in
> As a dog might, or a child, to touch your hand
> Or pluck your gown, and humbly mind you so
> Of presence and affection (I 640–4)

– a description that could apply to Marian, with her humble and affectionate nature, her likeness to 'dumb creatures'. Marian's is not a passionate sexuality – it is passive and unself-aware. She may remind Aurora of the sustenance of Nature – especially in her later devotion to her child; but she is also Nature exploited and abused: when Aurora meets her again in Paris, she recognises the eyes

> Which always had the brown, pathetic look
> Of a dumb creature who had been beaten once
> And never since was easy with the world. (VI 317–9)

Soon we discover that Marian has been raped.

These differences in the two women's sexuality, suggested by the Nature imagery, are extremely important to the significance of their friendship, and of the placing of their second meeting in the narrative, as I shall show later. What is most immediately striking about that second meeting is first, the frantic urgency with which Aurora, having glimpsed her face, seeks Marian out; and secondly, the instantaneous and unquestioned way she offers Marian a home. It is true that then the question of Marian's child arises, and delays the two women's acceptance of each other: Aurora's self-righteous attempts to preach at and 'reform' Marian to a proper sense of her 'sin' are undercut by Marian's indignant protestations of her innocence, and finally the story of the rape leaves Aurora humiliated and apologetic for her censorious attitude. Her offer of a home is then immediately renewed and is immediately accepted by Marian.

Aurora's frantic search for Marian through Paris is generalised into a more abstract search by the imagery: Aurora bumps into another preoccupied pedestrian, and meditates on how

> We shape a figure of our fantasy.
> Call nothing something, and run after it
> And lose it, lose ourselves too in the search,
> Till clash against us comes a somebody
> Who also has lost something and is lost [...] (VI 285–9)

This suggests Aurora is looking for something more than just a missing person – Marian represents 'something' important she has lost, and that has caused her to 'lose' herself. It is the discovery of this lost 'something' that explains Aurora's eager offer of a home to Marian, and Marian's trusting acceptance. It seems to me that it is female sisterhood itself, mutual mothering, that both women have lost – their coming together falls into place as inevitable, when it is read against the contrasting pattern of images of motherlessness and women's betrayal of other women in the narrative so far.[9] Aurora is motherless, and her childhood was haunted by 'a mother-want about the world', which left her 'seeking' (I 40–1). She is then imprisoned by a false mother, her rigid spinster aunt. Since then, the only offer of female friendship she has had is from the false Lady Waldemar (III 489), whose real motive is to use Aurora to break up Romney's marriage with Marian, so she herself can marry him. Marian's experience of other women has been even worse: her mother attempted to sell her to a man; and Lady Waldemar, posing as a friend, persuades her to give up Romney, which leads to her abduction and rape. Here, Lady Waldemar explicitly makes use of and betrays Marian's 'mother want':

'She wrapped me in her generous arms at once,
And let me dream a moment how it feels
To have a real mother, like some girls [...]' (VI 1001–3)

The further betrayal by Lady Waldemar's servant, who arranges for the rape, is seen by Marian as another monstrous perversion of motherhood:

'A woman ... hear me, let me make it plain ...
A woman ... not a monster ... both her breasts
Made right to suckle babes ... she took me off
A woman also [...]' (VI 1182–5)

After her experience of 'mothers', Marian's bitter conclusion is

'She served me (after all it was not strange,
'Twas only what my mother would have done)
A motherly, right damnable good turn.' (VII 8–10)

After the rape, a miller's wife is briefly kind to Marian, and finds her a place as a servant, but then her mistress, herself an adulteress, hypocritically turns her away when she is found to be pregnant. Again, the betrayal by a woman is what hurts: '"any woman, womanly,/Had thought of him who should be in a month,/ The sinless babe"' (VII 82–4). Against this background, the spontaneous coming together of two 'motherless' women is not surprising. Aurora uses the language of female sisterhood to Marian: '"I lost my sister Marian many days,/ And sought her ever"', '"Come with me, sweetest sister"' (VI 449–50; VII 117). There is also self-reproach in Aurora's decision: after her first meeting with Marian, she did not follow up the friendship, and has earlier reproached herself for that failure, as she might have 'kept her safe' from Lady Waldemar's 'traps' (IV 472–3).

Intervening between Aurora's two assertions of sisterhood with Marian is the difficult interview in which Marian's child is explained. The friendship is both instantaneous, inevitable, *and* a difficult, precarious achievement, reaching across class mistrust and sexual prejudices. The difficulty and saving importance of the

friendship is brilliantly conveyed by Barrett Browning in a twice
repeated metaphor. First Aurora leads the way to her house, while
Marian

> Turned round and followed closely where I went,
> As if I led her by a narrow plank
> Across devouring waters, step by step [...] (VI 481–3)

But after a mile, Marian refuses to go any further, as her baby is
waiting for her at home. They turn round, and Marian leads Aurora
to her house to see the baby:

> Then she led
> The way, and I, as by a narrow plank
> Across devouring waters, followed her,
> Stepping by her footsteps, breathing by her breath [...] (VI 500–3)

Each woman offers the other rescue, from the devouring waters of
female loneliness and betrayal – but the friendship is also a narrow,
precarious bridge across Marian's mistrust and Aurora's moralistic
prejudices. The pair of scenes also conveys the equality and
reciprocity that is necessary to a true friendship between the women:
Aurora first takes possession of Marian – they are to meet in
Aurora's world. But then Marian stands her ground, and leads
Aurora back to understand *her* world, and to accept her view of
herself and the child. The two images also suggest the way the
women will later take on aspects of each other's identity, taking
turns to follow each other's footsteps.[10] The reversal by which first
Aurora leads, and then Marian leads, prefigures the movement of
the next scene: from a superior, judgemental moral position, Aurora
is brought to acknowledge her mistake and Marian's superiority:

> But I, convicted, broken utterly,
> With woman's passion clung about her waist
> And kissed her hair and eyes, – 'I have been wrong,
> Sweet Marian' ... (weeping in a tender rage) ...
> 'Sweet holy Marian!' (VI 778–82)

Of course, this change is brought about by Aurora learning the true
story of the rape, not by a real change in her attitude to illicit sex.
Nevertheless, the scene does represent a revision of the standard

scenario in which the pure woman tries to 'save' the fallen woman:
there is even a hint of satire at Aurora's initial attitude, when she is
so shocked at Marian's delight in her illegitimate baby. Aurora
insists that love is behind her attitude, and Marian replies somewhat
wearily: '"Alas", she said, "you are so very good"' (VI 695).

Once Marian has been accepted on her own terms, with the baby,
the way is clear for the two women to set up house together. As they
journey towards Italy, there is an alternation of strength between
them, a reciprocity of support. At first, Aurora, losing her sense of
identity, is supported by her own need to support Marian:

> I was weak;
> I struggled for the posture of my soul
> In upright consciousness of place and time,
> But evermore, 'twixt waking and sleeping.
> Slipped somehow, staggered, caught at Marian's eyes
> A moment (it is very good for strength
> To know that someone needs you to be strong)
> And so recovered what I called myself,
> For that time. (VII 409–17)

But as Aurora muses sadly on the boat, Marian comes up to comfort
and sympathise with her loneliness:

> 'But now,' I said, 'you leave the child alone.'
> 'And you're alone,' she answered, – and she looked
> As if I too were something. Sweet the help
> Of one we have helped! Thanks, Marian, for such help.' (VII
> 511–14)

The household that they set up together is proposed by Aurora as a
self-sufficient women's house:

> 'I am lonely in the world,
> And thou art lonely, and the child is half
> An orphan. Come, – and henceforth thou and I
> Being together will not miss a friend,
> Nor he a father, since two mothers shall
> Make that up to him.' (VII 120–5)

As the Marxist-Feminist Literature Collective put it, Barrett
Browning suggests that 'Marian and Aurora could support each

other without men if necessary.'[11] This is certainly a revolutionary
suggestion: but it is important to face the fact that this is not what
actually happens in the rest of the poem. Barrett Browning's ideal of
female solidarity does not actually reach so far. It is not just that
Romney arrives to break up the idyll: it is that, despite Aurora's
brave proposal to Marian, she is not presented as finding any peace
or fulfilment in the relationship. Marian finds happiness – but then
she has the child (a boy) to make her complete: Aurora is still lonely,
discontent, and obsessed as never before with thoughts of Romney.
This is true even on the journey, and once they get to Italy, and set
up house together, we are given no more scenes of friendship
between the two women: Marian's only role seems to be to provide
the flowers and occasionally lend the baby (VII 930–52), and
Aurora seems to spend all her time walking around alone or sitting
alone, brooding about her lost past and unfulfilled present. Marian's
presence, with the baby, only serves to make Aurora more discontent
with her own life, by contrast: she hears Marian laughing in the
garden, and thinks,

> Laugh *you*, sweet Marian, – you've the right to laugh
> Since God himself is for you, and a child!
> For me there's somewhat less, – and so I sigh. (VIII 25–7)

There is a paradox here: Aurora was the more eager of the two
women for the friendship, yet now she has it, she is the less happy.
From Marian's past history, we would expect *her* to have been the
keener of the two on their friendship. Yet, as we saw, it was Aurora
who was frantically searching for Marian as the important
'something' she had lost; and on first finding her, speaks of her need
for Marian in terms of 'hunger':

> 'do we throw away
> The bread we worked and prayed for, – crumble it
> And drop it, ... to do even so by thee
> Whom still I've hungered after more than bread,
> My sister Marian?' (VI 451–5)

While it is Aurora who is so desperate to make contact with Marian,
we then find the relationship only increasing her feelings of
unhappiness and emptiness in her life. I think this paradox can be
explained if we investigate what Marian means to Aurora, in

relation to *Romney*. The function of her friendship with Marian is ultimately to bring Aurora together with Romney: Marian represents some aspect of her female identity that she has to come to terms with before that can happen. Thus the intensity of her search for Marian is not caused only by a need for female sympathy: it also arises from her problems with her sexual identity.

As we have seen, the Nature imagery hints at a difference between Marian and Aurora as sexual beings. Further hints about Marian's sexuality are conveyed by her physical description. Interestingly, she is no archetypal dark passionate woman or blonde temptress, or even suffering blonde saint. This is how she first appears to Aurora:

> Nowise beautiful
> Was Marian Erle. She was not white nor brown,
> But could look either, like a mist that changed
> According to being shone on more or less:
> The hair, too, ran its opulence of curls
> In doubt 'twixt dark and bright, nor left you clear
> To name the colour. Too much hair perhaps
> (I'll name a fault here) for so small a head,
> Which seemed to droop on that side and on this,
> As a full-blown rose uneasy with its weight [...] (III 809–18)

Marian's undefined mistiness seems appropriate to a woman who takes her being so much from men ('being shone on more or less'), as devoted slave-wife, rape victim, or mother.[12] A woman's hair is often used to signify her sexuality in Victorian literature,[13] and the way Marian's heavy hair drowns her face is a repeated detail:

> The small fair face between the darks of hair,
> I used to liken, when I saw her first,
> To a point of moonlit water down a well:
> The low brow [...] (VI 313–16)

The small head, the low brow, seem to indicate lack of intellect; the heavy hair hints at a sexuality that obscures Marian's individuality, and imposes a 'weight' of suffering on her. Overabundant and on display, it also suggests her sexual vulnerability. It is unlike Aurora's hair, which seems to have a life of its own, but is also under its owner's control:

My long loose hair began to burn and creep,
Alive to the very ends, about my knees:
I swept it backward as the wind sweeps flame,
With the passion of my hands. Ah, Romney laughed
One day ... (how full the memories come up!)
'– Your Florence fire-flies live on in your hair.'
He said, 'it gleams so.' Well, I wrung them out,
My fire-flies; made a knot as hard as life
Of those loose, soft, impracticable curls,
And then sat down and thought ... (V 1126–35)

Aurora's hair is turning electric here at the thought of Romney and
Lady Waldemar together: unacknowledged sexual jealousy is
implied. But the memory of Romney's admiration, of her hair
(sexuality) as a display for him, prompts her to wring it out and
knot it up – to conceal and restrain it. This hair-imagery extends to
the third woman in the story, Lady Waldemar. Appropriately, she
has snaky locks:[14]

Her maid must use both hands to twist that coil
Of tresses, then be careful lest the rich
Bronze rounds should slip [...] (V 614–16)

This artful coil is quite different from Aurora's practical 'knot' –
Lady Waldemar's sexuality involves artful scheming to catch her
man and deceive her rivals, and a careful balance between blatant
sexual allure and a concealment of her true rapacity.

That both Lady Waldemar and Marian Erle are parts of a
dramatisation of Aurora's problems of female identity, is signalled
early in the poem in the description of Aurora's mother's portrait.
Aurora's mother is dead, and Aurora has only the portrait to look at
for her female ideal. Onto the portrait she projects the various
possible images of woman provided by her culture, 'Whatever I last
read or heard or dreamed'.[15] Among these images are

Our Lady of the Passion, stabbed with swords
Where the Babe sucked; or Lamia in her first
Moonlighted pallor, ere she shrunk and blinked
And shuddering wriggled down to the unclean [...] (I 160–3)

It is clear that the suffering mother later takes form as Marian Erle, and the evil Lamia as Lady Waldemar. Somehow these two women are involved with Aurora's sense of her female identity,[16] and, I would argue, specifically her sexuality. Cora Kaplan remarks that Marian, in order to be presented as 'a "pure" victim of male violence', 'must be denied the self-generated sexuality which is permitted to upper-class women in *Aurora Leigh* but which taints all working-class women except Marian'.[17] This judgement, however, ignores the differences between Aurora and the 'upper-class' Lady Waldemar, and also the limitations of Aurora's 'self-generated sexuality'. While Aurora is presented as an intensely sexual woman, largely through her descriptions of Nature, she is not allowed to feel any sexual desires in relation to *men*. This purely 'self-generated' sexuality is not going to allow her to be a mother. As we see in her refusal of Romney, a relationship with a man is a threat to her independence and identity. But, in retrospect, she half regrets her refusal: if Romney had loved her,

> I might have been a common woman now
> And happier, less known and less left alone.
> Perhaps a better woman after all,
> With chubby children hanging on my neck
> To keep me low and wise. Ah me, the vines
> That bear such fruit are proud to stoop with it.
> The palm stands upright in a realm of sand. (II 513–19)

She regrets the loss of a possible identity as wife and mother, and it is interesting that this role is presented as something that weighs a woman down, keeps her 'low'. We are reminded here of Marian's head drooping with the weight of her man-directed sexuality. It is also significant that Aurora images her subsequent single life as a barren 'realm of sand'. After her rejection of Romney, her 'self-generated' sexuality disappears, and she figuratively knots up her hair, living a lonely and asexual existence (presumably her passion goes into her poetry). The choice presents itself to her as between a lonely independence, and a sexual relation with a man which blots out identity, as Marian's separate identity is blotted out by Romney, by the rapist, and by her son. The other possible way of relating sexually to men, is of course Lady Waldemar's way: she actively pursues Romney, and speaks coarsely and frankly of her 'love' as 'garlic' and as 'fever':

> 'Am I coarse?
> Well, love's coarse, nature's coarse – ah, there's the rub.
> We fair fine ladies, [...]
>       we have hearts within,
> Warm, live, improvident, indecent hearts,
> As ready for outrageous ends and acts
> As any distressed sempstress [...] (III 454–6, 461–4)

But, within the sexual ideology of the book, and of most Victorian literature, this possibility can only be rejected as evil – though we may suspect that Lady Waldemar carries out Aurora's secret wishes, in pursuing Romney and in foiling his marriage with Marian.[18]

Thus it is Marian who represents all that Aurora has cut out of her life by her refusal of Romney and her subsequent unconventional life as a single poetess; and Marian also represents all Aurora's fears about what giving up her singleness to a man might mean. Marian, as we saw, is the woman who made the bargain Aurora would not – who is ready to be Romney's slave-wife. That her eventual fate is rape, suggests that passive devotion to men and sexual exploitation by men are not that far apart. Nevertheless, Marian is rewarded for her sufferings by the prize of the child; though her sufferings suggest at what price maternity is to be bought. Given the terms of Aurora's refusal of Romney, and the terms in which she views her single life, it is not surprising that she has to meet and both reconcile herself to and differentiate herself from Marian before being able finally to marry him.[19] Her relationship with Marian is inextricably involved with her relationship with Romney. It is significant that the moment before she catches sight of Marian's face in Paris, her thought has been 'Yet Romney leaves me ...', and then 'God! what face is that?/O Romney, O Marian!' (VI 226–7) Similarly, as Marian tells her story, Aurora hears *Romney*'s voice:

>         It is strange,
> Today while Marian told her story like
> To absorb most listeners, how I listened chief
> To a voice not hers, [...]
>       one that mixed with mine
> Long years ago among the garden-trees,
> And said to *me*, to *me* too, 'Be my wife,
> Aurora.' (VII 174–81)

She reproaches herself now for her refusal, thinking she might have 'saved' him from Lady Waldemar. Then she recovers and reproaches herself for this emotional reaction, and the female fantasy of self-sacrifice to 'save' a man: 'It seems as if I had a man in me,/Despising such a woman.' (VII 213–14) The 'woman' in Aurora here is a woman like Marian: contact with Marian has brought her to life, and she is drawing her towards Romney, but Aurora also has a 'man-like' strength and independence that counters this tendency.

Aurora does not, however, have to become entirely 'woman', or entirely Marian, in order to win Romney; rather, a compromise must be reached between the 'man' and 'woman' in her, and between her and Romney.[20] Similarly, Marian has to take on some of Aurora's strength and independence – she learns how to refuse Romney, while Aurora learns to accept him. In the final scenes of the story, the two women take on something of each other's identities. Romney arrives, and first, conscientiously, proposes marriage to Marian. Marian speaks to him and to Aurora with a new strength, 'As one who has authority to speak,/And not as Marian' (IX 250–1). She tells how she has come to realise her own worth:

> 'I, who felt myself unworthy once
> Of virtuous Romney and his high-born race,
> Have come to learn, – a woman, poor or rich,
> Despised or honoured, is a human soul,
> And what her soul is, that she is herself,
> Although she should be spit upon of men [. . .]' (IX 326–31)

From this position of strength, she refuses Romney's proposal. Looking back at her former feelings, she is able to distinguish between 'love' and 'worship':

> 'Did I indeed
> Love once; or did I only worship? [. . .]
>     What was in my thought?
> To be your slave, your help, your toy, your tool.
> To be your love . . . I never thought of that:
> To give you love . . . still less.' (IX 362–3, 369–72)

Thus Marian discovers her separate identity: she is no longer just the passive worshipper or victim of men. The female fear of self-annihilation through sexual relationships with men has been exorcised. We must not, however, overemphasise Marian's independence from men here: she stresses she is only continuing to live for the sake of her son, and it is partly for his sake that she refuses Romney's offer.

Before her refusal, however, she asks Aurora if she should accept. Aurora gives her full support, offering her both Romney, and her own belief in Marian's purity: ' "Accept the gift, I say/My sister Marian" ', ' "Here's my hand/To clasp your hand, my Marian, owned as pure!" ' (IX 255–6, 268–9) The devotion of pure woman to fallen woman could hardly go further than this offer of the man she loves. In return, Marian gives Romney back to her:

> 'Most noble Romney, wed a noble wife,
> And open on each other your great souls –
> I need not farther bless you. If I dared
> But strain and touch her in her upper sphere,
> And say "Come down to Romney – pay my debt!" ' (IX 440–4)

The 'come down' is significant – Aurora has to acquire some of the qualities of the 'low and wise' Marian in order to relate to Romney. In their final scene together, she abases herself to him, and calls herself a failure in denying her love for him for the sake of her poetry: but he too has changed, and he gives her back her independence and power, by his belated admiration for her poetry and support for her vocation. He is also blinded – symbolically, he has lost some of his male power, making the relationship more equal.

Thus finally the contact between the two women results in a realignment, a balancing of qualities that were previously incompatible. Each woman moves away from the extreme – Marian from extreme sexual passivity and vulnerability, and Aurora from her extreme and lonely independence. Marian, while finding strength and belief in herself, retains her maternal devotion to her son; Aurora, while admitting her dependence on Romney, retains her powerful vocation, now fully sanctioned by him.

The resolution of *Adam Bede* is more conventional. Dinah gives up her independence, and is fully assimilated into society as wife of Adam and mother of his children. This transformation is brought about partly by her contact with Hetty – as Nina Auerbach points out, the two women 'drain each other's identities and exchange natures.'[21] While the overt story is one of Dinah's one-sided generosity and love towards Hetty, whom she 'saves', the image patterns suggest a 'covert' story, in which Dinah robs Hetty of those sexual qualities that she lacks, leaving Hetty with her own deathly qualities, and eliminating her from the story. The two extremes of purity and sexuality are now balanced in Dinah, and Hetty is no longer needed. In their first important scene together, in Hetty's bedroom, the two extremes are still widely separated:

> What a strange contrast the two friends made! ... Hetty, her cheeks flushed and her eyes glistening from her imaginary drama, her beautiful neck and arms bare, her hair hanging in a curly tangle down her back, and the baubles in her ears. Dinah, covered with her long white dress, her pale face full of subdued emotion, almost like a lovely corpse into which the soul has returned charged with sublimer secrets and a sublimer love.[22]

But, as Auerbach puts it, 'as an abandoned wanderer [Hetty's] flush will disappear, replaced by an intensifying pallor until she becomes the corpse Dinah resembles here. Correspondingly, Dinah will get rounder and ruddier, finally to marry Hetty's fiancé Adam and discard her Methodist garb.'[23] It is their embrace in the prison that marks the turning-point in this process. Once again, the embrace of two women is necessary before the plot can be resolved in marriage. Dinah is embracing sexual and procreative qualities that were previously eliminated from her life, and her female identity is changed by the contact. Auerbach sees the relationship between the two women as hinting a 'fundamental complicity between purity and fallenness';[24] but I would see it more as a process by which the two socially threatening female qualities of independence and sexuality are toned down, combined, and assimilated in marriage. The fallen woman can only be discarded in this process; while the independent woman picks up from her the sexuality that allows her capitulation to a man.

It is interesting that in both *Aurora Leigh* and *Adam Bede*, the independent woman's problems with sex and marriage are worked out through the contact not with a conventionally married friend, but with a 'fallen' woman. This may be because, in the conventions of Victorian literature, marriage does not seem to involve sex,

though courtship may hint at it. It is only illegitimate babies who
are produced by a sexual act: sex within marriage is a taboo subject.
The relationship with the 'fallen' woman brings out the independent
woman's fears of sex as weakness or as victimisation, fears which are
resolved through an interchange of identities.

If we read *Goblin Market* as a poem about a fallen woman rescued
by a pure woman, it seems to be suggesting an extreme of
sisterly solidarity, of shared identity, beyond anything in *Adam Bede*
or *Aurora Leigh*. The two sisters, Laura and Lizzie, live together in a
manless world. Laura succumbs to the temptations of eating the
forbidden fruits sold by the sinister goblins. Gilbert and Gubar point
out that the loss of the lock of hair that Laura gives to the goblins
can be read as the loss of her virginity, in exchange for the sexual
delights of the goblin fruit.[25] After she has eaten the fruit, Laura
falls into a decline – her fate is already foreshadowed by Jeanie,

> Who should have been a bride;
> But who for joys brides hope to have
> Fell sick and died.

Lizzie determines to save Laura – but not morally, as Dinah saves
Hetty, or financially, as Aurora saves Marian. Instead, she proposes
to go out and get her some more of the fruit for which she hungers,[26]
as the goblins now do not appear to her – they seem to reserve their
temptations for virgins. Lizzie never judges Laura, and Laura never
feels guilt, only 'baulked desire'. Lizzie heroically withstands the
goblins' efforts to make her eat the fruit, despite their violence:

> Though the goblins cuffed and caught her,
> Coaxed and fought her,
> Bullied and besought her
> Scratched her, pinched her black as ink,
> Kicked and knocked her,
> Mauled and mocked her ...

The goblins finally give up and take their fruit away. Lizzie has
retained her virginity – the 'penny' in her purse – and, running home
covered in the juice of the fruits the goblins have been pressing to her
lips, she offers herself to Laura: 'Eat me, drink me.' As sufferer and
rescuer she is not just a Madonna figure: she becomes a female
Christ, as she urges Laura to 'Eat me, drink me' and be saved. While

her spiritual influence can be compared to that of Dinah on Hetty, the effect of her embraces is the opposite. While Dinah gains 'bloom' from her contact with Hetty, and Hetty fades away, Lizzie imparts her own vitality to the fading Laura, and restores her to her former blooming state. Laura is saved and cured – the goblin juices now taste bitter to her, and she recovers. A moral rescue is implied here, though not consciously intended by Lizzie: Laura now sees the sensual delights for which she 'fell' as unwholesome and disgusting, though her 'fall' is still not seen in terms of 'sin'. The physical similarity between the sisters also implies a refusal to judge or condemn Laura, and an assertion of female solidarity. Before Laura's decline the two sisters are not divided into sensual and saintly or intellectual types, as are Hetty/Dinah and Marian/Aurora – they are both fair-haired angels, indistinguishable and inseparable:

> Golden head by golden head,
> Like two pigeons in one nest
> Folded in each other's wings,
> They lay down on the curtained bed:
> Like two blossoms on one stem . . .[27]

After Laura's rescue they return to this happy similarity, and both eventually become wives. The implication is that it is only chance that causes Laura rather than Lizzie to fall, and that Laura retains and can regain her underlying identity with Lizzie; while Lizzie, going out to face the goblins, literally puts herself in Laura's place in order to save her.

Female solidarity is also implied in the all-female world the sisters inhabit after Laura's rescue. It is true that both sisters eventually marry – their story is thus nominally fitted into the conventional narrative progression towards marriage. But the men they marry do not appear as characters in the poem, and the sisters only seem to produce female children, more 'sisters'.[28] Thus, as in *Aurora Leigh*, the fallen woman is reclaimed into a strong female–female manless alliance – but in *Goblin Market* there is no intrusive male lover as the real goal for one of the women, nor a male child as the *raison d'être* of the other. The goblins are the only males in the poem, and there is a strong contrast between their deceitfulness and violence, and the peaceful female world of the sisters. Thus we can read the poem as an extreme affirmation of solidarity between pure and fallen women – though the price for Laura's reintegration and regeneration as a flawless counterpart of the marriageable Lizzie seems to be a complete repression of her sexuality, instead of the pure woman's discovery of sexuality that we have seen in Dinah and Aurora. Lizzie rescues Laura specifically by her own *resistance* to the goblins' sexual temptations, as she stands

> Like a royal virgin town
> Topped with gilded dome and spire
> Close beleaguered by a fleet
> Mad to tug her standard down

In this action, Lizzie resembles characters like Sissy Jupe in Dickens' *Hard Times* or Molly Gibson in Gaskell's *Wives and Daughters*, who go out and brave a sexually powerful man in order to save their sexually-compromised (though *not* 'fallen') friends, Louisa Bounderby and Cynthia Fitzpatrick.[29] By their fearless innocence and asexuality, these heroines abash and defeat the men and save their friends for respectability.

These similarities suggest that it may be oversimplified to read Laura only as a 'fallen woman'. She is perhaps more like a sexually compromised but still redeemable and marriageable woman like Cynthia Fitzpatrick. Unlike the typical fictional fallen woman, Laura does not produce a child as a result of her 'fall', and the imagery of barrenness that attaches to the goblin fruit and its effect suggests that the fruit is an *imaginary* object of desire.[30] While other fallen women bloom into maternity as a result of their sexual encounters, Laura pines and fades from 'baulked desire': she resembles rather a frustrated spinster, able to imagine the sexual delights that she cannot have. As she dwindles and decays, she is like the Princess in Rossetti's *The Prince's Progress*, who fades and dies because the Prince is so slow in arriving. The Princess's decline too is presented in imagery of starvation, just as Laura hungers for the goblins' fruit: 'Her heart was starving all this while/You made it wait.' She too goes grey: 'silvery hairs showed in her locks/That used to be so brown.' Greying hair in Rossetti's poems seems to be always associated with sexual frustration, rather than mere ageing. Thus, the elder sister in 'The Lowest Room' also has grey hair, as opposed to her blonde sister. The elder sister, with her yearnings for an unobtainable Homeric dream-world, is also like Laura with her longings for the goblins' imaginary delights: again, Laura is more like a frustrated spinster than a fallen woman. Similarly, she resembles the spinster-figure in Rossetti's poem 'A Triad', who 'was blue with famine after love', and 'famished died for love', rather than the wife or the mistress.

Laura also resembles the 'starving' spinster-heroines of Charlotte Brontë's novels, in particular, Caroline Helstone in *Shirley*.[31] Caroline has allowed her imagination to become obsessed by her desire for Robert Moore, who, after initially encouraging her, rejects her. She wastes and pines like Laura, metaphorically deprived of 'bread', given a 'stone' instead. Interestingly, she is able to revive their relationship in *imagination*, but this unreal pleasure soon fades and leaves her desolate:

> Robert's features and form were with her; the sound of his voice was quite distinct in her ear; his few caresses seemed renewed. But these joys being hollow, were, ere long, crushed in: the pictures faded, the voice failed, the visionary clasp melted chill from her hand, and where the warm seal of lips had made impress on her forehead, it felt now as if a sleety rain-drop had fallen. She returned from an enchanted region to the real world. . .[32]

Like Laura coming back from this dream world, she is left with 'dim head and colourless tresses'. Later, we learn that she is especially tortured by the recollection that she forced a lock of her hair onto Moore in exchange for one of his own. For a woman to let a man have a lock of her hair undoubtedly has sexual implications,[33] but what it seems to mean here is that Caroline has compromised herself by revealing her desire for Moore, by showing her sexual availability before she was sure of him. The idea that a woman is betraying herself and her sister women if she reveals or even entertains sexual thoughts about a man before he has committed himself is taken for granted in the book, and explicitly stated by Shirley.[34] It is interesting that a lock of hair is used in a similar way by Jane Austen in *Sense and Sensibility*. Marianne has let Willoughby have a lock of her hair before they are engaged: she has committed and compromised herself. Thus, when he deserts her, she too fades, pines and nearly dies; and one of his worst actions is to write a letter implying that she forced the hair on him.

These parallels suggest that we could read Laura not as a 'fallen

woman', but as a frustrated, imaginative spinster, who has
inexcusably allowed herself to entertain thoughts of sexual delights
with no prospect of fulfilment in reality. Of course, her imaginings
have not been aroused by any particular man – they seem to be
self-generated, with the goblins as male equivalents of Keats'
imaginary 'Belle Dame Sans Merci'.[35] Nevertheless, we could say
that Laura is imaginatively exploring one of the pitfalls of male–
female sexual relationships – not that men may rape her, but that
they may arouse her and then withdraw. If we read Laura as a
character like Caroline Helstone or Marianne Dashwood, this will
obviously have an effect on the way we read her 'rescue' by Lizzie.
Caroline and Marianne are both saved by a sister and a mother.
Shirley leads Caroline into a private, natural world of female
friendship, and Elinor leads Marianne into a calm world of 'sense'
and emotional restraint. Mrs Pryor and Mrs Dashwood provide
Caroline and Marianne with the intense mothering they need to
make up for their emotional losses. The implications are that it is
the love and strength of other women that can save a woman from
the prison of unreciprocated sexual desire.

In *Goblin Market*, Lizzie combines these sister and mother roles.
Like Shirley, she takes Laura back into an all-female world, and like
Elinor she calmly resists the temptations of the imagination, and
demonstrates their 'bitterness' to her sister. She also offers Laura a
maternal physical contact, as she urges her to 'Hug me, kiss me, suck
my juices', and Laura 'kissed and kissed her with a hungry mouth'.
This scene is analogous to the many scenes of maternal cherishing
between female friends, often accompanied by images of
nourishment, that exist in nineteenth-century fiction by women.
The 'female Christ' reading is not inconsistent with this
interpretation: when Miss *Temple* feeds the starving Jane Eyre with
seed-cake, or *Diana* Rivers nourishes her with bread and milk,[36] a
spiritual nourishment from a transcendent female source is implied,
as well as a physical nourishment from a surrogate mother. Of
course, what Laura eats is not nourishing food but 'bitter' goblin
juices. Nevertheless, after the experience she is nourished, in that she
is restored to health, she is no longer 'hungry'. Thus, by her strength
and sustenance, Lizzie saves Laura from her extreme dependency on
men and what she imagines they can provide. Lizzie shows her that
she does not need these fantasies, and that she can survive without
them. The problem here is not, as in *Adam Bede* and *Aurora Leigh*,

how is the independent woman to recognise her sexual needs, but how is a helplessly dependent woman to regain an imaginative independence from her sexual desires.[37]

On the other hand, the price of Laura's rescue is repression, as I have suggested, of sexual desires and imaginative potential. We may feel the same about the subduing of Marianne in *Sense and Sensibility*; and what is remarkable about Shirley and Caroline is that they lead each other into an imaginative world of *female*-centred sexuality and female mythology, from which they can criticise the oppressions of male society.[38] But in *Goblin Market*, Lizzie firmly recuperates Laura for *domesticity*.[39] This is their everyday life, from which Laura falls:

> Neat like bees, as sweet and busy,
> Laura rose with Lizzie:
> Fetched in honey, milked the cows,
> Aired and set to rights the house,
> Kneaded cakes of whitest wheat,
> Cakes for dainty mouths to eat,
> Next churned butter, whipped up cream,
> Fed their poultry, sat and sewed,
> Talked as modest maidens should ...

This is like the world of Lucy Deane or of the younger sister in 'The Lowest Room'; and, like the elder sister, Laura is discontented:

> Lizzie with an open heart,
> Laura in an absent dream,
> One content, one sick in part...

That Lizzie should return Laura to contentment with this domestic world is as if the younger sister were to eliminate the elder sister's longings, or Lucy were to wipe out Maggie's passion and imagination and turn her into a complete replica of herself. Lizzie is the repressive angel-woman ideal, here successfully assimilating the deviant, sexual, imaginative woman.

As in *Mill on the Floss*, the friendship here thus seems both to celebrate female solidarity, and to repress female potentialities. Critics disagree as to which of these interpretations is dominant, whether 'it is ... a poem of bitter repression' or 'a fantasy of feminine freedom and self-sufficiency and a celebration of sisterly

and maternal love'.[40] But these two interpretations reflect the
structure of the conservative ideology of womanhood that Rossetti
shared with other writers such as Mrs Ellis. As we have seen, Mrs
Ellis was a firm believer in the idea of 'woman's sphere': woman
was to exercise moral influence in the home, while man dealt with
the outside world. While repressing women in one way, this
ideology also gives them a new domestic and moral power-base.
Female solidarity played an important part in this ideology,
maintaining the values of 'woman's sphere':

> A circle of young female friends, who love and trust each other, who
> mutually agree to support the weak in their little community, to confirm
> the irresolute, to reclaim the erring, to soothe the irritable, and to solace
> the distressed; what a realisation does this picture present of the brightest
> dreams of imagination, when we think what woman might be to her
> own sex, and to the community at large.[41]

At the end of *Goblin Market*, Laura admonishes her daughters in
strikingly similar terms:

> 'For there is no friend like a sister
> In calm or stormy weather;
> To cheer one on the tedious way,
> To fetch one if one goes astray,
> To lift one if one totters down
> To strengthen while one stands.'

For Rossetti, as for Mrs Ellis, sisterhood is powerful to keep women
in their place, but also to transform that place into a strong female
community.[42] Dorothy Mermin links the poem's vision of an all-
female community of women and children to Rossetti's attraction
to the Anglican sisterhoods – 'The Anglican sisterhoods, like the
central fantasy of *Goblin Market*, satisfied ... the need for a sphere
of significant activity, combined with emotional fulfilment, within
the limits of women's traditional roles.'[43] Thus repression of female
deviancy must coexist with celebrations of women's combined
strength, as functions of the female friendship in *Goblin Market*.

# Chapter Three

# Earnest Women and Heartless Flirts

The fashionable woman who uses her beauty and charm to gain masculine attention usually appears in fiction as the heroine's opponent or even enemy: for instance, Mary Crawford, Blanche Ingram, Lady Waldemar. The heroine's virtue, sincerity and artlessness are defined against these knowing schemers and charmers. It is surprising, therefore, to find a number of novels in which friendships between these two types are important: Lucy and Ginevra in *Villette*, Dorothea and Rosamond in *Middlemarch*, Molly and Cynthia in *Wives and Daughters*, and Marcella and Letty in Mrs Humphry Ward's *Sir George Tressady*. In these novels, the friendship with the flirtatious woman is used to dramatise the heroine's problems with questions of beauty and sexuality in forming her feminine identity. In this case, it is *conscious* beauty, deliberate attractiveness, not the flower-like innocent beauty of the 'angel' woman; and *active*, even predatory sexuality, not the passive, vulnerable sexuality of the fallen woman.

Of course, my categories overlap somewhat here: Hetty Sorrel is clearly a heartless flirt, quite conscious of her attractiveness to men as she poses in front of her mirror. But, unlike Hetty the soon-to-be-fallen woman, the flirts I am concerned with here are socially *successful*: they have the power to manipulate the men they want into marriage. They are not outcasts, but are only too adept at playing social games. This use of beauty and sexuality to manipulate men is a power that the heroines also lack – while it is, of course, the power that gains women any sort of economic or social status in a patriarchal society, this society also requires women to preserve an appearance of angelic innocence and passivity. Thus Victorian heroines are almost always totally unconscious of their feelings for the hero, and drastic coincidences and interventions are required to awaken them. The consciously attractive, manipulative friend may function here as an agent in this awakening, often by acting out the repressed desires of the heroine. This is true to some degree of all the 'flirts' I am discussing here. Just as the fallen woman can awaken the heroine to an acceptance of sexual vulnerability, so the flirtatious woman can awaken or embody her active desire for the man she loves. Thus Rosamond's intervention awakens Dorothea to her feelings for Will, and Cynthia's intervention awakens Molly to her feelings for Roger. Ginevra in her flirting with and her despising of Dr John enacts some of Lucy's feelings for him, and enables Lucy literally to 'act' in the play as a flirtatious *man*, robbing Dr John of Ginevra, paying him back for some of his neglect of Lucy as a woman. Letty provides Marcella's only acceptable route to Sir George – in 'making love' to the wife, she uses all the passionate expression and manipulative charm that Mrs Ward cannot allow her to use towards the husband.

Whilst the heroine can thus take on some of the qualities of the flirt, the contrast between them also enables an otherwise unconventional heroine to take on some of the qualities of the conventionally good, 'angel' woman, and try to 'save' her erring friend. Thus in *Middlemarch* and *Sir George Tressady*, Dorothea and Marcella can be shown as staunch supporters of marital fidelity, going off to 'rescue' their light-minded friends from committing adultery, and reconciling them to their wifely duties. The 'feminine', flirtatious woman, who thinks only of clothes, possessions and men, can be shown up as the real danger to society, while the serious-minded, educated heroine is not the threat she might seem. Mrs Ward in particular seems intent on creating an ungainsayable super-woman in Marcella, who has beauty, intelligence, political power, marital love, male admirers *and* virtue. Marcella and Letty's friendship is clearly an extended and simplified imitation of Dorothea's and Rosamond's:[1] George Eliot is doing something more complex than Mrs Ward. In particular, the scene between Dorothea and Rosamond turns into a *mutual* rescue, unlike the totally one-sided 'saving' of Letty by Marcella's superior moral influence; the 'saving' effect of Dorothea on Rosamond is also more problematic – Rosamond soon reverts to type. A similar disbelief in such conversions appears in *Villette* and *Wives and Daughters* – Lucy and Molly accept Ginevra and Cynthia for what they are – in the former case with humorous cynicism, in the latter, with loving understanding. Molly does 'save' Cynthia from the scandalous consequences of her liaison with Mr Preston, but it is practical, not moral help that Molly gives.

The flirt, of course, always has her own marriage plot. It is part of her character that she makes a socially successful marriage. But her marriage, for rank and/or money, is always contrasted with the heroine's love-match, which is made to seem unconventional by contrast – just as the heroine's marriage is also often contrasted with the sentimental marriage of the 'angel' woman. Again, the women intrude into each other's love-plots – Cynthia, Rosamond and Ginevra carry the heroes away into their world of superficial attractiveness, before giving them back to a more earnest relationship with the heroines; Marcella unwittingly intrudes her earnest relationship with George into Letty's superficial marriage with him, and has to recreate Letty as an earnest woman as well as giving George back to her. In *Middlemarch* and *Wives and Daughters* too, we have this familiar and important device of the female rival giving the man back to his rightful mate.

In this chapter, I concentrate on the female friendships in three novels, *Wives and Daughters*, *Middlemarch* and *Sir George Tressady*. The similarities between *Sir George Tressady* and *Middlemarch* emphasise an important pattern: through her friendship with the flirtatious woman, the earnest heroine, who because of her interests and her exceptionality is more drawn to friendship with men, is led back towards women's traditional roles. A solidarity is discovered between exceptional and 'ordinary' women, within 'women's sphere': here the heroine can demonstrate her acceptability, and discover a position of power. Various strategies are used to contain the revolutionary implications of the friendships, which are presented as remarkably intense and passionate transgressions of social convention. In *Wives and Daughters* female friendship is less exceptional and less momentous; Mrs Gaskell's types are not so starkly polarised, and the society she portrays encompasses a wider range of acceptable female identities. On the other hand, as her types are less extreme, their assimilation to social norms is less problematic.

\* \* \*

Mrs Gaskell's sympathetic treatment of Cynthia's character in
*Wives and Daughters* is unexpected, and has been praised as
something entirely new in fiction.[2] Cynthia is charming,
manipulative, both fickle and indiscreet in her relations with men,
and incapable of love. But this combination of dangerous traits is
presented as the result of her deprivation of maternal love in her
childhood. Not only is the reader led to understand this, but
Cynthia herself has a refreshing self-understanding and, at times,
self-acceptance. She knows her limitations, and that she cannot
change. Our sympathy for her is also helped by the contrast with her
mother, a frivolous, fashionable woman who demonstrates all the
folly and selfishness that Cynthia lacks, without any of Cynthia's
charm and tact. But what most inclines us to like Cynthia is her
usually trusting and mutually supportive friendship with the
heroine, Molly, who is also not a simple stereotype.[3] Since Molly
accepts Cynthia as she is, so do we. It is only through Cynthia's
confidences to the sympathetic Molly that we learn of her loveless
childhood and her self-understanding – an understanding which is
partly brought on by a comparison of her own character and
circumstances to Molly's goodness and love-surrounded existence.

In her presentation of the two women's characters, Mrs Gaskell is
explicitly breaking up and confusing stereotypes. Other characters
refer to Molly as Una and Cynthia as Duessa, but this polarity is
shown to be oversimplified. It is Molly's father, in his emotional
over-reaction to her first admirer, who protests that Molly should be
allowed to move among the young men in his house 'as unharmed as
Una herself' (p. 86).[4] Mr Gibson is being unrealistic in his
expectation of perpetual purity and innocence in Molly. Towards
the end of the book, Roger Hamley, now Cynthia's rejected lover,
calls her a 'false Duessa', in contrast to Molly, whom he is now
beginning to love (p. 699). Again, this is an emotional over-
reaction: Mr Gibson, wiser by now, replies 'Come, come! Cynthia
isn't so bad as that. She's a very fascinating, faulty creature' (p.
700). Mrs Gaskell varies and complicates the standard characteristics of the flirtatious woman in her portrayal of Cynthia. Cynthia
knows that she is beautiful, but that very awareness makes her
behave *un*selfconsciously: 'Cynthia was very beautiful, and was so
well aware of the fact that she had forgotten to care about it; no one
with such loveliness ever appeared so little conscious of it. Molly
would watch her perpetually as she went about the room, with the

free stately step of some wild animal of the forest' (p. 255). Cynthia
is not, like Rosamond Vincy, an accomplished *actress* – she is here
associated with Nature, not art. The 'wild animal' image alerts us to
her sexuality, and also to a certian *anti*-social element in her. As she
later says to Molly, ' "I have grown up outside the pale of duty and
'oughts'. Love me as I am, sweet one, for I shall never be better" ' (p.
261). There is thus much in the presentation of Cynthia's character
that approximates her to a rebellious, unconventional woman like
Maggie Tulliver.[5] She compares herself to the 'good' Molly as
Maggie compared herself to the 'good' Lucy:

> 'Nonsense, Molly! You are good. At least, if you're not good, what
> am I? There's a rule-of-three sum for you to do! But it's no use talking; I
> am not good, and I never shall be now. Perhaps I might be a heroine still,
> but I shall never be a good woman, I know.'
> 'Do you think it easier to be a heroine?'
> 'Yes, as far as one knows of heroines from history. I'm capable of a
> great jerk, an effort, and then a relaxation – but steady, everyday
> goodness is beyond me.' (p. 258)

Like Cynthia, Maggie also can only be 'good' in short bursts of
heroism; and both women briefly 'steal' the lovers of their 'good'
friends. They are both disruptive characters.

On the other hand, other Maggie-like qualities are given to
Molly. Molly's appearance is rough, dark and unfashionable, like
Maggie's – only in her case it is curly hair, not straight hair, that is
objected to by her fashion-conscious step-mother: ' "And as for your
hair! it's worse than ever. Can't you drench it in water to take those
untidy twists and twirls out of it?" ' (p. 496). Molly also behaves in
tomboyish ways:

> 'I don't think you would have called Molly a lady the other day, Miss
> Browning, if you had found her where I did: sitting up in a cherry-tree,
> six feet from the ground at least, I do assure you.'
> 'Oh! but that wasn't pretty,' said Miss Browning, shaking her head at
> Molly. 'I thought you'd left off those tom-boy ways.' (p.276)

Like Maggie too, Molly has passionate feelings: 'She had often
been called naughty and passionate when she was a child; and she
thought now that she began to understand that she really had a
violent temper' (p. 356). Molly's anger here at her step-mother's

insulting treatment of Roger Hamley is, of course, caused by her unacknowledged love for him. Cynthia lacks this capacity for passionate feeling, either anger or love – this is what differentiates her from Maggie and Molly, and makes her like Rosamond, Ginevra and Letty. Like other flirts, Cynthia is very concerned with and expert at the art of dress – 'With regard to dress, Cynthia soon showed that she was her mother's own daughter in the manner in which she could use her deft and nimble fingers' (p. 255). Yet again this touch of artifice is presented as a 'natural' grace or talent, and we learn that Cynthia 'was generally dressed with careless grace', while it is Molly 'who was delicate neatness itself' (p. 277), despite her alleged 'tomboy ways'.

Thus Mrs Gaskell breaks up and reconstructs in Cynthia and Molly elements of more polarised types like Maggie and Lucy. Part of the effect of this is to make the disruptive tendencies represented by a heroine like Maggie less threatening, more assimilable. Molly's tomboyish wildness and passionate feelings are tempered by the neatness and dutifulness of a Lucy; Cynthia's disruptive sexual charm is tempered by her lack of deep feeling, and her respect for appearances: in the end, a non-passionate marriage to a man of the right status and appearance, is what she really wants. But, on the other hand, the combination of characteristics in the two women, and their friendship, also mean that Mrs Gaskell can present a much greater range of acceptable female behaviour within the limits of society. There is no one deadly standard of insipid female goodness to which women have to try to conform.

The presentation of the women's characters and their friendship in *Wives and Daughters* contrasts markedly with the much simpler treatment of women friends in Mrs Gaskell's earlier novels. In both *Mary Barton* and *Sylvia's Lovers*, we have the central heroine flanked by a bad, flirtatious friend (Sally, Molly) and a good, earnest friend (Margaret, Hester). As the heroine becomes a better woman, she switches her allegiance from the bad friend to the good friend. Each friendship works simply as a moral influence and a moral indicator. Molly and Cynthia's friendship has no such simple significance. Molly does not influence or change Cynthia, though she does help her to evade some of the worst consequences of her actions; neither does friendship with Cynthia degrade Molly, though she is falsely suspected of Cynthia's own sexual indiscretion because of her attempts to help Cynthia recover her letters from Mr Preston.

Here, Molly takes on Cynthia's role as a sexually compromised woman, but only in order to save her: the pattern is reminiscent of Lizzie's saving of Laura in Christina Rossetti's *Goblin Market*. Molly faces and vanquishes Mr Preston as Lizzie faces and vanquishes the goblins: in both cases the virtuous woman braves a sexual situation undefiled, and returns with what will save her sister. The difference is, of course, that Molly is saving Cynthia's reputation, not her soul or her virtue. As Molly briefly takes on Cynthia's role in order to help her, so Cynthia takes on Molly's role as the lover of the earnest Roger Hamley. But both these roles are miscast – Molly's virtue is revealed; and Cynthia realises the inappropriateness of Roger for her: both women revert to type. Cynthia's playing of Molly's part here, however, also inadvertently helps her friend, forcing Molly gradually to become aware of her true feelings for Roger, whom she had previously thought of only as a brother. Thus the two women do operate to assimilate each other into acceptable marriages – Molly saves Cynthia for respectability and Mr Henderson, and Cynthia both arouses Molly's feelings for Roger, and puts her through various tests of her virtue, which show her to be the best wife for him.

Molly and Cynthia's friendship has an interesting structural parallel in the friendship between the brothers Osborne and Roger Hamley. Here, as with the women, we have a charming but morally weak friend, and a plain, awkward, morally strong friend. Roger supports and helps Osborne with the problem of his secret marriage, as Molly helps Cynthia with the problem of her secret relationship. Men, it seems, can be as devoted as women; but what is interesting is that in order for this friendship to be plausible, one of the friends must be presented as a *feminised* man: as the Squire says, Osborne is ' "always in his element talking to women. I sometimes think he's half a woman himself, he spends so much money and is so unreasonable" ' (pp. 438–9). This is not just the Squire's prejudice: the narrator remarks, 'Osborne, on the contrary, was, what is commonly called "fine"; delicate almost to effeminacy in dress and manner; careful in small observances' (p. 288). The closeness of his friendship with Roger is attributed to this 'effeminacy': 'When Roger came home Osborne did not let a day pass before telling his brother of his plans. He never did conceal anything long from Roger; the feminine part of his character made him always desirous of a confidant, and as sweet sympathy as he could extract' (p. 301). It is

only when one of the partners is thus feminised that a relationship
between men can show some of the closeness and tenderness of a
relationship between women – though Osborne and Roger's
friendship has none of the *physical* closeness and maternal intensity
of Molly and Cynthia's. The two men are also less involved with
each other's lives: they are not rivals for the same woman, and they
do not take on each other's identities or change the direction of each
other's plot.

When Cynthia first appears in Molly's life, the instantaneous
welcome Molly gives her, and the immediate friendship that is
formed, are both striking. As in *Aurora Leigh*, two mother-deprived
women form an immediate and necessary bond. Molly is in love
with the *idea* of Cynthia, even before she meets her: 'Was Cynthia
coming at last? Oh, what a pleasure it would be to have a
companion, a girl, a sister of her own age!' (p. 250). Molly's delight
at this idea contrasts strongly with her immediate *dismay* at the
early news of her father's intention to remarry. A step-mother can
only be a repellent idea to Molly, an intruder into her loving
relationship with her father. But while Mrs Gibson arrives as a
persecutor and hindrance to Molly, Cynthia arrives as a rescuer: an
equal companion who will relieve Molly's isolation, deprived as she
is now of mother and of father. Cynthia also turns out to be an ally
*against* Mrs Gibson, giving voice to Molly's suppressed feelings of
dislike for her step-mother: Cynthia 'was a most sympathetic
listener to all Molly's innocent confidences of joys and sorrows,
sympathising even to the extent of wondering how she could endure
Mr Gibson's second marriage, and why she did not take some active
steps of rebellion' (p. 260). While Cynthia arrives as a rescuer and
ally in Molly's life, Molly fills a much bigger gap in Cynthia's,
offering a sympathetic love and closeness that Cynthia has never
experienced before:

> I do believe I love you, little Molly, whom I have only known for ten
> days, better than anyone.'
> 'Not than your mother?' said Molly, in grave astonishment.
> 'Yes, than my mother!' replied Cynthia, half-smiling. 'It's very
> shocking, I daresay; but it is so. Now, don't go and condemn me. I don't
> think love for one's mother quite comes by nature; and remember how
> much I have been separated from mine!...'
> '... Somehow, I cannot forgive her for her neglect of me as a child,
> when I would have clung to her.' (pp. 257, 261)

Later, when Cynthia confides her problems with Mr Preston to Molly, Molly takes on an explicitly motherly role towards Cynthia, acting as her protector from unwanted male attention (as Mr Gibson had hoped Mrs Gibson would protect Molly), and as her comforter – the grown-up and accomplished Cynthia suddenly becomes a little child: 'Cynthia began to cry, out of weariness of body and despair of mind. Molly's arms were round her in a minute, and she pressed the beautiful head to her bosom, and laid her own cheek upon it, and hushed her up with lulling words, just as if she were a little child' (p. 524). When Cynthia is depressed after her decision to give up Roger, the scene is repeated: 'She took Cynthia into her arms with gentle power, and laid her head against her own breast, as if the one had been a mother, and the other a child' (p. 602).[6] All this one-sided mothering is rather a strain on Molly, and we notice that she in turn is rescued by Lady Harriet, as Cynthia at this point is incapable of providing reciprocal support.

Cynthia does not often take on a nurturing or protective mother role towards Molly, but we could see her as representing the mother as sexually attractive, mature woman. It is interesting that just before the first occasion when Molly takes Cynthia into her arms as a child, Cynthia has appeared strangely 'aged and careworn' (p. 517), a woman of experience. Just as Molly cannot keep up her strong, protective mother role, but needs further mothering from Lady Harriet, so Cynthia cannot keep up her woman-of-the-world role, and collapses into a little child. Each woman is trying out her grown-up roles. It is as beautiful, charming, implicitly sexual woman that Cynthia first attracts Molly. On first meeting, 'Molly was absorbed in the contemplation of Cynthia's beauty.... Molly fell in love with her, so to speak, on the instant' (p. 253). It is significant that Cynthia first appears in Molly's life as she reaches adolescence and begins to be attractive to men.[7] Just as Lucy helps with Maggie's 'coming out', so Cynthia helps with Molly's.[8] As I have suggested, it is Cynthia who awakens Molly to the sexual possibilities of her feelings for Roger: 'The short conversation had been very pleasant, and his manner had had just the brotherly kindness of old times; but it was not quite the manner he had to Cynthia; and Molly half thought she would have preferred the latter' (p. 280). Cynthia, by charming Roger, reveals to Molly a new way of relating to him. We could say that Cynthia, in first attracting Roger sexually, is acting out what Molly unconsciously wishes to do. When Roger leaves for Africa, it is the perceptive Cynthia who reads Molly's feelings aright: '"Why Molly!. . . what's the matter with you? One might think you cared for him yourself"' (p. 422). When Cynthia gives up Roger, and Molly 'mothers' her, she repays Molly by correctly predicting '"Molly, Roger will marry you! See if it isn't so!"' (p. 602), thus giving him to her friend, and allowing the plot to resolve itself in a happy marriage.[9]

While Cynthia, at first unawares, forwards Molly's relationship with Roger, she does of course also act as the main obstacle to that relationship for about half the book. As I have said, she first appears as a rescuer in Molly's life, a companion who mitigates the isolation brought on by her father's second marriage, an ally against the step-mother. But she also introduces problems and trials into Molly's life, and into the plot, that were not there before. These trials are connected with sexuality – Molly's virtue is tried in the confrontation with Mr Preston, and in extricating Cynthia from that relationship, and tried again in her pain over Cynthia's relationship with Roger. Both these trials are caused by Cynthia's sexual allure. Cynthia is the means of confronting the heroine with the dangers of female sexuality. Cynthia's collapse into a little child during the Mr Preston incident, and her eventual handover of Roger to Molly, signify the capitulation of beauty to goodness, the superior strength and worth of Molly's virtue. On the other hand, Cynthia suffers no permanent eclipse or conversion, and bounces back to marry Mr Henderson, and to remain Molly's friend. In fact, rather than being 'converted' by Molly, Cynthia undergoes a slight revulsion from the pressure of Molly's extreme goodness – she becomes temporarily alienated from Molly when she is concealing her troubles about Mr Preston, and again after she has revealed them and feels she has fallen in Molly's estimation. But after a brief trip to London, the friendship is restored as soon as Cynthia comes back:

If Molly had thought her manner of departure was scarcely as affectionate and considerate as it might have been – if such a thought had crossed Molly's fancy for an instant, she was repentant for it as soon as ever Cynthia returned, and the girls stood face to face, with all the old familiar affection, going upstairs to the drawing room with their arms round each other's waists, and sitting there together hand in hand. (pp. 585–6)

The trials Cynthia puts Molly through are not only trials of her virtue, they are also trials of her love and loyalty to Cynthia as a female friend. Though Cynthia's relationship with Roger arouses the possibility of jealousy between the two friends, values of female loyalty are continually affirmed: 'Now Molly's love for Cynthia was fast and unwavering, but if anything tried it, it was the habit Roger had fallen into of always calling Cynthia Molly's sister' (p. 355). As we saw, it is Cynthia who eventually presents Roger to Molly; this operates as a kind of reward for Molly's earlier, unselfish, giving up of Roger to Cynthia:

> As long as Roger was drawn to Cynthia, and sought her of his own accord, it had been a sore pain and bewilderment to Molly's heart; but it was a straightforward attraction, and one which Molly acknowledged, in her humility and great power of loving, to be the most natural thing in the world. She would look at Cynthia's beauty and grace, and feel as if no one could resist it. (p. 389)

Molly's admiration for Cynthia's beauty and charm is unreserved – she does not devalue it as Lucy does Ginevra's or Jane Eyre does Blanche Ingram's. Cynthia, in return, generously uses her art to transfer some of her attractiveness to Molly: 'She brought down her pretty artificial flowers, plucked out of her own best bonnet to put into Molly's, saying they would suit her complexion, and that a knot of ribbons would do well enough for her' (p. 259). This is like Lucy Deane's delight in dressing up Maggie. We know that Molly herself has an appalling dress-sense, as witness her choice of the dreadful plaid gown to wear on her first visit to the Hamleys. It is Cynthia who enlivens grown-up occasions like going to a ball for Molly, as Molly tells Roger:

> 'You will enjoy it very much – going together?'
> For the first time during this little conversation she glanced up at him – real honest pleasure shining out of her eyes.
> 'Yes, going together will make the enjoyment of the thing. It would be dull without her.' (p. 309)

While Molly does not devalue Cynthia's attractiveness, the narrator does sound a warning note. Molly, on their first meeting, is described as 'captivated' by Cynthia's 'unconscious power of fascination' – 'A woman will have this charm, not only over men

but over her own sex; it cannot be defined, or rather, it is so delicate
a mixture of many gifts and qualities that it is impossible to decide
on the proportions of each. Perhaps it is incompatible with very high
principle' (p. 254). This raises the possibility that Molly has been
*duped* by Cynthia, but interestingly, this possibility is not
developed. We never feel that Molly's love for and loyalty to
Cynthia is wrong-headed, and she is never disillusioned about
Cynthia in the way Cynthia's male admirer, Roger, is. Nor do we
feel that Cynthia does not really value and love Molly: her
friendship with Molly seems to be her sole genuine and deep
relationship. Molly's loyalty to and solidarity with Cynthia goes to
extreme lengths. When Cynthia has revealed to Molly the truth
about her relationship with Mr Preston, and Molly has tried to help,
Cynthia accuses Molly of secretly judging and criticising her –
Cynthia is afraid she has now fallen in Molly's estimation. Molly
breaks down in tears at these accusations, and Cynthia is filled with
remorse:

> '. . . I know it is the truth, and I deserve it – but I need not reproach
> you.'
> 'You did not reproach me!' said Molly, trying to smile. 'I have
> thought something of what you said – but I do love you dearly – dearly,
> Cynthia – I should have done just the same as you did.' (p. 535)

Cynthia replies, 'No, you would not. Your grain is different,
somehow', and this corresponds to what we know of Molly. But
nevertheless, Molly's avowal of complete identification with
Cynthia here is striking. Instead of the 'good' woman reproaching
and trying to reform the erring woman, Molly offers practical help,
uncritical love (whatever unspoken criticisms she may have made),
and a sympathetic identification with Cynthia's actions and
problems. As I have said, this help and identification goes so far as
Molly taking on herself the gossip and scandal that should rightly
attach to Cynthia. She uses her purity and innocence in Cynthia's
service. It is her lack of sexual awareness that disarms Mr Preston,
and defuses the sexual situation between him and Cynthia:

> There [Molly] stood, frightened, yet brave, not letting go her hold on
> what she meant to do, even when things seemed most against her; and
> besides, there was something that struck him most of all perhaps, and
> which shows the kind of man he was – he perceived that Molly was as

unconscious that he was a young man, and she a young woman, as if she had been a pure angel of heaven. (p. 533)

This scene is reminiscent of Sissy Jupe braving and defeating James Harthouse, to protect Louisa Gradgrind in Dickens' *Hard Times*, as well as of *Goblin Market*. The pure woman protects her sexually indiscreet sister from the male sexual threat. Molly helps Cynthia to be more reputable, while Cynthia, unawares, helps Molly to be more sexual in her feelings for Roger.

Cynthia also, however, gives some more conscious proofs of reciprocal loyalty to Molly. When Molly falls ill, having worn herself out in coping with the problems of the Hamley family, Cynthia returns unexpectedly from London as soon as she hears of Molly's illness: ' "I never knew Molly had been so ill, or I would have come directly." Her eyes were full of tears. Mr Gibson was touched; he shook her hand again, and murmured, "You are a good girl, Cynthia" ' (p. 640). The friendship with Molly allows Cynthia to display a 'goodness' that is not evident in her dealings with men. Cynthia now takes on, in her own fashion, a quasi-maternal, nurturing role towards Molly – she uses her charm and tact to revive the invalid:

Cynthia's tact made her talkative or silent, gay or grave, as the varying humour of Molly required. She listened, too, with the semblance, if not the reality, of unwearied interest, to Molly's continual recurrence to all the time of distress and sorrow at Hamley Hall.... Cynthia instinctively knew that the repetition of all these painful recollections would ease the oppressed memory ... (p. 641)

Earlier, she has offered a similar tactful sympathy when Mrs Hamley died: 'Cynthia came softly in, and taking Molly's listless hand, that hung down by her side, sat at her feet on the rug, chafing her chilly fingers without speaking. The tender action thawed the tears that had been gathering heavily at Molly's heart, and they came dropping down her cheeks' (p. 256). Cynthia's tenderness and concern for Molly finally reconcile Lady Harriet, Molly's other friend, to her – again, the action of taking Molly's hand is significant:

But when she heard her mother quickly recapitulating all the details of the plan for Molly, Cynthia's eyes did sparkle with gladness; and almost to Lady Harriet's surprise, she thanked her as if she had conferred a personal favour upon her. Lady Harriet saw, too, that, in a very quiet way, she had taken Molly's hand, and was holding it all the time, as if loath to think of their approaching separation – somehow, she and Lady Harriet were brought nearer together by this little action than they had ever been before. (p. 667)

This sympathetic and affectionate hand-holding typifies Cynthia's attachment to Molly – it is not as intense as Molly's maternal embraces of Cynthia, more a gesture of sisterly sympathy and attachment.

Unlike the female friendships in *Aurora Leigh* and *Mill on the Floss*, the sisterly loyalty between Molly and Cynthia is not seen as an isolated instance against a background of inter-female rivalry and betrayal. Molly has what Jacqueline and Laura Berke call 'a whole constellation of deeply concerned, warmly affectionate mother-surrogates',[10] including Lady Harriet, Mrs Hamley and the two Miss Brownings. In fact, Mrs Gibson's unsympathetic mothering of both Cynthia and Molly is the exception. Molly's friendship with Lady Harriet is an interesting inter-class relationship, with Molly bravely criticising Lady Harriet for her impertinent attitude to the classes below her – ' "your ladyship keeps speaking of the sort of – the class of people to which I belong as if it was a kind of strange animal you were talking about" ' (p. 196). Lady Harriet provides a strong and positive image of a single woman[11] – she has recently annoyed her parents by refusing a suitable match. She and Molly are alike in their honesty and directness of speech: on their first meeting they are also united in a dislike of Mr Preston and his familiar ways. Lady Harriet here voices some of Molly's misgivings. It is significant that later it is Lady Harriet who rescues Molly from the imputation of a clandestine relationship with Mr Preston – she brings the truth to light, and squashes the rumours by her patronage of Molly. She represents the strong singleness that can deal with sexual threats like Mr Preston, and which Molly too manifests in her scenes with him. The Miss Brownings, unlike Lady Harriet, believe the rumours about Molly, and take it on themselves to upbraid her. While Lady Harriet takes on a supportive maternal function in relation to Molly, the Miss Brownings take on the maternal role of guardian of morals. But what is interesting is that the female gossip about and disapproval of Molly is not treated with the sort of scorn and anger that George Eliot uses for a similar situation in *The Mill on the Floss*. These women are not hypocritical betrayers of their sex; they are rightly concerned about Molly's morals. When misunderstandings have been righted, Molly is quickly reinstated in their esteem. Mrs Gaskell is much more accepting of the female social world than was George Eliot. The standards of female behaviour are not oppressive to her.[12] This is reflected in the large tolerance and essentially unproblematic nature of Molly and Cynthia's friendship. The friendship of these two types, whom we might suppose to be enemies, takes place *within* society, not outside, it, or during some temporary suspension of social rules, as with Aurora and Marian, or Dorothea and Rosamond, or Dinah and Hetty.

George Eliot's and Mrs Ward's flirtatious women are much more typical than Cynthia; and female friendship is presented in *Middlemarch* and *Sir George Tressady* as much more rare and difficult than it is in *Wives and Daughters*. Rosamond and Letty, the flirts, are by definition hostile or indifferent to other women, directing their behaviour exclusively to gain male attention. The earnest women, Dorothea and Marcella, are more exceptional and gifted than Mrs Gaskell's Molly, and they too thus have reasons for preferring male company and finding friendship with 'ordinary' women unsatisfactory or difficult. For friendship to take place between these two types of women, they both have to change their perspectives: the friendship is a hard-won and climactic breakthrough. Nevertheless, the female solidarity demonstrated in the friendships is contained within a narrative centring on marriage – and in both novels, the purpose of the friendship is for the earnest woman to 'convert' the flirt into a good wife, thereby demonstrating her own moral superiority and social acceptability. In *Middlemarch*, the power and intensity of the friendship between the two women is further contained by being presented as a totally exceptional occurrence, a necessarily temporary lifting of social conventions and restrictions.

Dorothea and Rosamond can hardly be called friends: they only meet three times in *Middlemarch*: nevertheless, they share one of the most intense and emotional scenes of female friendship in Victorian literature. Though they met so seldom, they are continually compared together by the narrator and by other characters, but entirely for the purpose of presenting them as opposing types of womanhood. A man's moral worth is measured by which one he prefers: Lydgate at first makes the wrong choice, preferring Rosamond, but he comes to revise this judgement of their relative worth; Ladislaw is always sure which of the two is most valuable. On first meeting Dorothea, Lydgate thinks '"She is a good creature – that fine girl – but a little too earnest. . . . It is troublesome to talk to such women"' (p. 119).[13] He is 'already conscious of being fascinated by a woman strikingly different from Miss Brooke' – Rosamond, whom he thinks '"is grace itself: she is perfectly lovely and accomplished. That is what a woman ought to be"' (p. 121). The narrator remarks ominously that he 'might possibly have experience before him which would modify his opinion as to the most excellent things in woman' (p. 120), and, as predicted, by the end of the book he sees in Dorothea '"a heart large enough for the Virgin Mary"' (p. 826), as she helps to rescue his marriage with the narrow-hearted Rosamond. Earlier, when his marriage troubles begin, he contrasts Rosamond's cold indifference towards him with what he has seen of Dorothea's self-sacrificing devotion to her husband. These comparisons work to assimilate Dorothea, the unusual, gifted woman, to social norms – Rosamond *appears* to be the socially acceptable 'angel' woman, but really, we are shown, it is Dorothea who has the 'angelic' qualities of self-sacrifice, devotion to wifely duty, and maternal sympathy.

Gilbert and Gubar argue ingeniously that, despite the overt contrast between the two women, there is a sub-text that links them in a subversive complicity.[14] Rosamond, in her stealthy but stubborn defiance of Lydgate, enacts the anger Dorothea would not allow herself to express against her 'marriage of death' with Casaubon. According to Gilbert and Gubar, there is a husband-killing rage at work in *Middlemarch* – the actress Laure literally kills the husband who bores her; Rosamond metaphorically flourishes on the murder of Lydgate's brains, and he appropriately dies young, freeing her for a second marriage; Dorothea suppresses her anger against Casaubon, and is ready to sacrifice her life to him – but this behaviour is quickly rewarded by the plot killing off Casaubon. However, this secret complicity is very heavily disguised – both the narrator and Lydgate give strong emphasis to the contrast between Dorothea's wifely submissiveness and attempts to rescue her mistaken marriage, and Rosamond's narrow selfishness as she works to wreck hers. The two women's complicity in anti-male anger also does not affect their interaction – we never see Dorothea actually taking on any of Rosamond's qualities of resistance and opposition, as, for instance, Dinah took on Hetty's sexual qualities. What does happen is that Rosamond, briefly, takes on some of Dorothea's qualities of goodness and self-sacrifice. What Dorothea takes from Rosamond is an increased awareness of the sexual element in her relationship with Will – two of their meetings operate to awaken her in this way. Here we could say that Rosamond, in exerting herself to charm Will, is enacting Dorothea's secret wishes, as well as forwarding the relationship by the crisis she provokes.

The two women are first compared by Mr Chichely, at the party in Chapter 10. Mr Standish has called Dorothea '" an uncommonly fine woman"', and Mr Chichely replies,

> 'Yes, but not my style of woman: I like a woman who lays herself out a little more to please us. There should be a little filigree about a woman – something of the coquette. . .'
> . . .'And I like them blonde, with a certain gait and a swan neck. Between ourselves, the mayor's daughter is more to my taste than Miss Brooke or Miss Celia either.' (p. 115)

Rosamond is here presented as a typical flirt. Mrs Ellis, writing on female friendship in *The Daughters of England*, defines flirtation as 'all that part of the behaviour of women, which, in the art of pleasing, has reference only to men'. More particularly, it can be detected when 'the bland and beaming smile is put on for the occasion; when expressive looks are interchanged; when glittering curls are studiously displayed; when songs are impressively sung.'[15] All this we can recognise in Rosamond's later behaviour towards Lydgate. Interestingly, Mrs Ellis sees this sort of behaviour as one of the greatest threats to female friendship – a test of a flirt is to see 'whether, in mixed society, she is the same to women as to men':

> . . .I have often seen a drooping countenance suddenly grow animated, an oppressive headache suddenly removed, and many other symptoms of an improved state of health and spirits as suddenly exhibited, when the society of ladies has become varied by that of the nobler sex; and never does female friendship receive a deeper insult, than when its claims are thus superseded by those, perhaps, of a mere stranger.[16]

We see something of this neglect of women for men in

Rosamond's scene with Mary Garth at Stonecourt, where
Rosamond is more concerned at adjusting her own appearance in the
mirror, and asking questions about the stranger, Lydgate, than in
attending to Mary's concerns. Once Lydgate is there, her behaviour
changes, and she even simulates friendship with Mary in order to
interest him:

> Nothing escaped Lydgate in Rosamond's graceful behaviour: how
> delicately she waived the notice which the old man's want of taste had
> thrust upon her by a quiet gravity, not showing her dimples on the
> wrong occasion, but showing them afterwards in speaking to Mary, to
> whom she addressed herself with so much good-natured interest, that
> Lydgate, after quickly examining Mary more fully than he had done
> before, saw an adorable kindness in Rosamond's eyes. But Mary from
> some cause looked rather out of temper. (p. 144)

Soon after this the narrator comments damningly, 'Every nerve and
muscle in Rosamond was adjusted to the consciousness that she was
being looked at' (p. 144). As we have seen, this self-consciousness is
absent from Cynthia's character in *Wives and Daughters*; and
Cynthia also charms men *and* women equally: 'She exerted herself
just as much to charm the two Miss Brownings as she would have
done to delight Osborne Hamley, or any other young heir. That is to
say, she used no exertion, but simply followed her own nature,
which was to attract everyone of those she was thrown amongst' (p.
261). This equality of treatment means Cynthia is, in Mrs Ellis'
terms, less of a threat to female friendship than the typical flirt.
    Rosamond's combination of self-conscious acting to please men,
and corresponding disregard of women and the claims of female
friendship, is also seen in Gwendolen Harleth, heroine of *Daniel
Deronda*:

> In the ladies' dining-room it was evident that Gwendolen was not a
> general favourite with her own sex; there were no beginnings of intimacy
> between her and other girls, and in conversation they rather noticed what
> she said than spoke to her in free exchange. Perhaps it was that she was
> not much interested in them, and when left alone in their company had a
> sense of empty benches. Mrs Vulcany once remarked that Miss Harleth
> was too fond of the gentlemen; but we know that she was not in the
> least fond of them – she was only fond of their homage – and women
> did not give her homage.[17]

Louise Bernikow, in her book on female friendship, *Among Women*, takes this passage as an example of the typical nineteenth-century attitude to female friendship, showing that women alone together are always presented as waiting for men to arrive to initiate any significant interaction.[18] But this interpretation ignores the implicit criticism of Gwendolen's attitude in the passage. 'Empty *benches*' especially implies that Gwendolen's social behaviour is always, like Rosamond's, a theatrical *performance* for a male audience. Her inability to relate to women is one sign of what is wrong with her character. George Eliot in her novels shares with Mrs Ellis a disapproval of female behaviour exclusively directed towards attracting men. On the other hand, George Eliot spoke of her own preference for the company of men to that of women[19] – presumably, it was men as intellectual companions, rather than as admirers of her charm, that she meant. Similarly, in *Middlemarch*, one of Dorothea's unusual attributes is that she can be *friends* with men – Sir James Chettam finds himself enjoying with her that 'frank kindness and companionship between a man and a woman who have no passion to hide or confess' (p. 97), and Lydgate remarks to himself, ' "She seems to have what I never saw in any woman before – a fountain of friendship towards men – a man can make a friend of her" ' (p. 826). Here, George Eliot differs from Mrs Ellis, who insists that women's 'best friends, as friends only, will ever be found amongst their own sex. There is but one relation in life in which any of the men whom they meet with in mixed society can be anything to them.'[20]

Thus both Rosamond and Dorothea would seem to have reasons for preferring male to female company – Rosamond because she wants admiration, and Dorothea because she wants intellectual companionship. Though we are told of Rosamond and Mary's friendship, after the scene at Stonecourt we never see them together again. Rosamond's usual relationship with other women is typified by the scene in which her aunt comes to warn and advise her about her flirtation with Lydgate. Her aunt's visit is directed solely by considerations of propriety, not by any real care for Rosamond, and Rosamond is hostile to such interference. The two women are mainly interested in each other's clothes:

Nevertheless, the quilling inside Rosamond's bonnet was so charming that it was impossible not to desire the same kind of thing for Kate, and

Mrs. Bulstrode's eyes, which were rather fine, rolled round that ample
quilled circuit, while she spoke.
    'I have just heard something about you that has surprised me very
much, Rosamond.'
    'What is that, aunt?' Rosamond's eyes also were roaming over her
aunt's large embroidered collar. (p. 330)

Relationships between women in Middlemarch are largely of this
sort: there is no supportive, a maternal female community as in
*Wives and Daughters*. Mrs Bulstrode appears in this scene as the
voice of the sort of female public opinion that was castigated in *Mill
on the Floss*. Rosamond's initial reactions to Dorothea are governed
by superficial or conventional considerations: she cannot be
impressed by Dorothea's unfashionable clothes, but she *is* impressed
by her rank and possessions, as one of the 'county divinities' (p.
470), and as 'mistress of Lowick Manor with a husband likely to die
soon' (p. 327). When Dorothea comes to 'save' Rosamond,
Rosamond can only at first take the conventional view and think of
her as a hostile female rival who has come to triumph over her.
    Dorothea, unlike Rosamond, does have a close, continuing female
friendship, with her sister Celia. Celia, with her practical common-
sense, serves as a contrast to Dorothea's idealism, bringing her down
to earth. But Celia's lack of vision, and her acceptance of her
conventional destiny as Sir James's wife, also function as the norm
from which Dorothea understandably deviates. Celia's devotion to
her baby may be pretty, but eventually it becomes boring to
Dorothea, who longs to get away and involve herself in more active
concerns. The friendship with Celia pulls Dorothea back into the
conventional female world of 'mothering' – the way forward seems
to lie in the men's world of thought and action. This ideal of male
intellectual companionship is of course proved delusive in her
marriage to Casaubon; but we see Dorothea forming strong,
practical alliances with Sir James, Lydgate and Caleb Garth. Her
relationship with Will begins in discussions of life and art, and ends
with her supporting his political career. No woman in the book
offers Dorothea the sort of interesting or active companionship she
gets from some of the men; on the other hand, no other relationship,
not even that with Will, offers the emotionalism, intensity and
physical closeness of her last meeting with Rosamond.
    When Dorothea first meets Rosamond, the narrator emphasises the
contrast between them, 'a contrast that would certainly have been

striking to a calm observer' (p. 470) – though as the observer is Will, he is too preoccupied with Dorothea to reflect on this contrast. Dorothea's simple, unfashionable clothing associates her with purity, nature, timeless heroism, and saintliness:

> Let those who know, tell us exactly what stuff it was that Dorothea wore in those days of mild autumn – that thin white woollen stuff soft to the touch and soft to the eye. It always seemed to have been lately washed, and to smell of the sweet hedges – was always in the shape of a pelisse with sleeves hanging all out of the fashion. Yet if she had entered before a still audience as Imogene or Cato's daughter, the dress might have seemed right enough: the grace and dignity were in her limbs and neck; and about her simply parted hair and candid eyes the large round poke which was then in the fate of women, seemed no more odd as a head-dress than the gold trencher we call a halo. (p. 470)[21]

Here, the associations of the 'angel' woman are skilfully combined with the heroic or mythic associations of her usually rebellious counterpart – the elder sister in 'The Lowest Room', or Maggie in *The Mill on the Floss*. Rosamond's appearance, by contrast, is merely expensive and fashionable, and associates her with artifice and trivial social pretension:

> They were both tall, and their eyes were on a level; but imagine Rosamond's infantine blondness and wondrous crown of hair-plaits, with her pale-blue dress of a fit and fashion so perfect that no dressmaker could look at it without emotion, a large embroidered collar which it was to be hoped all beholders would know the price of, her small hands duly set off with rings, and that controlled self-consciousness of manner which is the expensive substitute for simplicity. (pp. 470–1)

In their climactic scene together, Dorothea's naturalness is to break through Rosamond's social conventionality, and take her briefly into Dorothea's realm of heroic action.

But in this scene, something of the opposite happens, some of Rosamond's self-consciousness and social awareness is transferred to Dorothea, who loses some of her innocence in regard to Will, and becomes more aware of how their relationship might look to outsiders. Dorothea has just interrupted Rosamond and Will together, making music – she leaves with a feeling of 'vague discomfort':

Now that she was alone in her drive, she heard the notes of the man's voice and the accompanying piano, which she had not noted much at the time, returning on her inward sense; and she found herself thinking with some wonder that Will Ladislaw was passing his time with Mrs. Lydgate in her husband's absence. And then she could not help remembering that he had passed some time with her under like circumstances, so why should there have been any unfitness in the fact? But Will was Mr Casaubon's relative, and one towards whom she was bound to show kindness. Still, there had been signs which perhaps she ought to have understood as implying that Mr Casaubon did not like his cousin's visits during his own absence. 'Perhaps I have been mistaken in many things,' said poor Dorothea to herself, while the tears came rolling and she had to dry them quickly. She felt confusedly unhappy, and the image of Will which had been so clear to her before was mysteriously spoiled. (p. 472)

Dorothea's next meeting with Rosamond is to be a more intensified replay of this one – she will find Rosamond and Will in an even more explicitly sexually suggestive intimacy. In her reaction this time, she is fully awakened to her own feelings for Will, imagining she has lost him to Rosamond: 'now, with a full consciousness which had never awakened before, she stretched out her arms towards him and cried with bitter cries that their nearness was a parting vision: she discovered her passion to herself in the unshrinking utterance of despair' (p. 844). Rosamond, we know by now, has been consciously plotting to vary the monotony of her marriage by a relationship with Will – doing deliberately what we are to suppose Dorothea once did in all innocence. Rosamond both acts out Dorothea's suppressed desire, and functions as a scapegoat to protect Dorothea's purity: by contrast with Rosamond's manoeuvrings, Dorothea's attitude is childishly innocent. Dorothea finally goes to Rosamond to 'save' her from adultery, to argue for the bonds of marriage, once again exonerating herself from any such imputations about her own relationship with Will. The scenes with Rosamond both make Dorothea more aware of the sexual element in her relationship with Will, and put her through tests of her own purity, so that the contradictory demands of the plot can be met – that the heroine should marry, but that she should also remain innocent.

While Rosamond does thus function as a scapegoat for Dorothea's sexuality, and as an indication, by contrast, of the earnest woman's moral worth and attractiveness, in Dorothea and

Rosamond's final scene together a powerful and valuable bond of
female sympathy and solidarity is created between them. Just as in
*Mill on the Floss*, there is a contradiction between this valuable
solidarity, and the symbolic reading of the friendship, in which one
image of the feminine triumphs over the other. Rosamond may be
wrong to think that Dorothea has come to triumph over her, but the
narrator cannot help reminding us that this is in fact what is
happening – that the scene demonstrates Dorothea's superior
goodness – though Dorothea's goodness consists in her entire
unawareness of any superiority to Rosamond.

Rosamond and Dorothea's final scene together has rightly been
called 'the climax of *Middlemarch*'. Dorothea's overcoming of her
own jealousy, and her outgoing sympathy to Rosamond,
demonstrate her final attainment of the book's moral ideal,
symbolised in her famous 'vision' from her window: 'Far off in the
bending sky was the pearly light; and she felt the largeness of the
world and the manifold wakings of men to labour and endurance.
She was a part of that involuntary palpitating life, and could neither
look out on it from her luxurious shelter as a mere spectator, nor
hide her eyes in selfish complaining' (p. 846). Dorothea has escaped
from the prison of egoism that entraps characters like Casaubon or
Rosamond. Her outgoing is to humanity, not specifically to women
– on the road outside the window she sees both 'a man with a
bundle on his back and a woman carrying her baby'; and her
climactic decision is to suppress her own pain, and 'think of those
three' – Rosamond, Lydgate and Ladislaw. Nevertheless, it is to
Rosamond that she goes: for obvious reasons, she cannot go to betray
Rosamond and Will to Lydgate, and this would also not involve the
sort of heroic self-suppression that sympathy with Rosamond
demands; propriety debars any meeting with Will, the lover who
has, she thinks, rejected her. But, apart from these practical
considerations, it is significant that George Eliot should have chosen
to show the saving operation of sympathy through the influence of
one woman on another. It is true that in the novel we also see
examples of a woman 'saving' a man (Mary Garth and Fred), and a
man 'saving' another man (Mr Farebrother and Fred – and here
self-sacrifice by the 'rescuer' is also involved). But in both these
cases, it is warning and example that operate rather than
sympathetic identification,[22] which is the keynote of Dorothea and
Rosamond's meeting. The situation is also so constructed that

Rosamond is able to reciprocate, to act unselfishly and 'save' Dorothea's relationship with Will by revealing the truth. It is interesting that Dorothea is unable to produce any such effect on Mr Casaubon, another 'narrow' nature with which she comes in contact. The sort of emotional appeal that works with Rosamond only produces repulsion in him – the only moment of tenderness she wins from him is the product of silent waiting. Her self-suppression produces no reciprocation from him, but only a plan to exploit her further. It seems it is only between two women that a sympathetic merging and transformation can occur.

Dorothea's vision of sympathy with common humanity on the road represents an abandonment of her earlier heroic ideals: her marriage has shown her it is impossible to lead an 'epic' life, and has taught her sympathy with the common troubles that arise from social bonds and restrictions. On the other hand, paradoxically, her vision *is* heroic – a new kind of heroism, manifested in what the narrator at the end calls 'unhistoric acts' (p. 896). As the practical manifestation of her vision, Dorothea's outgoing to Rosamond represents both a sympathy with the commonplace social bonds and restrictions of women's lives, and heroic transcendence of social barriers and conventions that usually keep apart women who are rivals, and who are of different classes. As we learnt earlier, Mr Brooke 'would not have chosen that his nieces should meet the daughter of a Middlemarch manufacturer, unless it were on a public occasion' (p. 116). Dorothea herself, however, is usually unaware of class distinctions, but her initial jealousy of Rosamond as a rival is a bigger barrier. In her first reaction, she sees Rosamond as 'the lying woman' in the Judgement of Solomon:

> There were two images – two living forms that tore her heart in two, as if it had been the heart of a mother who seems to see her child divided by the sword, and presses one bleeding half to her breast while her gaze goes forth in agony towards the half which is carried away by the lying woman that has never known the mother's pang. (p. 844)

This describes the point in the Biblical story where the real mother must be imagining ('seems to see') the result of the judgement; what happens next, we know, is that she gives up her claim on the child, in order to save it. This is the resolution Dorothea reaches – by the time she goes to see Rosamond, she has let go of all hope of happiness for herself, and only wants to 'save' everyone concerned. This does not, however, involve giving Will (the baby) to Rosamond (the false mother) – a cynical interpretation of her actions would be that she then goes to make sure her rival also cannot have the man, to take him away from her – though her motives are presented as an entirely unselfish desire to save Lydgate and Rosamond's marriage, and rescue Rosamond from 'the misery of false incompatible bonds' (p. 854). It is interesting that the same Biblical story is used, more orthodoxly, in *Wives and Daughters* to describe Molly's feelings about her rival Cynthia: 'Her constant prayer, "O my lord! Give her the living child, and in no wise slay it," came from a heart as true as that of the real mother in King Solomon's judgement' (p. 460). Molly's concern is all for Roger's safety and happiness – she is afraid he may die in Africa. As we have seen, she surrenders him gladly to her rival. In both novels, true to the Biblical story, the 'real mother' is finally rewarded for her unselfishness and given back her 'baby' – though not by some masculine judge, but by the other woman herself.

Mrs Gaskell leaves the implication that Cynthia is 'the lying woman' unspoken and unchallenged, but Dorothea soon revises her opinion of Rosamond. Her first efforts at unselfishness are directed towards her rival:

Was she alone in that scene? Was it her event only? she forced herself to think of it as bound up with another woman's life ... that base prompting which makes a woman more cruel to a rival than to a faithless lover, could have no strength of recurrence in Dorothea when the dominant spirit of justice within her had once overcome the tumult and had once shown her the truer measure of things. (pp. 845–6)

Dorothea identifies Rosamond not as a rival, but as a woman with a problem whom she can help. It is a short step from this changed perspective to changing the way Rosamond sees her.

Dorothea's approach to Rosamond is both sisterly and motherly, as shown in her opening gesture:

But Dorothea, who had taken off her gloves, from an impulse which she could never resist when she wanted a sense of freedom, came forward, and, with her face full of a sad yet sweet openness, put out her hand. Rosamond could not avoid meeting her glance, could not avoid putting her small hand into Dorothea's which clasped it with gentle motherliness; and immediately a doubt of her own prepossessions began to stir within her. (p. 851)

Dorothea's spontaneity and 'naturalness' reach across whatever artificial barriers lie between the two women – 'The cordial, pleading tones which seemed to flow with generous heedlessness above all the facts which had filled Rosamond's mind as grounds of obstruction and hatred between her and this woman, came as soothingly as a warm stream over her shrinking fears' (p. 852). Dorothea's 'natural' emotion reaches its climax in tones 'like a low cry from some suffering creature in the darkness' (p. 853), and breaks down Rosamond's defences entirely, opening her out to a direct, unselfconscious, emotional encounter: 'When Rosamond's convulsed throat was subsiding into calm, and she withdrew the handkerchief with which she had been hiding her face, her eyes met Dorothea's as helplessly as if they had been blue flowers. What was the use of thinking about behaviour after this crying?' (p. 854). The withdrawing of the handkerchief corresponds to Dorothea's initial removing of her gloves; the 'blue flowers' of Rosamond's eyes correspond to the 'suffering creature' in Dorothea's voice, as images of naturalness, appropriate to each woman's nature. The barriers of convention are down, and the two women meet in a 'natural' place beyond social restrictions.

Nevertheless, it is of social restrictions that Dorothea begins to talk to Rosamond – her message is about the bonds of marriage, not about the liberating influence of female friendship: ' "Marriage is so unlike everything else. There is something even awful in the nearness it brings. Even if we loved someone better than – than those we were married to, it would be no use" ' (p. 855). Dorothea speaks out of her own experience of the awful closeness of marriage, and the new pain of giving up Will – 'filled with the need to express pitying fellowship rather than rebuke, she put her hands on Rosamond's and said with more agitated rapidity – "I know, I know that the feeling may be very dear – it has taken hold of us unawares – it is so hard, it may seem like death to part with it – and we are weak – I am weak –" ' (p. 855). This is like Molly's sympathetic identification with Cynthia – the difference being that Dorothea actually has, at different times, experienced the feelings she is attributing to Rosamond – discontent with her marriage, love for a man she cannot have. From her experience of the restrictions and trials of a woman's life, she can identify with another woman's similar experience – it is their common suffering that brings women together. Mrs Ellis would agree – in *The Women of England*, she attributes the closeness of women's friendship to 'their mutual knowledge of each other's capability of receiving pain'.[23] Mrs Ellis would also approve of the advice Dorothea gives Rosamond – to sacrifice her love, to save her marriage. Women's friendship works to maintain the status quo, to assimilate women safely into marriage. Rosamond, of course, less deliberately, also does this for Dorothea: by revealing the truth, she clears the way for Dorothea's assimilation into marriage with Will.

As Gilbert and Gubar point out, 'While Dorothea goes to save Rosamond by an act of self-sacrifice, Rosamond actually makes the sacrifice and thereby saves Dorothea.'[24] But this reciprocation of Rosamond's is severely undercut throughout the scene – Rosamond is 'taken hold of by an emotion stronger than her own' (p. 856), and even this sympathetic response is undercut by her other motive, anger at Will's reproaches, which have wounded her self-esteem: 'She had begun her confession under the subduing influence of Dorothea's emotion; and as she went on she had gathered the sense that she was repelling Will's reproaches, which were still like a knife-wound within her" (p. 856).[25] The narrator gratuitously continues to diminish the merit of Rosamond's action: Dorothea's gratitude is the result of 'her usual tendency to over-estimate the good in others', since what she thinks of as Rosamond's 'generous effort' was only 'a reflex of [Dorothea's] own energy' (p. 857). In later commentary, the narrator refers to the scene as showing 'the saving influence of a noble nature, the divine efficacy of rescue that may lie in a self-subduing act of fellowship' (p. 861), rather than the reciprocal friendship and mutual rescue of two women. Instead, Dorothea's goodness triumphs over and briefly transforms Rosamond's narrowness, confirming that Dorothea's type of womanhood is the better.

The commentary also emphasises the extraordinary nature of what has occurred: 'But it is given to us sometimes even in our everyday life to witness the saving influence of a noble nature' (p. 861). The coming together of the two women takes place in an extraordinary moment, outside the everyday world: 'this moment was unlike any other: she and Rosamond could never be together again with the same thrilling consciousness of yesterday within them both' (p. 854). Their final embrace takes place in a climactic 'minute': 'for a minute the two women clasped each other as if they had been in a shipwreck' (p. 856). The 'shipwreck' of their normal lives licenses such abnormal behaviour. As I have said, they meet at a place of natural emotions and ahistorical heroism, outside the confines of society; but this sort of contact, by definition, cannot be sustained when they return to their social roles and everyday lives. Rosamond reverts to type, though she always remembers Dorothea with gratidute. Neither woman makes any move to sustain their relationship with each other. Its very abnormality is what makes the relationship so intense and significant, an unrepeatable turning-point in the two women's lives, which operates to assign them securely to their respective mates, and to allow the resolution of Dorothea's plot into marriage.

The friendship between Letty and Marcella in Mrs Humphry Ward's *Sir George Tressady* imitates and expands aspects of Rosamond and Dorothea's friendship in *Middlemarch*.[26] Once again, an earnest woman is contrasted with a heartless flirt, and the earnest woman's sympathy and moral influence 'convert' the flirt into a good wife in a scene of passionate emotion. Unlike in *Middlemarch*, the friendship then continues, and the conversion becomes permanent – all witnessing to the superior morality and wifeliness of the earnest woman. Letty Tressady is a typical flirt – hard-hearted, narrow-souled, mercenary, full of tricks for making men interested in her. She inveigles Sir George into marriage. He is amused and challenged by her, and has, as he later confesses, a low opinion of women: ' "I said to myself, one mustn't let women count for too much in one's life. And the idea of women troubling their heads with politics, or social difficulties, half amused, half disgusted me" ' (p. 425).[27] Of course, he is confessing this to a very different sort of woman ( ' "Then I came to know you" '), having had, like Lydgate, to revise his opinion on 'the most excellent things in woman' (*Middlemarch*, p. 120). Like Lydgate too, he is disillusioned by Letty's lack of sympathy for his work and for his financial difficulties. Sir George is determined to pursue a political career, and he finds himself attracted to Marcella Maxwell, the wife of the leader of the opposing party, Aldous Raeburn, Lord Maxwell. Marcella, 'one of the most famous women of her time' (p. 538), is a powerful political figure, though, in line with Mrs Ward's views,[28] her power is not exercised directly, but through her 'influence' on her husband and his supporters. The opposing party is similarly inspired behind the scenes by another powerful woman, Mrs Allison. Marcella and Mrs Allison like and respect each other. Marcella, in her beauty, charm, goodness and strength is described as an almost overwhelming figure – she is the powerful ideal Mrs Ward believed women could attain by keeping to their traditional role and exercising power through men. The traditional definition of women's role as moral influence is made use of as an avenue to power. As one of the male characters says, ' "The women who matter just now – and you women are getting a terrible amount of influence – more than you've had any time this half-century – are the women who sit at home in their drawing-rooms, wear beautiful gowns, and attract the men who are governing the country to come and see them" ' (p. 369).

Lest we should think there is anything unwomanly, or threatening to the status quo in such a powerful woman as Marcella, Mrs Ward insists on her utter devotedness and intellectual indebtedness to her husband:

> With the natural conceit of the shrewd woman, she would probably have maintained that her social creed came entirely of mother-wit and her own exertions – her experiences in London, reading, and the rest. In reality it was in her the pure birth of a pure passion. She had learnt it while learning to love Aldous Raeburn; and it need astonish no one that the more dependent all her various philosophies of life had become on the mere personal influence and joy of marriage, the more agile had she grown in all that concerned the mere intellectual defence of them. She could argue better and think better; but at bottom, if the truth were told, they were Maxwell's arguments and Maxwell's thoughts. (p. 126)

There is no need to fear women having independent thoughts: men are still needed as the intellectual initiators. Having grasped Maxwell's beliefs, however, Marcella can go on to use her moral influence (not just 'mere' intellectual argument) to convert others. In particular, she influences Sir George, by her moral conviction and her womanly sympathy, until he abandons his party at a crucial vote. Contact with Marcella reveals the poverty of George's marriage with Letty. Marcella sees this at once: 'It was plain to her woman's instinct that he was at heart lonely and uncompanioned. Well, what wonder with that hard, mean little being for a wife!' (p.

235). The intelligent, political woman also has the most womanly
sympathy. Letty is later galled by her 'discernment of the way in
which – at least since their honeymoon – he must have been
criticising and judging her – judging her by comparison with another
woman' (p. 348). Sir George of course falls in love with Marcella,
who is horrified, as she has been doing everything for her husband's
sake. Her first reaction is to think of his wife:

> 'Sir George!' – she put out her hand timidly and touched him – 'may I
> tell you what I am thinking of? Not of you nor of me – of another
> person altogether!'
> He looked up.
> 'My wife?' he said, almost in his usual voice. (p. 427)

Suddenly Marcella's power of sympathy is turned on Letty,
imagining how she herself would feel in a similar situation:

> A sudden perception leapt in Marcella, revealing strange worlds. How
> she could have hated – with what fierceness, what flame! – the woman
> who taught ideal truths to Maxwell! She thought of the little self-
> complacent being in the white satin wedding-dress, that had sat beside
> her at Castle Luton – thought of her with overwhelming soreness and
> pain. (p. 427)

This 'sudden perception' shows us Marcella's power of sympathy,
but also reveals a certain blindness to another woman's feelings in
her actions so far – a blindness that has been rather acidly
commented on by Letty. When Marcella invites George but not
Letty to visit her, Letty comments, '"She's not a woman's woman –
that's all"' (p. 88), and later she is more damning: '"she is just a
superior kind of flirt. She is always making women anxious about
their husbands under this pretence of politics. Heaps of women hate
her, and are afraid of her"' (p. 337). Of course, we have been
assured that Marcella is not a 'flirt', and that there is no sexual
motive or consciousness in her relationships with men other than her
husband. But we have here a legitimate grievance, and grounds for a
divisive split between 'ordinary' women, and those educated women
who enjoy conversing as equals with men on 'male' subjects.
Marcella is aware of some uneasiness in her relations with other
women:

She understood vaguely, without vanity, that she was a power in this English society, that she had many warm friends, especially among men of the finer and abler sort. But when a woman loved her, and insisted, as it were, on making her know it – and, after all, the experience was not a rare one – Marcella received the overture with a kind of grateful surprise. She was accustomed, without knowing why, to feel herself ill at ease with certain types of women; even in her own house she was often aware of being furtively watched by hostile eyes. . . . (p. 131)

The 'certain types' are presumably types like Letty, jealous of Marcella's power over men. The problem is defined as their hostility – Marcella herself is shown as ready and grateful for female friendship, and not lacking in it. In particular, she has a close friendship with Lady Betty Leven. But after her experience with Sir George, she is to realise that she may have caused some of the hostility by her own blindness, and she is to make a determined effort to bridge the gulf between her and the 'certain types'; though a more cynical interpretation would be that even these hostile types are to be made to acknowledge her predominance and come under her spell.

Despite Letty's criticisms of Marcella, she herself is not a 'woman's woman' either. There is a painful little scene in which she snubs her former friend Mrs Hawkins, the vicar's wife. Mrs Hawkins is presented as vulgar, awkward and ambitious, but her friendship with Letty had been genuine: 'When Letty had been a brilliant child in short frocks, the vicar's wife, who was scarcely six years older, had opened her heart, had tried to make herself loved by Mrs Watton's niece. There had been a moment when they had been "Madge" and "Letty" to each other' (p. 30). Now Letty's mind is set on higher things. 'From head to foot she breathed affluence, seduction, success – only the seduction was not for Mrs Hawkins and her like' (p. 29). Ironically, Letty's snobbery is going to make it especially impressive to her when such a 'famous' woman as Marcella offers her friendship. Here the condescension is all on Marcella's side, and the vulgarity on Letty's

What prompts Marcella to go to Letty is a spiteful letter Letty sends to Marcella's husband, denouncing Marcella and Sir George. Maxwell shows the letter to Marcella, who reacts like this: ' "I shall go to her," she said simply. "I must see her!" ' (p. 436). From this point onwards, the problem is to be resolved between the two

women: Sir George fades into the background. The resolution does
not depend on his choice between the two women, but on Marcella's
giving him back to Letty, and her persuasion of Letty to take him.
Marcella's first motives in going to Letty are explanation and
apology, now she has come to sympathise with Letty's feelings as a
wife: 'She knew nothing of the real Letty Tressady. It was the wife
as such, slighted and set aside, that appealed to the imagination, the
remorse of this happy, this beloved woman' (p. 467). She
apologises, in the name of marriage: '"Married people" – she spoke
hurriedly, her breath rising and falling – "are not two, but, one –
and my first step should have been to come – and – ask you to let me
know if you too – to find out what your feelings were, whether you
wished for a friendship – that – that I had perhaps no right to offer
to Sir George alone"' (p. 465). Like Dorothea, she comes with a
message about the sacredness and inescapability of marriage,
though, unlike Dorothea, she speaks from experience of a happy
marriage. We are not shown two women sympathising about
marriage as a painful bond: instead, the happily married one brings
the good news to the unhappily married one and, as we shall see,
converts her too into a good and happy wife. That it is the powerful
political woman who is also the defender and upholder of
matrimony reinforces Mrs Ward's message about the potential of
women's traditional role, and the social acceptability of powerful
women.

Letty, of course, like Rosamond, initially reacts with hostility –
'first, hatred of her beauty, then triumph in the evident nervousness
with which her visitor approached her' (p. 464) – but also like
Rosamond she begins to be abashed by Marcella's humble manner
and superior worth, 'this mingling of self-abasement with an
extraordinary moral richness and dignity . . ., which began almost to
intimidate her' (p. 468). She does not, however, break down at
once, but strikes back at Marcella by proclaiming her own intention
to commit adultery with another admirer, and blaming Marcella
and George – '"It's your doing and George's, you see, if he doesn't
like it!"' (p. 469). Marcella recoils in horror at this revelation of
how much she has undermined the sanctity of marriage, but Letty's
assertion also gives her the upper hand in moral terms. Now her
mission can be to 'save' Letty's marriage. 'Raving' about her
unhappy marriage and her proposed lover, Letty has an hysterical
breakdown, and Marcella is ready with motherly care: 'Marcella

knelt beside her, the tears running down her cheeks. She put her arms – arms formed for tenderness, for motherliness – round the girl's slight frame' (p. 472). With what would have been arrogance in Dorothea, Marcella consciously resolves to 'convert' Letty – 'she had passionately determined that this blurred and spoiled marriage could and should be mended, and that it lay with her to do it; and in the spirit of her audacious youth she had taken upon herself the burden of Letty's character and fate, vowing herself to a moral mission, to a long patience' (p. 473). The two women's positions have reversed – Marcella is no longer the self-abasing transgressor come to apologise, and Letty now feels 'a new and clinging need' – Marcella's presence has 'begun to thrill and subjugate her', though we are reminded that Letty could have been converted by nothing less than 'a Marcella at her feet' (p. 477). Mrs Ward thus presents the friendship in terms of power-relations, depending on concepts like 'abasement' and 'subjugation'. It is a contest, which Marcella has won – Marcella 'had devoted herself first to the understanding, and then to the capturing, of the smaller, narrower life' (p. 538), and Letty, her defeated captive, is now 'within a moral grasp she was never again to shake off' (p. 478). The conversion of Letty has illustrated Marcella's moral predominance.

The experience is also supposed to have opened Letty's eyes to the possibilities of female friendship, but this enticing vision is clouded by her sense of her own unworthiness:

...Letty was conscious of a strange leap of something till then unknown, something that made her want to sob, that seemed to open to her a new room in the House of Life. Marcella had not kissed her since the day of their great scene. ... But sometimes when Marcella stood beside her ... a half-desolate intuition would flash across the younger woman of what it might be to be admitted to the intimate friendship of such a nature, to feel those long, slender arms pressed about her once more, not in pity or remonstrance, as of one trying to exorcise an evil spirit, but in mere love, as of one asking as well as giving. The tender and adoring friendship of women for women, which has become so marked a feature of our self-realising generation, had passed Letty by. She had never known it. Now, in these unforeseen circumstances, she seemed to be trembling within reach of its emotion; divining it, desiring it, yet forced onward to the question, 'What is there in me that may claim it?' (p. 488)

But Letty never attains this sort of reciprocal relationship with

Marcella, who continues to admonish her by letter. This passage is
quoted from by Vineta Colby and by Elaine Showalter as
characteristic of Mrs Ward's attitude to female friendship, without
making it clear that it is describing a state *not* attained in the novel,
and that the very wording of the passage emphasises the idea of a
female hierarchy of moral worthiness that underlies Letty and
Marcella's passionate scene of friendship. Vineta Colby sees such
passionate scenes in Mrs Ward's novels as 'decorous outlets for her
characters' passions', and feels it necessary to defend them from a
lesbian interpretation: 'What her novels reflect, therefore, is far
more romantic convention than sexual perversion or repression.'[29] It
is true that while Marcella cannot legitimately express any passion
for Sir George, she can find an 'outlet' in a scene with another
woman. It is even hinted that her later letters to Letty contain a
secret message for George: 'Strange! – as he read the letters George
felt his own heart beating. Were they in some hidden way meant for
him too? – he seemed to hear in them a secret message – a woman's
yearning, a woman's response' (p. 539). But this diversion of passion
from man to woman is not just there because of 'romantic
convention' – by this transference, the disruptive potential of
adulterous relationships can be contained and diverted in a scene of
passionate female conversion to marriage. The scene is also necessary
to the apotheosis of Marcella as heroine, the completion of her
identity as perfect woman.

Elaine Showalter also disagrees with Colby's implication that the
female friendships in Mrs Ward's novels are merely 'decorative', but
she sees them as reflecting 'the intense bonds of the female
subculture. . . . Bonds of loyalty, empathy, charity, and love between
women are her answer to female oppression.'[30] This seems rather a
sentimental view of what is happening in *Sir George Tressady*, from
which Showalter quotes here. Letty is not presented as oppressed,
except by her own narrow attitudes, and Marcella brings her the key
to female power through acceptance of the bonds of marriage. The
result of Marcella's letters to Letty is 'that the ugly house on the hill
had in truth ceased to be in the least dull or burdensome to her.
George went in and out of it. And for the woman that has come to
hunger for her husband's step, there is no more *ennui*' (p. 541). All
Letty's sense of oppression has been removed, and she has given up
her own existence to that of her husband. On the other hand,
Marcella herself illustrates what power such a woman can wield.

While conservative writers like Mrs Ellis or George Eliot present female friendship as a bond between sufferers, produced by their common recognition of their suffering, and designed to strengthen them to bear it, Mrs Ward's conservatism is different. For her, women in their traditional roles are not sufferers, they are glamorous figures of power, who can attract and influence other women as followers.[31]

Marcella's friendship with Letty is seen as a turning-point in her relations with other women. Lady Betty predicts:

'I see exactly what fate is going to happen to you in middle life. Women couldn't get on with you when you were a girl – you didn't like them, nor they you; and now everywhere I hear the young women beginning to talk about you, especially the young married women; and in a few years you will have them all about you like a cluster of doves, cooing and confessing, and making your life a burden to you.' (p. 483)

Again, these are not reciprocal relationships – these are 'daughters' rather than 'sisters', followers and worshippers rather than equals. Lady Betty herself, of course, is presented as Marcella's equal, but, interestingly, their friendship has none of the emotional or physical intensity of Marcella's friendship with Letty. Instead, it is presented through light-hearted conversations which comment on the action, and in which Lady Betty often makes gentle fun of Marcella's idealistic aspirations. Thus her reading of the friendship with Letty is affectionately cynical: '"How like her!"' she thought to herself, "to forget the wife's existence to begin with, and then to make love to her by way of warding off the husband!"' (p. 485). Though more cynical than the 'moral rescue' explanation, this interpretation does protect Marcella from the implication that she might be cultivating Letty's friendship in order to *continue* the relationship with George. Once again, the friendship is seen as *preventing* adulterous consequences and upholding marriage.

The friendship with Letty is Marcella's triumph, and the climax of the plot. Afterwards, everyone is restored to their right places, preparatory to the ending. As the main characters are already married, the novel cannot end with a marriage[32] – so a death is used instead: Sir George is killed while trying to rescue men from an accident in one of his coal mines. Letty is not good enough to be left with a happy and successful marriage; and Sir George, having once

loved and lost Marcella, is ready for death, which involves a final
vision of her as he dies. Thus, indirectly, Marcella does take George
from Letty, as Dorothea takes Will from Rosamond. Marcella
triumphs on all fronts: the friendship between her and Letty is
primarily designed to show the entire predominance of one type of
female identity over another.

# Chapter Four

# *Shirley:*
# Disruption
# and Containment

The presentation of the female friendship in *Shirley*, and the way it relates to the narrative structure, is radically different from all the examples I have dealt with so far. For once, female friendship is central to the novel, and this necessarily disrupts the conventional structure, revealing that existing conventions cannot fully contain or portray an autonomous female friendship. The structure of *Shirley* has often been criticised for its loose and fragmentary qualities,[1] but this very looseness is both caused by and allows a more sustained and central exploration of female friendship for its own sake than is usual in the well-structured marriage-plot. Unlike the female friendships in any of the other novels I have discussed, this friendship is not designed to assimilate either of the women to marriage, in fact, it leads *away* from marriage, into a peaceful, manless, female world of Nature. Rather than negotiating a socially acceptable female identity, the friends discover an asocial position of strength from which they can make subversive criticisms of the social and cultural oppression of women.

The double marriage ending, which puts a stop to the exploration of this subversive female alternative, is forced and hurried,[2] and the narrator draws attention to its arbitrary, 'fictive quality';[3] as Gilbert and Gubar put it: 'Brontë calls attention to the ridiculous fantasy that is the novel's end by entitling her final chapter "The Winding-Up". As if that were not enough to qualify the happy ending, she ties up loose ends and proclaims, "I think the varnish has been put on very nicely".'[4] The ending is clearly there just to satisfy convention. The narrator's awareness of what she is doing here

indicates that her real interest is in the less conventional parts of the
novel, the themes that convention will not allow her to develop
fully,[5] as Shirley says about the depiction of female characters in
literature: '"If I spoke all I think on this point; if I gave my real
opinion of some first-rate female characters in first-rate works,
where should I be? Dead under a cairn of avenging stones in half an
hour"' (p. 343).[6] In the presentation of Caroline and Shirley's
friendship there are several hints that the female world they belong
to cannot be represented fully in terms of current conventions. Thus
though the female friendship is developed more than in other novels,
it nevertheless gives the sense of something that can never fully take
place – the friends never make their expedition to Nunnwood, and
the nunnery there is in ruins anyway; they never take their sea voyage
to the Isles,[7] and the current 'stories' about women in Milton and in
the Bible limit and diminish the female roles they can play. The
friendship carries a strong aura of nostalgia, for another more
'natural' and therefore more female time – the friendship sharpens
the awareness of loss and alienation in the two women.

The partial exploration of an alternative, lost female world, a
different type of story, is put a stop to by the reimposition of the
love-plots and the conventional ending. But at the very end, we have
a momentary return of nostalgia, for the 'fairishes' and the natural
world that have been obliterated by industrial development – a
development that Shirley and Caroline become part of by their
marriages to the brothers Moore. The narrator converses with her
old housekeeper about the heroines' marriages:

> 'What was the Hollow like then, Martha?'
> 'Different to what it is now; but I can tell of it clean different again:
> when there was neither mill, nor cot, nor hall, except Fieldhead, within
> two miles of it. I can tell, one summer-evening, fifty years syne, my
> mother coming running in just at the edge of dark, almost fleyed out of
> her wits, saying, she had seen a fairish (fairy) in Fieldhead Hollow; and
> that was the last fairish that ever was seen on this country side.... A
> lonesome spot it was – and a bonnie spot – full of oak trees and nut
> trees. It is altered now.' (p. 599)

This evocation of an earlier, magical, natural world links back to
the world in which Shirley and Caroline meet, or wish they could
meet – autonomous female friendship is part of a lost world outside
social (and novelistic) convention.

In order to deal with this world at all, the novel has had of course to break with convention. As Janice Swanson says, Brontë 'upends conventions, keeping one leading man at a distance and the other entirely absent during most of the novel.'[8] The structure of the novel is notable for its unconventional postponement and inactivity in the love-plots. Thus we could say that the female friendship serves to fill in the time before the 'inevitable marriages', providing a substitute for romance; but it is this very substitution that becomes the subject of the novel.[9] The lives of unmarried women become the centre, and romance is relegated to the periphery. The absence of the men allows Brontë to explore both the suffering, empty life of Caroline as a single woman, and the enjoyment and fullness of Shirley's independent life. These two poles of single womanhood then meet in a sustaining female friendship that flourishes by the exclusion of the male. That Brontë intended to 'upend conventions' in her plotting is several times indicated by the narrator. She begins the book by warning the reader not to expect 'passion, and stimulus, and melodrama'. Instead, she promises 'something unromantic as Monday morning' (p. 39). Later, this kind of warning is attached especially to Caroline's 'narrative': 'at eighteen the true narrative of life is yet to be commenced. Before that time, we sit listening to a tale, a marvellous fiction' (p. 121). But this 'true narrative' has structural problems: the whole point about Caroline's life from now on is going to be that *nothing happens* to her: 'passion, and stimulus, and melodrama' are missing.

Something 'exciting' is of course introduced into the book with the industrial troubles and the attack on the Mill; but, in contrast, the friendship between Shirley and Caroline is defined by its peacefulness, its exclusion from and of male violence and excitement. As Linda Hunt says, 'Brontë equates affection between women with repose':[10] the presence of gentlemen, Shirley and Caroline agree, would dispel the 'quietude' of their expedition to Nunnwood, producing instead 'more elation and more anxiety: an excitement that steals the hours away fast, and a trouble that ruffles their course' (pp. 221, 222). Hunt sees Brontë as also wanting these 'more vigorous emotional satisfactions'[11] for her heroines, and therefore reintroducing the marriage plots and the conventional ending, instead of allowing the friendship to develop as a substitute for marriage. But it is also true that the trouble and excitement of male–female interaction are necessary to give the plot shape and direction, given that female friendship has been defined solely as 'repose': narrative, as well as emotional considerations dictate the intrusion of the men into Caroline and Shirley's idyll, and the conventional ending. This may be why the women's excursions to Nunnwood and the Isles do not take place – they would lead away from novelistic action into a contemplative realm conventionally more suited to nature poetry. The narrative conventions that thus curtail and contain the friendship are not, however, just a matter of form – the conventions embody what is considered socially significant or acceptable: that male–female 'excitement' is more interesting than female–female 'repose'; that marriage is the only acceptable and fulfilling destiny for a woman.[12] On the other hand, as I have suggested, the tongue-in-cheek quality of the ending hints that Brontë is questioning these conventions.

The presentation and interaction of the two women as 'types' also undermines convention. We could see them as another variant on the angel/monster, Lucile/Corinne opposition, with Caroline as the blonde, conventional, womanly heroine, and Shirley as the dark, unconventional, gifted woman. It is true that Caroline seems to have all the qualities of the 'angel' woman:

> What her brown eyes and clear forehead showed of her mind, was in keeping with her dress and face – modest, gentle, and, though pensive, harmonious. It appeared that neither lamb nor dove need fear her, but would welcome rather, in her look of simplicity and softness, a sympathy with their own natures, or with the natures we ascribe to them. (pp. 291–2)

As Janice Swanson puts it, Caroline 'embodies every virtue belonging to the Victorian ideal of femininity – patience, docility, obedience or submissiveness, and modesty'.[13] We often see her diligently engaged in sewing – either her own clothes, or clothes for the poor. Shirley, by contrast, cannot concentrate on her 'needle': 'She takes her sewing occasionally: but, by some fatality, she is doomed never to sit steadily at it for above five minutes at a time. . . . After tea Shirley reads, and she is just as tenacious of her book as she is lax of her needle' (pp. 372, 373). Like the elder sister in Rossetti's 'The Lowest Room', like Maggie Tulliver or Dorothea Brooke, Shirley is the bookish heroine, who belongs to a world of myth and heroism: it is she who fantasises about the original 'woman-Titan'. Like Corinne, she is a woman of artistic genius, though she is too lazy to write down the imaginative visions she creates.

But here the resemblances of the heroines to the Lucile/Corinne pattern end. Caroline's 'angelic' nature does not ensure her the social acceptability and marriageability that attend Lucile, the younger sister in Rossetti's poem, Lucy Deane or Paulina Home. Her agonised boredom and emotional starvation as she forces herself to her sewing remind one rather of Maggie than Lucy. She is an angel-woman tortured by the self-sacrifice and silence required of the conventional woman's role. Some critics, misled by the stereotypical descriptions of Caroline, have seen her protests against her fate as out of character.[14] Robert Bernard Martin, insisting on reading the two women as a 'contrast between the modern woman and the womanly woman', is forced to attribute Caroline's protest to an intrusion by the author, and to exaggerate her dissension from Shirley's feminist opinions.[15] But an intelligent questioning of social behaviour is part of Caroline's character from the start, as when she implicitly criticises Robert Moore's attitude as an employer in the 'Coriolanus' chapter. Her resignation to Robert's rejection and her prospective role as old maid is always accompanied by suffering and questioning. We are never shown any angelic glad submissiveness in her consciousness. On first describing Caroline, Brontë signals clearly that we are not to take her at face value: 'So much for Caroline Helstone's appearance; as to her character or intellect, if she had any, they must speak for themselves in due time' (p. 102). Caroline's predicament consists precisely in the disjunction between her insignificant, girlish appearance, and her sharp inner thoughts and fierce inner emotions.

While Caroline reveals unexpected pitfalls in the angel-woman's path, Shirley, on the other hand, faces none of the difficulties endured by unconventional women like Corinne, the elder sister, Maggie, Lucy Snowe or Dorothea. She is a social and romantic success, happy and attractive in her unconventionality. This rearrangement of roles affects the significance of the friends' interaction, and the questions about female identity that it raises. Caroline does not appear as a monitory image to dampen down the unconventionality of Shirley and make her feel guilty or deprived by contrast. Rather, the opposite happens: Shirley appears as an image of female freedom and strength who encourages and voices Caroline's discontent with the limitations of her conventional

female role, and enacts her repressed wishes. Similarity in female
discontent and a distinctively female outlook are brought out by the
friendship, rather than a contrast of 'good' and 'bad' types of
woman.[16] This effect is heightened by the timing of Shirley's
appearance in the book. She is introduced when Caroline is at her
lowest point of deprivation and self-suppression, but also when
Caroline has begun to formulate an inward protest at the conditions
of her life as a single woman. Caroline's inward discontent takes
outward form in Shirley: Gilbert and Gubar are surely right to see
Shirley as acting out Caroline's repressed desires, especially in
controlling or punishing the men who oppress her.[17] Thus Shirley is
able to manipulate Caroline's unsympathetic uncle, Mr Helstone; to
act as an equal in business affairs with Robert Moore, and as a
superior in lending him money; to attract the proposal from him
that he would not make to Caroline, and then to punish his
arrogance and mercenariness by refusing; and to eject from her house
Mr Donne, one of the curates whose arrogant and dominating
behaviour always torments Caroline. With her money, she is also
able to put substance and action into Caroline's concern for the
plight of the workers, a concern that is part of Caroline's attack on
Robert's unfeeling attitude in the 'Coriolanus' chapter.

   Though Shirley thus operates as a projection of Caroline's desires,
and though she is introduced comparatively late into the book, I do
not think we are justified in regarding her as a less important or
central character.[18] It is true that we see into Caroline's
consciousness, but not into Shirley's, but, as Swanson says, this is
because Shirley 'can speak for herself while Caroline, forced on
inwardness and burdened by "palsifying faculties", must have her
thoughts presented'.[19] If we take the two women to be equally
important, this is another way in which their friendship is different
from the female friendships I have discussed so far: instead of a
friendship between the heroine and another, less important
character, we have a friendship between two equal heroines. The
presence of two heroines, with two separate love plots, of course
further fragments the novel: but the friendship of the two women is
what holds it together.

   While the female friendship has this central structuring role, it is
also sharply differentiated from all the other relationships in the
book. It is almost as if it takes place in a different kind of reality, an
alternative world of 'repose', which, as I have suggested, cannot be

satisfactorily portrayed within the conventions of the novel. It is portrayed as an island of peace and understanding in a predatory world, and it offers subversive feminist criticisms, both implicit and explicit, of that world. These criticisms suggest lines of action and modes of revisionary representation that, as I shall show, also cannot be developed within current social or novelistic conventions. Becauses of its specialness, the friendship is powerless to affect the rest of the action: it is separate from the male world of machinery, violence and history, and there is also no wider solidarity between women in the novel which could lend some power to the friends' criticisms of the male world.

As in many other novels, the friendship is presented very much as an isolated occurrence among the other female–female relationships in the novel. As Shirley says to Caroline, 'I have never in my whole life been able to talk to a young lady as I have talked to you this morning' (p. 226), and Caroline later remarks on how Shirley is 'so different to everyday young ladies' (p. 265). Their friendship contrasts with Caroline's knowledge and avoidance of such 'commonplace young ladies':

> Commonplace young ladies can be quite as hard as commonplace young gentlemen, – quite as worldly and selfish. Those who suffer should always avoid them; grief and calamity they despise: they seem to regard them as the judgments of God on the lowly. With them to 'love' is merely to contrive a scheme for achieving a good match: to be 'disappointed' is to have their scheme seen through and frustrated. They think the feelings and projects of others on the subject of love, similar to their own, and judge them accordingly.
>
> All this Caroline knew, partly by instinct, partly by observation: she regulated her conduct by her knowledge, keeping her pale face and wasted figure as much out of sight as she could. Living thus in complete seclusion, she ceased to receive intelligence of the little transactions of the neighbourhood. (p. 206)

It is at this low point of isolation from female company that her uncle comes in and takes her off to visit Shirley for the first time. The commonplace young ladies are imprisoned in a uniform conventionality, but divided from each other as a set of competitive schemers. Though Caroline is able to avoid them here, she later comes in for the sort of attack she dreads from them, from Mrs Yorke, who accuses her both of being a silly romantic girl, and of scheming to ensnare Robert Moore. As in *Mill on the Floss*, women here are pitiless in their judgements of each other. We do not see women doing each other actual harm, as in *Aurora Leigh* – it is hardness and lack of motherly or sisterly sympathy that is shown, rather than deception and betrayal. Instead of the sustaining mother-substitutes that Molly has in *Wives and Daughters*, Caroline only has the harsh Mrs Yorke and the self-centred, nagging Hortense Moore. Shirley, of course, does have a loving mother-substitute in Mrs Pryor, who later turns out to be Caroline's real mother: the three of them form an island of female sympathy. Shirley too is repelled by 'commonplace young ladies' – in her case, the Sympson sisters, with their stifling conformism: 'They knew by heart a certain young-ladies-school-room code of laws on language, demeanour, &c.; themselves never deviated from its curious little pragmatical provisions; and they regarded with secret, whispered horror, all deviations in others' (p. 428). Again, uniformity characterises ordinary female behaviour:[20] but these young ladies do not have the power over Shirley that the Misses Wynne and Sykes had over Caroline – they cannot hurt her, or cause her to moderate her unconventional behaviour. With Shirley's appearance, and her friendship with Caroline, the balance of power has shifted – the censorious female community is here matter for laughter, not fear; and even Caroline stands up to Mrs Yorke and her criticisms.

Before Shirley arrives, however, Caroline has attempted to make contact with other lonely single women – the 'old maids', whose ranks she is afraid she will have to join. As opposed to the 'commonplace young ladies', these women are eccentric and therefore isolated: Caroline has to work through a barrier of prejudice and ridicule to discover their humanity. Caroline discovers the suffering and deprivation that lie behind Miss Mann's censoriousness, and the saint-like benevolence that lies behind Miss Ainley's ugliness. She resolves to keep visiting Miss Mann, and to help Miss Ainley in her charitable work; but she gains no sustenance from these contacts. Miss Mann and Miss Ainley are only too grim warnings of what sort of future lies before her. They illustrate Caroline's previous thoughts about the exploitation of old maids:

> '... certain sets of human beings are very apt to maintain that other sets should give up their lives to them and their service, and then they requite them by praise: they call them devoted and virtuous. Is this enough? Is it

to live? Is there not a terrible hollowness, mockery, want, craving, in that existence which is given away to others, for want of something of your own to bestow it on? I suspect there is. Does virtue lie in abnegation of self? I do not believe it.' (p. 190)

It is not surprising that her efforts for Miss Ainley 'brought her neither health of body nor continued peace of mind: with them all, she wasted, grew more joyless and more wan' (p. 199). To join in self-forgetful sisterhood with Miss Ainley can only represent a kind of suicide for Caroline. In her first discovery of Miss Ainley's virtues, she 'momently' repudiates her own larger needs:

What was her love of nature, what was her sense of beauty, what were her more varied and fervent emotions, what was her deeper power of thought, what her wider capacity to comprehend, compared to the practical excellence of this good woman? Momently, they seemed only beautiful forms of selfish delight; mentally she trod them under foot. (p. 198)

It is these very qualities and interests – love of nature, fervent emotions, deep thoughts – that will form the shared centre of her friendship with Shirley. It is a friendship in which her mental and emotional qualities are developed and revealed, not repressed. Friendship with Miss Ainley also cannot satisfy Caroline's need for love: 'she still felt with pain that the life which made Miss Ainley happy could not make her happy: pure and active as it was, in her heart she deemed it deeply dreary because it was so loveless – to her ideas, so forlorn' (p. 198). This need for love, for 'something of her own', is eventually satisfied by Mrs Pryor, rather than by Shirley: Mrs Pryor provides the intense mothering that compensates for Caroline's emotional deprivation, and Shirley provides the sisterly congeniality of tastes and ideas that allows her nature to expand.

It is interesting that friendship with Miss Ainley is equated with becoming *like* Miss Ainley, living her sort of life. There is no question that Caroline could contribute any variety to Miss Ainley's life – for instance, take her for a walk in Nunnwood.[21] Miss Ainley's character has been defined in such a way as to make this impossible: she is *only* self-sacrificing goodness, she has no other faculties such as 'love of nature' or 'power of thought': this is why she is able to be so happy in her limited life. She operates as a monitory image of what Caroline *should* but cannot be – 'After all,

[Caroline] was an imperfect, faulty human being: fair enough of form, hue, and array: but, as Cyril Hall said, neither so good nor so great as the withered Miss Ainley' (p. 292). To ally herself with Miss Ainley would thus represent for Caroline a conformity, a capitulation, to the stifling code of female self-sacrifice that is already killing her.[22]

The friendship with Miss Mann rather drops from sight after Caroline's first visit: we do not have Caroline comparing herself with Miss Mann, and wondering if she could live such a life. The possibilities Miss Mann represents are perhaps too unpleasant and too unacceptable to be openly dealt with: but she does offer another path Caroline could take. She is dying of a painful disease – as Caroline is wasting away from her lack of love – and her pain makes her censorious: 'she allowed scarcely any one to be good; she dissected impartially almost all her acquaintance' (p. 195). This may at first seem very far away from Caroline's sweetness of disposition, but we have also seen Caroline thinking very bitter thoughts, and, till Shirley comes, disliking most of her acquaintance among the ordinary young ladies and gentlemen of her society. If the young ladies are inclined to judge her, she is certainly censorious in her cutting evaluation of them. The alternative to the self-sacrificing benevolence of Miss Ainley is a self-destructive bitterness and misanthropy. Thus neither of these old maids offers Caroline a model to be followed, or a valuable and sustaining friendship: in this, they differ from the old maid Miss Marchmont in *Villette*, who offers Lucy both.

While the relationships among women in the book, apart from the triad of Shirley, Caroline and Mrs Pryor, are either hostile or debilitating, relations among men, and between men and women, are also variously antagonistic or unsatisfactory. In the central third of the novel, the development of the peaceful friendship between Caroline and Shirley is contrasted by the violent attacks of men and masters on each other; and the concerted female plan to bring charitable relief to the workers, is contrasted by the concerted male plan to defend the Mill by force.[23] This episode ends in the male sphere with further reprisals and revenge; in the female sphere, we have the loving reconciliation of Caroline and Mrs Pryor. As well as the violence and hostility of the clash between men and masters, the 'masters' are also divided among themselves. Yorke, Helstone and Moore all disagree over politics, and the rift between Helstone and

Moore is only healed when they make common cause against the rioting workers. Friendship between men seems to be non-existent – the narrator satirises the pseudo-friendship between the three curates. They are continually 'rushing back and forwards' to visit each other, but 'what attracts them, it would be difficult to say. It is not friendship; for whenever they meet they quarrel' (pp. 40–1). 'Quarrelling' is endemic among the book's male characters.[24] Male-female relations fare no better – as Linda Hunt points out, 'Throughout the novel marriage is presented in a negative light.'[25] Mr Helstone and Mrs Pryor, from their experiences of marriage, inveigh against it; and Mr Yorke's marriage, while workable, scarcely seems pleasant. His family is full of dissension, between his wife and his children, and between his sons – though not, significantly, between his daughters. Mr Yorke has been disappointed in his love for Mary Cave, but later he admits to Robert Moore that if he could have had her easily, he probably would not have wanted her; the man she does marry, Mr Helstone, makes her life miserable by his neglect. After her death, he proceeds to treat his niece, Caroline, with the same coldness and lack of sympathy.

Caroline is also, of course, treated coldly by Robert Moore, the man she will later marry. She gets no emotional sustenance from the men in her life, until Robert has finally been 'feminised' by his wound and subsequent isolation and enclosure. Shirley's relationship with her lover, Louis Moore, though emotional, is more of a power-struggle than a sympathetic mutuality. Both heroines' relationships with their lovers are characterised by misunderstanding, evasion, concealment and manipulation.[26] Janice Swanson sees the friendship between Shirley and Caroline as an implied criticism of the heterosexual relationships in the book: 'Shirley and Caroline draw each other out in ways which imply a failure of communication between the sexes and a criticism of marriage as a means for these women to experience the continuation of a kind of growth fostered through friendship.'[27] The only exceptions to this lack of communication between the sexes are Mr Hall's friendship with Caroline, and William Farren's friendship with the two heroines. William Farren, as a working man, inhabits the same world of deprivation and exclusion as the women;[28] Mr Hall, happily living with his sister, avoids the pitfalls of marriage. Significantly, we also see him as a friend of Miss Ainley and of William Farren. He is able to identify with the excluded. On the other hand, a working man

like the overseer Joe Scott, who identifies with the interests of his
master Robert Moore, is shown as a thoroughgoing misogynist.

In the midst of the personal and social antagonisms of the book,
the heroines' friendship does therefore show up as an island of peace,
a rare and precious discovery. Their mutual sympathy in ideas and
tastes is stressed:

> In Caroline, Miss Keeldar had first taken an interest because she was
> quiet, retiring, looked delicate, and seemed as if she needed some one to
> take care of her. Her predilection increased greatly when she discovered
> that her own way of thinking and talking was understood and responded
> to by this new acquaintance.... Caroline's instinct of taste, too, was
> like her own: such books as Miss Keeldar had read with the most
> pleasure, were Miss Helstone's delight also. They held many aversions
> too in common....
>     ... The minds of the two girls being toned in harmony, often chimed
> very sweetly together. (pp. 230, 231)

This is like the harmony Jane Eyre finds with the Rivers sisters, and
Shirley moves quickly from a position as Caroline's protector, to an
appreciation of her as an equal and a likeness, as the sisters do
towards Jane. Like the sisters and Jane, the women here share an
intense appreciation of nature. Their first private conversation is on
a walk on the 'extensive and solitary' Nunnely Common, and they
begin by comparing memories of moorland and storm weather (pp.
218–19). Like Jane Eyre's paintings, these extreme and violent
scenes suggest an intense and turbulent inner life, shared by the two
women. As the scene progresses, the 'Nature' they appreciate and
identify with becomes more nurturing and explicitly female, but
also associated with ruins and the distant, vanishing past. The
projected expedition to Nunnwood promises entry to a secret,
secluded female space, a long-lost female world. Nunnwood is 'the
sole remnant of antique British forest in a region whose lowlands
were once all sylvan chase' (p. 220), and in its centre, says Caroline,
'"is a dell; a deep, hollow cup, lined with turf as green and short as
the sod of this Common: the very oldest of trees, gnarled mighty
oaks, crowd about the brink of this dell: in the bottom lie the ruins
of a nunnery"' (p. 221). The ruined nunnery evokes a lost world of
female community – the women agree that the natural magic of the
wood would be destroyed by male company. What Linda Hunt calls
'the vaginal imagery of this passage'[29] also makes it a place of female

sexuality. Not surprisingly, the wood is fertile, and Caroline, Caliban-like, offers to show Shirley its natural riches: '"I know where we could get nuts in nutting time; I know where wild strawberries abound"' (p. 221). Like Caliban, excluded from the conversation and projects of her 'betters', Caroline has nevertheless her own kind of knowledge.

Earlier, we have heard of her feeding Robert Moore with nuts and berries, and spending an afternoon with him in Nunnwood – clearly this symbolises her sexual feelings for him, and her allowing him to make use of and invade them. This shared feast with Robert has left her pining and wasting away, like Laura in *Goblin Market*. Later, we also learn that she has given Robert a lock of her hair. With Shirley now, she admits that even at the time her visit to Nunnwood with Robert left '"its own peculiar pain"' (p. 222), produced by her masochistic sense of unworthiness in his presence. The two women are agreed that the presence of men would spoil their enjoyment of the wood:

'We were going simply to see the old trees, the old ruins; to pass a day in old times, surrounded by olden silence, and above all by quietude.'

'You are right; and the presence of gentlemen dispels the last charm, I think. If they are of the wrong sort ... irritation takes the place of serenity. If they are of the right sort, there is still a change – I can hardly tell what change, one easy to feel, difficult to describe.'

'We forget Nature, imprimis.'

'And then Nature forgets us; covers her vast, calm brow with a dim veil, conceals her face, and withdraws the peaceful joy with which, if we had only been content to worship her only, she would have filled our hearts.'

'What does she give us instead?'

'More elation and more anxiety: an excitement that steals the hours away fast, and a trouble that ruffles their course.' (pp. 221–2)

Here we have the equation of female friendship with quietude that I have discussed; and the quietude is associated with the past ('old times ... olden silence'), and with a communion with a female Nature. The personification of Nature here turns her into a goddess, the 'Great Mother'. Female friendship is given an appropriate theology: but the insistence on Nunnwood as a place of the past, of ruins and remnants, suggests that the power of the Great Mother, and of female community, is a thing of the past, a lost power that can only exist 'outside' the male-dominated machine age.

As I have suggested, the women's friendship in its peaceful world of Nature contrasts with the violence taking place in the men's world of industry. The women's world offers an implied criticism of the men's action, but is totally separate from it, and powerless to affect it. This is most clear when the women watch the riot – ' "we shall see what transpires with our own eyes: we are here on the spot, and none know it ... we stand alone with the friendly night, its mute stars, and these whispering trees" ' (pp. 334–5). In this secret, natural place the women are safe, and their embrace contrasts with the assault taking place below, and assimilates them even further to Nature – 'Shirley put her arms around her: they stood together as still as the straight stems of two trees' (p. 335) – but they are also excluded from the history the men are enacting. Their female friendship is as vulnerable to this male history as are the trees uprooted at the end of the book to make room for Robert's new factory town, or the ruined nunnery.

Nevertheless, Nunnwood offers an imaginative meeting-place for Shirley and Caroline. The imagery suggests that the women are elaborating a fantasy, a symbol of their inner worlds – if this is so, perhaps it does not matter that the expedition never 'actually' takes place. Nunnwood operates as a code through which they can communicate, a secret, female language of Nature that they share.[30] The same is true of their imaginings about their projected sea-voyage, which can be read as an extended shared fantasy about female sexuality. And both of these female fantasies lead on to some sharp criticism of either the social rules or the dominant fantasies of the male world. Shared female feeling leads on to shared subversive thoughts – as Shirley suggests later, 'we are alone: we may speak what we think' (p. 314). This implies that the thoughts have always been there, unspoken and concealed – the presence of another, sympathetic woman, and the absence of men allows the unaccept-able to be spoken, and a specifically female perspective on male institutions to be elaborated.

The discussion of the Nunnwood expedition and the advisability of excluding men, develops into a discussion of men's characters, and the advisability of marriage, from a woman's point of view. Caroline reveals the domestic harshness of her uncle, and Shirley ' "can well conceive" ' that Mr Helstone, whom she was disposed to admire, is devoid of ' "indulgence ... warmth of heart ... sympathy and considerateness" ' (p. 223). The conversation continues:

'I often wonder, Shirley, whether most men resemble my uncle in their domestic relations . . .'
'I don't know: I can't clear up your doubts. I ponder over similar ones myself sometimes. But, to tell you a secret, if I were convinced that they are necessarily and universally different from us – fickle, soon petrifying, unsympathizing – I would never marry. I should not like to find out that what I loved did not love me. . . . That discovery once made, what should I long for? To go away – to remove from a presence where my society gave no pleasure.'
'But you could not, if you were married.'
'No, I could not, – there it is. I could never be my own mistress more. A terrible thought! It suffocates me! . . . Now, when I feel my company superfluous, I can comfortably fold my independence round me like a mantle, and drop my pride like a veil, and withdraw to solitude. If married, that could not be.' (pp. 223–4)

As we have seen, the way most of the men behave in most of the book renders the women's fears here justified. Shirley's pride and strength in her independence are also notable here: marriage, rather than the desirable aim of the plot, seems a dangerous risk, involving a loss of freedom and integrity. It is true that the conversation moves away from a conclusion so subversive to novelistic and social convention. The two women describe their ideal man, the 'exception' – though Caroline's remark that '"I suppose we each find an exception in the one we love, till we *are* married"' (p. 224) turns these descriptions into hopeful fantasy, and hints at disappointment to come. More pious hopes are expressed by Shirley:

'. . .when they *are* good, they are the lords of creation. . .
Indisputably, a great, good, handsome man is the first of all created things.'. . .
'But are we men's equals, or are we not?'
'Nothing ever charms me more than when I meet my superior – one who makes me sincerely feel that he is my superior.'
'Did you ever meet him?' (pp. 225–6)

The course of their conversation follows the shape of the novel: as Shirley's fantasies about her 'superior' are brought in here to put an end to the women's doubting speculations about marriage, and their shared tranquillity without men, so is Louis Moore belatedly introduced into the plot to embody this 'superior', and put an end to the women's friendship and Shirley's proud singleness. Even once she is engaged to Louis however, Shirley still has ' "dreams of her wild woods, and pinings after virgin freedom" ' (p. 584); and we never see enough of either Shirley or Caroline after their marriages to judge whether Caroline is not right in her fears of what happens to illusions about men's exceptionality or superiority when 'we *are* married'. The doubts and fears the women raise about men and marriage here cannot be unspoken. They do not ultimately affect the plot, but they suggest an unacted alternative story, in which the possibilities of tranquil female community, or strong female singleness, would be explored.

The same is true of Caroline's speculations about the more productive possibilities that could and should be offered to single women, and the related conversation between her and Shirley, in which Shirley asks.

> 'Caroline, . . . don't you wish you had a profession – a trade?'
> 'I wish it fifty times a-day. As it is, I often wonder what I came into the world for. I long to have something absorbing and compulsory to fill my head and hands, and to occupy my thoughts.' (p. 235)

Again, this is an unacted possibility – the society of the novel cannot accommodate such a demand. In talking of Nunnwood, the women fantasise about a lost past world of female power, and here they wish for an unattainable future world of female activity. It is interesting that in this conversation we see Shirley voicing and helping Caroline to voice what have been Caroline's solitary, inward, privately rebellious thoughts. The women's friendship provides a space in which they can explore female consciousness and question male social assumptions.

The women's conversation about their projected sea-voyage also develops into a questioning of male attitudes – specifically, of male images of women. Shirley proposes the voyage as a substitute for Caroline's plan to go away as a governess. Caroline is putting forward this plan because of her secret conviction that Robert will marry Shirley – she cannot bear to stay and witness their love-making, though she bears Shirley no ill-will. A man is intruding and spoiling the friendship. Shirley's proposal is a reinstatment of the female world she shares with Caroline. Caroline – who has just said ' "I *do* like Shirley: I like her more and more every day; but that does not make me strong or happy" ' (P. 246) – finds the prospect of the journey 'not only pleasant, but gloriously reviving' (p. 248). It is to be an all-female expedition, comprising the two friends and Mrs Pryor. Like the Nunnwood excursion, it is to take them far from society, and Caroline again imagines it in imagery of tranquillity and female fertility: '"I will fancy seals lying in the sunshine on solitary shores, where neither fisherman nor hunter ever come: of rock-crevices full of pearly eggs bedded in sea-weed; of unscared birds covering white sands in happy flocks"' (p. 248). Caroline also introduces a more exciting, male presence, when she imagines the whole sea swaying 'above a herd of whales rushing through the livid and liquid thunder ... rolling in the wake of a patriarch bull', but Shirley dismisses the image of any such male disturbance of their idyll: '"I hope our bark will meet with no such shoal ... I should not like to be capsized by the patriarch bull"' (p. 249). Shirley, as we are to see in her relationship with Louis, is much less passively susceptible than Caroline to the power and fascination of male sexuality, more likely to see it as something external that may 'capsize' her independent presence, than to allow it to take possession of her, as Caroline allows her feelings for Robert to invade her consciousness, like the herd of whales in the sea.

That the subtext of their conversation is sexuality is confirmed by Shirley's subsequent fantasy about the mermaid. Here, she imagines the women confronting a male fantasy about their sexuality:

'I see a preternatural lure in its wily glance: it beckons. Were we men, we should spring at the sign, the cold billow would be dared for the sake of the colder enchantress; being women, we stand safe, though not dreadless.... Temptress-terror! monstrous likeness of ourselves! Are you not glad, Caroline, when at last, and with a wild shriek, she dives!'

'But, Shirley, she is not like us: we are neither temptresses, nor terrors, nor monsters.'

'Some of our kind, it is said, are all three. There are men who ascribe to "woman," in general such attributes.' (pp. 249–50)

Here a male image of woman, with which the women cannot identify, is faced and questioned – later, Shirley is to proceed to revise such male myths. While Caroline is more aware of the social injustices that are done to women, Shirley is more aware of the way male-centred myths and stories oppress them with alien identities. As Shirley says later,

'If men could see us as we really are, they would be a little amazed; but the cleverest, the acutest men are often under an illusion about women: they do not read them in a true light: they misapprehend them, both for good and evil: their good woman is a queer thing, half doll, half angel; their bad woman almost always a fiend. Then to hear them fall into ecstasies with each other's creations, worshipping the heroine of such a poem – novel – drama, thinking it fine – divine! Fine and divine it may be, but often quite artificial – false as the rose in my best bonnet there.' (p. 343)

At this point Shirley does not risk giving her 'real opinion of some first-rate female characters in first-rate works', but earlier she has done just that in her criticism and revision of Milton's Eve, in Chapter 18. The mythic figure that Shirley creates here both criticises the limitations of Milton's conception of archetypal womanhood, and reinforces the connection between Nature and woman's lost power. Significantly, Shirley elaborates her criticisms of Milton after the two friends have decided not to enter the church, where the rest of their society is gathered, and the men are making speeches, but to stay outside and enjoy the ' "pleasant and calm" ' natural scene. The place is right for a revisionary female mythology to be created: this is where Shirley says ' "we are alone: we may speak what we think" .' Shirley imagines that ' "Nature is now at her evening prayers.... I will tell you what she is like: she is like what Eve was when she and Adam stood alone on earth" .' As the scene progresses, the question of how far Caroline shares Shirley's ideas arises – but here it is Caroline who immediately insists, ' "And that is not Milton's Eve, Shirley" ' (p. 314). Shirley agrees – ' "Milton tried to see the first woman; but, Cary, he saw her not" ' (p. 315). She dismisses his Eve as a cook or a housekeeper. Instead, she invents a 'woman-Titan', mixing elements of Christian and pagan mythology. This powerful figure is not just a remote progenitor: Shirley imagines her present now, as Nature, a mother goddess with whom she can commune. She is proposing a female mythology and a female spirituality which are alternatives to patriarchal religion:

'... Come, Shirley, we ought to go into church.'
'Caroline, I will not: I will stay out here with my mother Eve, in these days called Nature. I love her – undying, mighty being! ... She is taking

me to her bosom, and showing me her heart. Hush, Caroline! you will see her and feel her as I do, if we are both silent.' (p. 316)

It is the fact that she is alone with another woman that emboldens Shirley to create this vision. Women alone together in Nature can express a female consciousness that must be hidden when they are in church, or in society. Caroline, however, instead of joining in the elaboration of Shirley's vision, responds with gentle criticisms and deflating remarks: '"you have got such a hash of Scripture and mythology into your head that there is no making any sense of you. You have not yet told me what you saw kneeling on those hills"'; '"She is very vague and visionary! Come, Shirley, we ought to go into church"'; '"I will humour your whim; but you will begin talking again, ere ten minutes are over"' (pp. 315–16). It would be a mistake to read too much into Caroline's criticisms here, and to imagine a radical disagreement between the two women, with Caroline as the 'womanly' woman and Shirley as the opposing 'modern' woman.[31] As we have seen, Caroline shares Shirley's bond with a maternal Nature; and at the end of this scene, it is she who completes the revision of patriarchal religion, by attacking Joe Scott's misogynistic quotations from St Paul. Partly, she is poking fun at Shirley's rhapsodical style here – her own style is different, more descriptive and less visionary. Partly, her deflating remarks operate to reassure the reader: in one sense the women are alone and can say what they think; in another, they may be sharing the scene with a male reader. To make gentle fun of Shirley deflects severer criticism, and makes her expression of her views more acceptable. Caroline performs a similar function in the later scene when Shirley attacks men's illusions about women:

'Shirley, you chatter so, I can't fasten you: be still. And after all, authors' heroines are almost as good as authoresses' heroes.'

'Not at all: women read men more truly than men read women. I'll prove that in a magazine paper some day when I've time; only it will never be inserted: it will be "declined with thanks," and left for me at the publisher's.'

'To be sure: you could not write cleverly enough; you don't know enough; you are not learned, Shirley.' (p. 343)

It is important to notice that Caroline's criticisms do not have the effect of silencing Shirley: she is encouraged to further elaborations, sometimes even with explicit invitations from Caroline, as in ' "You have not yet told me what you saw kneeling on those hills" ' (p. 315).

Caroline, as I have suggested, is more aware of the social conditions that oppress women, while Shirley, being more independent in her social position, is more aware of the myths and stories that have no place for a strong woman like herself. Thus, Shirley's talk of her visionary mother Nature, makes Caroline think of her real mother: 'Shirley had mentioned the word "mother": that word suggested to Caroline's imagination not the mighty and mystical parent of Shirley's visions, but a gentler human form – the form she ascribed to her own mother; unknown, unloved, but not unlonged-for' (p. 316). Caroline wants to contact her mother on the social, not the mythic plane, and her mother, Mrs Pryor, when she does appear, is an exemplar of the sufferings of women in a patriarchal society, not an unfettered woman-Titan existing before and outside society. The difference between these two mother figures reflects the difference between Shirley's happy independence and Caroline's painful deprivation, between women's potentialities as represented in Shirley and her visions, and the waste of that potential in Caroline's imprisoned life and her protests.

The two friends combine, however, at the end of the chapter in attacking and laughing at the misogynistic Joe Scott. Joe quotes St Paul to support his views: ' "Let the woman learn in silence, with all subjection. I suffer not a woman to teach, nor to usurp authority over the man; but to be in silence" ' (p. 322). While both women question and tease him, it is interesting that it is Caroline who provides the revisionary reading of St Paul, in the form of a humourous inversion:

'. . . I dare say, if I could read the original Greek, I should find that many of the words have been wrongly translated, perhaps misapprehended altogether. It would be possible, I doubt not, with a little ingenuity, to give the passage quite a contrary turn; to make it say, "Let the woman speak out whenever she sees fit to make an objection;" – "it is permitted to a woman to teach and to exercise authority as much as may be. Man, meantime, cannot do better than hold his peace," and so on.' (p. 323)

It is appropriate that Caroline should take the lead here, as the argument with St Paul is about social rules and prescriptions, while the argument with Milton was about images and archetypes.

A more serious reason for finding flaws in the friendship than any imagined disagreement about women's position, is the disruption caused by Robert Moore. Critics have suggested that the element of rivalry and misunderstanding that he introduces seriously undermines the women's friendship. It seems to me, however, that the friendship triumphs over this test, and reaffirms the value of female–female over female–male bonds. As in the other novels I have discussed, Caroline is ready to give up her lover to her rival and friend: but Shirley does *not* here reciprocate and give Robert back to her in any sense: instead, she reasserts the primacy of their female friendship, and attacks the 'intrusion' of the male. This intrusion begins when Caroline imagines that Robert and Shirley will marry each other, and suffers acutely. This suffering puts in question the value of the friendship, and the quality of support she gets from Shirley. When Shirley first appears in Caroline's life, she comes as a rescuer, bringing relief and strength, to save Caroline from the isolation that Robert's rejection has forced her into:

> Miss Helstone's new acquaintance soon became of value to her: their society was acknowledged a privilege. She found she would have been in error indeed to have let slip this chance of relief – to have neglected to avail herself of this happy change: a turn was thereby given to her thoughts; a new channel was opened for them... (p. 229)

But the relationship between Robert and Shirley throws her into worse than her original misery:

> 'This is the worst passage I have come to yet: still I was quite prepared for it. I gave Robert up, and gave him up to Shirley, the first day I heard she was come: the first moment I saw her – rich, youthful, and lovely.... They will both be happy, and I do not grudge them their bliss; but I groan under my own misery ...' (pp. 239–40)

Her misery does not make her hate Shirley – she gives up Robert to her without jealousy – but the friendship loses its power to sustain her. As she says, '"I *do* like Shirley, ... but that does not make me strong or happy"' (p. 246). As I have suggested, however, Shirley is aware of this falling-off, and introduces the idea of the sea-voyage to restore both Caroline's strength and the friendship. This pattern continues – the next time Caroline falls into a pit of despair about Shirley and Robert, Shirley again restores the friendship, this time

with an explicit attack on Robert as an intruder into their shared
female world.

Robert in fact has arrived at Shirley's house just as Shirley finishes
fantasising about the mermaid. The mermaid intruded a male
fantasy into their female voyage; Robert now intrudes his male
presence and demands into their shared fantasy. Even though he
walks Caroline home afterwards, she interprets his conversation
with Shirley as love-making, and wakes the next day in despair
again, resolved that she must leave as soon as Shirley and Robert are
married. But Shirley seeks her out to put things right:

> 'I feel indignant, and that is the long and short of the matter,' responded
> Miss Keeldar. 'All my comfort,' she added presently, 'is broken up by his
> manoeuvres. He keeps intruding between you and me: without him we
> should be good friends; but that six feet of puppyhood makes a
> perpetually recurring eclipse of our friendship. Again and again he
> crosses and obscures the disk I want always to see clear: ever and anon he
> renders me to you a mere bore and nuisance.' (p. 264)

The 'eclipse' imagery links to a pattern of female moon imagery in
the book.[32] As in *Jane Eyre*, the moon is a representative of the
'Great Mother'. Just as Nature, the women agree, 'conceals her face'
from her female worshippers when a man is present, so here the
intruding man 'obscures' the moon of female companionship.
Shirley wins from Caroline a declaration of the value of their
friendship, and a reaffirmation of the tranquil, exclusively female
world where they meet:

> 'Shirley, I never had a sister – you never had a sister; but it flashes on
> me at this moment how sisters feel towards each other. Affection twined
> with their life, which no shocks of feeling can uproot, which little
> quarrels only trample an instant that it may spring more freshly when
> the pressure is removed; affection that no passion can ultimately
> outrival, with which even love itself cannot do more than compete in
> force and truth. Love hurts us so, Shirley: it is so tormenting, so racking,
> and it burns away our strength with its flame; in affection is no pain and
> no fire, only sustenance and balm. I am supported and soothed when you
> – that is, *you only* – are near, Shirley. Do you believe me now?' (p. 265)

Here, female friendship is explicitly set up as an equal 'competitor'
with heterosexual love. Caroline also affirms that the friendship can

survive the 'shocks of feeling', the hidden 'quarrels' that her fears about losing Robert to Shirley have created: true to her words, the friendship is even now 'spring[ing] more freshly when the pressure is removed'. Robert's intrusion tests the friendship, but it survives the test, with its value enhanced and recognised.

From now on, Shirley's presence only seems to strengthen Caroline. Some of Shirley's self-confidence and strength is transferred to her. She is no longer afraid of the 'trial' of her public appearance at the Whitsuntide celebrations:

> But this year Shirley was to be with her, and that changed the aspect of the trial singularly – it changed it utterly: it was a trial no longer – it was almost an enjoyment. Miss Keeldar was better in her single self than a host of ordinary friends. Quite self-possessed, and always spirited and easy; conscious of her social importance, yet never presuming upon it, it would be enough to give one courage only to look at her. (p. 291)

On this occasion, Caroline becomes more like Shirley:

> ...instead of sitting down in a retired corner, or stealing away to her own room till the procession should be marshalled, according to her wont, she moved through the three parlours, conversed and smiled, absolutely spoke once or twice ere she was spoken to, and, in short, seemed a new creature. It was Shirley's presence which thus transformed her ... (p. 294)

Later, when the two friends go out in the dark to warn Robert of the approaching rioters, Shirley imparts her courage to Caroline – she offers to carry Caroline across the narrow plank over the beck, as 'Caroline had never yet dared to risk the transit'. But Caroline is transformed: 'Caroline, without pausing, trod forward on the trembling plank as if it were a continuation of the firm turf: Shirley, who followed, did not cross it more resolutely or safely' (p. 332). This shared courage does not, however, lead them to influence or participate in the male action, as they are hoping: they are too late, and arrive instead at their usual meeting-place in the isolation of Nature. At this point, Shirley has so released Caroline's inhibitions, that she is about to rush down to the Mill and reveal her carefully concealed and suppressed love for Robert. Shirley has to change role, and physically restrain Caroline, knowing such a move would end in disaster.

Shirley thus is fully in the secret of Caroline's love for Robert. She often introduces his name into the conversation, to give Caroline the relief of speaking of him: 'She always felt a sort of shy pleasure in following Miss Keeldar's lead respecting the discussion of her cousin's character: left to herself, she would never have touched on the subject; but when invited, the temptation of talking about him of whom she was ever thinking was irresistible' (p. 275). Some critics have seen Shirley as failing Caroline by encouraging Robert's attentions to herself, and by not telling Caroline that she is not in love with him. Gilbert and Gubar remark that

> Shirley does not provide the release she at first seems to promise Caroline ... she gratuitously flirts, thereby inflicting pain on Caroline, who is tortured by her belief that Shirley is a successful rival for Robert Moore's love. Indeed, Shirley manages to rob Caroline of even a modicum of pleasure from Moore's presence ...[33]

Craik also criticises Shirley's conduct here: 'she is clearly intended to understand Caroline's situation and sympathise with her, yet she must apparently be ignorant of how her friendship with Robert increases Caroline's misery; serious limitations are thus implied, in her perception and in the very sympathy we are supposed to admire.'[34] But, as I have shown, the initial promise of the relationship, though threatened by Robert's intrusion, is restored and strengthened, precisely by Shirley's efforts, and her awareness that Robert is a threat. What then of her behaviour towards him? Though she is aware that his effect on Caroline separates the friends, she does not seem aware of Caroline's misreading of her relationship with him. But we must remember how distorted by her obsession Caroline's perception is – that Shirley loves and encourages Robert is *her* reading, as the narrator reminds us: 'What I have just said are Caroline's ideas of the pair: she felt what has just been described' (p. 254). And even Caroline does not see any flirtation in Shirley's behaviour: 'there was nothing coquettish in [Shirley's] demeanour: whatever she felt for Moore, she felt it seriously' (p. 254). Shirley, though sympathising with Caroline's feelings, cannot be expected to enter fully into her obsessive perspective; and she is also shown as a victim of the misinterpretations a woman is vulnerable to if she cultivates a genuine friendship for a man.

It is not Robert who divides the friends, it is Louis. At the Whitsuntide events the women's friendship is at its strongest, and, as I have shown, Caroline is most strengthened by Shirley's influence. But soon after, they are separated by the advent of the conventional Sympsons. Shirley gives in surprisingly readily to their imposition on her hospitality. Later, we find it is because she is hoping that Louis will come and join them. After the separation, Caroline declines rapidly, and is on the point of death when rescued again by a female friend – Mrs Pryor, who turns out to be her mother. While the friendship with Shirley provides her with Shirley's man-like strength, courage and outspokenness, and also the tranquillity of their shared female world, it does not provide the intense mothering we have seen other mother-deprived heroines obtaining from their female friends. In *Shirley*, an actual mother is brought in to provide this. The intensity and physicality of Mrs Pryor's love seems to restore to Caroline whatever she lost in losing Robert's love – once more she blooms, once more she has an object all of her own to love. Gilbert and Gubar point out that when Caroline goes to visit and revive the sick Robert at *Briar*mains, the Sleeping Beauty story is reversed: the heroine rescues the hero.[35] But when Mrs Pryor revives the 'statue'-like Caroline at *Briar*field, the story has already been revised – the heroine is awakened from her death-like trance, not by the hero, but by her mother. This revival by another woman is very like the way Lizzie revives Laura in *Goblin Market* – like Laura, Caroline is wasting away from 'baulked desire', and is restored by physical, maternal contact. But the relationship is also reciprocal: 'the child lulled the parent, as the parent had erstwhile lulled the child' (p. 412). Before the revelation that Mrs Pryor is her mother, it is only with Caroline that Mrs Pryor can drop some of her defences:

> Mrs Pryor liked a quiet walk ... when once she got away from human habitations, and entered the still demesne of Nature, accompanied by this one youthful friend, a propitious change seemed to steal over her mind and beam in her countenance. When with Caroline – and Caroline only – her heart, you would have said, shook off a burden, her brow put aside a veil, her spirits too escaped from a restraint... (pp. 360-1)

Interestingly, this meeting between the two women can only take place in Nature, the secluded female world where Caroline and Shirley also meet and are most free to be themselves.

Once Caroline has been revived by Mrs Pryor, the friendship with Shirley is restored, despite the continuing presence of the Sympsons,

and now Louis. But the friends do not interact in any important
way, apart from Caroline discovering the secret of Shirley's feelings
for Louis. Shirley, however, now Louis is present, does become more
like Caroline: her power is dimmed, and she conceals her feelings.
Most notably, when she conceals her fears about the dog-bite, she
literally enacts the advice the narrator had earlier given to Caroline,
and all 'disappointed' women:

> You held out your hand for an egg, and fate put into it a scorpion. Show
> no consternation: close your fingers firmly upon the gift; let it sting
> through your palm. Never mind: in time, after your hand and arm have
> swelled and quivered long with torture, the squeezed scorpion will die,
> and you will have learned the great lesson how to endure without a sob.
> (p. 128)

Shirley is as firm in repressing her feelings as ever Caroline was, and
like Caroline, she begins to waste away. On the other hand, Shirley
is concealing her feelings more out of pride than because she has been
rebuffed: her love for Louis is threatening to her independence. The
dog-bite is an interesting metaphor: Gilbert and Gubar link it to the
dog-bite that 'initiates Catherine Earnshaw into the prison of
gender'[36] in *Wuthering Heights* – it is an image of a sexual fall. But
the dog in *Wuthering Heights* is insistently *male*: the dog who bites
Shirely, however, is a female, called 'Phoebe'. She is probably not
really mad, but has been driven frantic by her ill-treatment by her
male master, Sam Wynne. Her name associates her with the moon-
goddess; and her story suggests that Shirley is about to fall prey to
the sort of female suffering that characterises Caroline and Mrs
Pryor. Love and ill-treatment by a male 'master' are inseparable, and
it is a necessary part of being female to experience this, though of
course Louis turns out to be a 'good' master. Shirley's proud,
independent 'masculinity' is undermined by this female madness, the
suffering that love imposes on women. Thus Shirley is debilitated as
Caroline regains her strength. Caroline's experience with Mrs Pryor,
however, suggests a female strength that may lie on the other side of
such suffering: but Shirley never gets so far.
    The introduction of Louis to 'tame' Shirley, and the symbolic
dog-bite that saps her strength, are both somewhat arbitrary and
extreme. Shirley does not gradually learn to be like Caroline, as
Aurora learns to be like Marian, or Maggie painfully tries to be like
Lucy. Caroline is not her model, nor does she carry out Shirley's

secret desires, in the way that Shirley carries out Caroline's. The friendship has been leading in quite another direction, towards increasing female independence and detachment from men for both women. Drastic measures are needed to defuse the friendship and bring the plot to an acceptable if arbitrary conclusion.

# Chapter Five

# New Women?

One would expect the so-called 'New Woman' novelists to give female friendship and solidarity a greater role in the structure of their narratives than did earlier Victorian novelists, and to take further the kinds of development we have seen in *Shirley*. But often there is a disappointing disjunction between overt protestations about the value of female solidarity, and a narrative which implies quite opposite meanings. This pattern can be illustrated in Ella Hepworth Dixon's *The Story of a Modern Woman*, and in Olive Schreiner's fiction. Solidarity is shown to be impossible, or ineffective, leading to female weakness and isolation, not strength. Strong female friendship is longed for and idealised, but never achieved. It is undermined by class barriers, or by the conventional association of female bonding with the status quo, with assimilation into traditional female roles. A more consciously political solidarity *against* the patriarchy rarely appears: perhaps it is, strangely, most strongly portrayed in anti-feminist novels like Mrs Lynn Linton's *The Rebel of the Family* (1880), or Mrs Ward's later *Delia Blanchflower* (1915), where it plays a powerful role in the narrative as a disruptive threat to order. In the attempt to create 'New Woman' as a fictional type, she was often constructed as a heroic *individual*: the odds she had to battle against increased the impression of the injustices done to women, and her isolation increased the impression of female heroism. Close and supportive bonds with other women would only lessen both impressions. The main alternative to the male–female ending is thus the woman-alone ending. But many New Woman stories do still make use of the male–female romance plot as their dominant structure: New Woman writers were concerned not to overturn women's traditional roles of marriage and motherhood, but to reform them and to take them *more* seriously, emphasising women's worth, dignity and even superiority in these roles. Where this is the case, we do find female friendship functioning as before, as a transforming interchange which assimilates women to their traditional roles, through a process of negotiation about acceptable female identity. The difference is that some rather more radical positions are reached through this process, but always involving very careful negotiations between old and new ideals: startlingly new female roles are often contained and made acceptable by conventional narrative structures. Examples of this kind of pattern can be found in Annie Holdsworth's *Joanna Traill, Spinster*, and in George Egerton's stories.

Difficulties in incorporating an idea *about* female solidarity into a narrative can be seen in Ella Hepworth Dixon's *The Story of a Modern Woman*.[1] The author wrote to W. T. Stead to say that her novel was intended as 'a plea for a kind of moral and social trades-unionism among women'.[2] The story is self-consciously *not* a conventional narrative ending in marriage: in order to survive as a writer, the heroine, Mary, accepts a commission to write a three-volume novel ' "on the old lines – a ball in the first volume; a picnic and a parting in the second; and an elopement, which must, of course, be prevented at the last moment by the opportune death (in a hospital) of the wife, or the husband – I forget which it is to be – in the last." ' This contrasts with the 'realistic' but unpublishable novel she would like to write: ' "It would be a bit of real life; it would have twenty-seven years of actual experience in it" ' (p. 149). This, we assume, is the novel we are reading. The major subject of the novel is Mary's attempts to survive as an independent woman, first as an artist, and then as a writer, rather than her romances; and the romances she has are not conventional: she refuses a proposal from an affectionate but totally unsuitable and vulgar painter, and she is deserted by the weak-willed intellectual Vincent Hemmings, who marries a rich heiress. Mary loves Vincent, not because he is particularly worthy, but because in the sexual ideology of the novel, once a man has embraced a woman, she is irrevocably tied to him by her feelings. Later, Vincent returns and proposes an elopement, but she resists. His wife does not opportunely die. The novel ends not

with marriage or death, but with the heroine alone, having lost
parents, lover and friend, still struggling on to make her living. The
final image is ominous, suggesting the failure of her attempt to
'stand alone': 'Standing alone, there on the heights, she made a feint
as if to grasp the city spread out before her, but the movement ended
in a vain gesture, and the radiance of her face was blotted out as she
began to plod homewards in the twilight of the suburban road' (p.
269). The dark ending reminds us that as a child, Mary had been
fascinated by Charlotte Brontë's *Villette*: though at least Lucy
Snowe was allowed a successful career.

The revisions of the conventional plot thus seem designed to show
the utter hopelessness of the 'modern woman's' lot.[3] Though, as we
shall see, professions of female solidarity are made, female solidarity
does not strengthen the heroine, or alleviate her isolation. Instead, it
seems to weaken her and further isolate her. Mary does have a
female friend, Alison Ives, who, rather implausibly, provides her
with contact with both the world of the fashionable aristocracy, and
the world of fallen women in the East End. Alison is strikingly
beautiful, stunningly dressed, and devotes her time to rescuing fallen
women. She seems, like Mrs Ward's Marcella, to be an attempt to
reconcile womanliness and political action. We are assured that she
'hated playing the man', and people are attracted at once by 'her
womanliness, her lack of snobbishness, her real desire to be in
sympathy with her own sex' (p. 39). She has also worked in a
sculptor's studio in Paris, 'could interpret Chopin like an artist, and
always had her hair exquisitely dressed' (p. 39). The 'modern
woman' can be all things – artist, social worker, and also,
reassuringly, fashion–conscious beauty. It is Alison who articulates
the 'modern' creed of female solidarity: ' "If women only used their
power in the right way! If we were only united we could lead the
world" ' (p. 213). Mary replies, ' ". . . we shall be by and by. All we
modern women are going to help each other, not to hinder" ' (pp.
213–14). Earlier, we have seen Mary's sympathy for a seamstress
who seems to her to be the embodiment of the traditional female
role: 'the figure of woman at her monotonous toil' (p. 13).

This sympathy does not, however, lead to any attempt to help or
befriend the actual seamstress – and Mary is divided from the actual
women she comes in contact with by a class snobbery that is
nowhere criticised in the text. At the Central London School of Art,
Mary is isolated, because 'she dreaded the confidences of the young

ladies, some of whom had prosperous flirtations, carried on in neighbouring pastry-cooks' shops' (p. 65). These women are described as 'of the lower middle-class; the daughters of retail shopkeepers' (p. 64), and so quite impossible as friends for the refined Mary. Alison does actually 'rescue' women of an even lower class, but the one case who appears as a character, Evelina, is similarly ridiculed for her vulgarity, especially her cheap, soiled, white wedding dress, which she insists on wearing at the wedding Alison fixes up for her. Both Alison and Mary are to perform acts of self-sacrifice for 'vulgar' women, but no prolonged contact is allowed – Mary never even meets Vincent's vulgar wife, and the 'tawdry' ex-mistress of Alison's suitor is on the point of death when Alison meets her. There is no possibility of reciprocity, or continued friendship. Female solidarity is an abstract idea, not a lived experience.

Their acts of solidarity also, in effect, destroy both Alison and Mary. Alison is engaged to be married to an eminent doctor: 'she supposed she should have to marry some day – the later the better – because it was absurd to suppose that old maids had any influence on people's lives; and Power, to put it plainly, was what the modern woman craved' (p. 78). Dr Strange, Alison's fiancé, takes the two women on a tour of his hospital, and there they come upon a dying fallen woman who turns out to be his ex-mistress. She also turns out to be the 'tawdry-looking girl' (p. 122) Mary had seen in the park waiting for a man who did not turn up, while Mary is also waiting for Vincent, who also disappoints her. Mary subconsciously identifies with the woman: "Oddly enough, the face of the girl she had seen in the Regent's Park rose up again and again. And yet what had they in common?' (p. 128). The woman is another symbol of female suffering for Mary: ' "If that tawdry-looking girl could write down her story . . . we should have another masterpiece! It is because they suffer so that women have written supremely good fiction" ' (p. 122). But no actual contact is made: women are isolated sufferers. Alison's contact with the woman comes too late: ' "If I had only known her earlier, who knows? I might have been her friend; I might have saved her from –" ' (p. 205). Alison shows her solidarity, however, by breaking off her engagement: this decision is explicitly presented as being due not to jealousy or anger, but sympathy. Alison's mother, thinks Mary, would not 'comprehend her daughter's extremely modern sympathy for this woman' (p.

217). For readers of Mrs Gaskell's *Ruth*, or Elizabeth Barrett Browning's *Aurora Leigh*, this sympathy does not seem so very modern, nor so whole-hearted as it was in those earlier books. And while Gaskell and Barrett Browning show solidarity with a fallen woman enriching the lives of other women characters, and strengthening both pure and fallen woman, here first the fallen woman dies, and then Alison also dies as the result of her decision. The shock to her emotions brings on a fatal illness. The physical weakness of women in the book is striking – Mary's nerves are continually overstrained by the effort of earning her own living, and the robust and vital Alison collapses immediately when deprived of a man. Women are feeble victims, and female solidarity, far from leading to power, only leads to useless self-sacrifice.

The same is true of Mary's refusal to run off with Vincent. This too, is presented as an act of female solidarity – ' "But it's the other woman – your wife. I can't, I won't, deliberately injure another woman. Think how she would suffer! Oh, the torture of women's lives – the helplessness, the impotence, the emptiness!" ' (pp. 254–5). Mary's decision is also a kind of death: 'After today it would all be a blank. And the impotence, the helplessness of woman's lot struck her with irresistable force' (p. 254). Women's weakness, not women's strength, is affirmed by female solidarity. As Mary walks alone along the street, another interpretation of her action strikes her – the houses she passes all 'represented the Family – that special product of civilisation for which she, as an individual, was to be sacrificed' (p. 259). As with the earlier women writers, female solidarity is seen as confirming and strengthening marriage and the family, but here there is no longer any belief in the value of those institutions, nor is there a conception of a new kind of female friendship that would work against them. In this case, female solidarity can only be debilitating and destructive to the independent woman.

Both *The Story of A Modern Woman* and Annie Holdsworth's *Joanna Traill, Spinster*[4] were featured in W. T. Stead's 1894 article, 'The Novel of the Modern Woman'. Stead introduces his review of Holdsworth's novel with the remark, 'I now come to a story of how one Modern Woman did help another with the best results',[5] implying that Ella Hepworth Dixon's theory is here put into practice. It is true that a sustaining female solidarity is integral to the structure of Holdsworth's novel. The plot involves a meek spinster who finds her independence and gives meaning to her life by befriending and rehabilitating a fallen woman, whom she takes into her house as a companion and equal. But Joanna Traill is presented throughout not as a daring 'Modern Woman', but as endearingly old-fashioned; and the way the relationship between the two women is presented has many echoes of the earlier novels I have discussed. Most importantly, the friendship transforms both women, in ways that assimilate both of them to marriage: the friendship is set within a double romance plot. So while Holdsworth does revise the conventional Madonna/Magdalen plot, in that she allows her fallen woman to marry, and it is the 'pure' woman, Joanna, who dies at the end, the primacy of male–female romance is not challenged, and both women are assimilated into traditionally 'womanly' roles.

From the beginning, Joanna's needs and strengths are presented as essentially 'womanly' – she is 'a woman with a woman's infinite craving for love, to be loved' (p. 8), and it is this need which is to be filled by her adoption of Christine, the fallen woman. This project is not initiated by her – instead, she is inspired by the forceful, philanthropic Mr Boas (a portrait of Stead?): her 'woman's heart had been possessed by his man's enthusiasm' (p. 30). Traditional 'womanly' qualities are what Boas is looking for, to implement his 'modern' philanthropic schemes:

> 'What these poor creatures want is not sisterhoods, but sisters.... They want women to go among them, with the tender touch of women for their bleeding hearts, and the tears of women for their unutterable wrongs.... Women who will love them and live with them, and work with them, and teach them the mighty possibilities of womanhood.' (pp. 26–7)

Joanna's possession of the right qualities for this work is implicitly linked to her old-fashionedness, and contrasted with the coldness and superficiality of the relentlessly 'modern' and fashionable Mrs Crane and Mrs Prothero, her actual sisters, who see Joanna as 'sadly behind the times' (p. 17) in her tastes. They are cultivating Boas merely as a fashionable curiosity, since 'enthusiasm is the catch word ... if you fly at anything, no matter if it's dogma or paupers or trades unions, you are at once in the fashion. Just now society is sacrificing to sincerity' (p. 20).

This superficial modern patronage of 'enthusiasm' contrasts with the 'enthusiasm' Boas awakens in the dowdy, unfashionable Joanna. Thus her characterisation is firmly distanced from the dangerously unorthodox image of the 'New Woman' – her motivations are motherly love for Christine, womanly veneration and later romantic love for Boas, and, it is hinted, religious belief: 'she had an old-fashioned belief in the assistance of another power that strengthened her own weakness' (p. 82). It is these traditional values, rather than any 'modern' ideas about sisterly solidarity that sustain her. Of course, by showing the development of sisterhood between this old-fashioned, necessarily pure, acceptably womanly spinster, and a 'fallen' woman, the book makes a powerful argument for the reacceptance and rehabilitation of such outcasts as Christine – Joanna's

> purity made her face and forgive the sin less spotless women would have shunned and condemned. Evil, that would have roused their disgust had only touched her womanliness and pity. She claimed sisterhood with the fallen, and yearned to reach hands of help to them. (pp. 65–6)

The romance with Boas, and Christine's eventual marriage, could also be seen as setting an unconventional message within a reassuringly conventional narrative structure. The sisterhood between pure and fallen does not produce a more feminist consciousness in either: instead, both are transformed in ways that make them more suitable for marriage. Joanna's contact with the youthful and blooming Christine restores some of her own bloom, and makes her more attractive to Boas. This effect is initially brought about by the help of Christine's superior skill in the art of dressing attractively, in an important scene that begins by contrasting their appearances. Joanna is dressing for dinner:

> . . . for the first time in her life she was dissatisfied with her appearance.
> She had never before given a thought to her dress. Now she discovered that the gown she wore, Mrs. Crane's choice, was ugly and middle-aged.
> The black silk fitted her with cruel exactness, and showed her angular outlines with uncompromising severity.
> The square at the neck was finished by a jet embroidery that made the face above it hard and colourless. There was no softness about her, and Joanna, vaguely conscious of a want, threw a lace shawl across her shoulders – a fatal act that stamped 'old maid' on her whole appearance.

'It is no use fighting against it,' she thought meekly to herself. 'I am not young – I am only a plain, middle-aged woman.' But she sighed as she turned from the glass.

Then her face changed at the sight of Christine in the doorway, and she forgot her own disadvantages in pleasure at the girl's appearance.

The simple gown had transformed Christine into a dainty child. She stood shyly under Miss Traill's scrutiny, her eyes big with excitement; and Joanna studied her from head to foot, and was well satisfied.

She had brushed out her elaborate fringe, and the hair waved naturally from her forehead, making the face more childlike and refined.

Her dress fell in straight folds from her waist, and she had fastened a spray of copper-beech in her belt – a detail that gave character to the whole costume.

'Do you think he [Boas] will think I look nice?' she asked artlessly.

'I am sure he will,' said Joanna. And with the words a pang shot through her, a cry for her own vanished youth.

'I am glad,' said Christine frankly, in turn scrutinising Joanna. She tipped her head on one side and pondered before she spoke again. 'Why do you wear that shawl? Is that the way at dinner?'

'No; but my dress wanted relief. It is too severe.'

'So it is; but that is not right. Please let me. Where's a pin?' (pp. 82–4)

'With a few deft touches', and some flowers, Christine transforms Joanna's appearance. Joanna looks in the mirror again:

Miss Traill did not recognise herself there.

The angles and leanness of her figure had disappeared with the hard surface of the silk. The belt outlined a waist still young and round, and the face with its light of pleasure and excitement was distinctly good to look at.

She was no longer a grim and unrelenting spinster, but a woman with undreamed-of treasures of feeling dimly shadowed in her face.

She blushed at the reflection of herself.

'What a clever little woman you are, Christine. Who taught you to do this?'

The girl shrugged her shoulders in a little foreign fashion. 'I never was taught – it seems to come natural. My grandmother was a French woman. . . .' (p. 85)

The effect is not lost on Boas: '"Heavens! how that little witch has brightened her up," he thought. "She was a dowdy old maid when I met her at Croydon. Now she is actually good-looking"' (p. 86).

Put crudely, Joanna's sexual charms are brought out by the help of an ex-prostitute; but this effect is rendered acceptable by the prior transformation in Christine from the artificial to the natural and childlike – 'She had brushed out her elaborate fringe, and the hair waved naturally from her forehead, making the face more childlike and refined'. The 'arts' by which she transforms Joanna 'come natural', an inheritance from her French grandmother – a paradox that neatly reconciles all the sexual charge of 'French' and the innocence of 'natural'. Thus the external change in Joanna's dress is not just a matter of artful exterior manipulation: it reveals her inner nature more clearly, her 'undreamed-of treasures of feeling'. Just as Christine's innate innocence is revealed by her change of clothes, so Joanna reveals an unsuspected sexuality, 'no longer a grim and unrelenting spinster'. Later, this revelation of Joanna's sexuality is explicitly linked to her *love* for Christine – Christine runs away to her old haunts, and, after a night of frantic searching, Joanna returns to find Christine at home asleep in Joanna's own bed: 'Joanna could restrain herself no longer. The pent-up passion of the night burst in a rush of sobs. She caught the girl in her arms, and sobbed and laughed and wept, wild in her great happiness' (p. 164). Again, this scene of assimilation between the two women issues in a sexual recognition from Boas: 'He had expected to find her pale and suffering from fatigue. Instead, she was sparkling, more animated than he had ever seen her. Her face was flushed; her eyes danced; her mouth took tender curves. Emotion made her beautiful' (p. 166). Joanna's passion for Christine is made acceptable because it is celebrating Christine's *rescue* from sexual transgression; and the clearly sexual transformation that Boas notes is explained as 'emotion'. A careful, and acceptable, blend of sexuality and selfless emotion, purity and allure is being concocted, by means of the friendship between the two women.

The way in which Joanna's embrace of Christine transfers Christine's bloom, in acceptable form, to the previously 'spinsterish' Joanna, is very reminiscent of Hetty's effect on Dinah in *Adam Bede*. But, unlike Hetty, Christine is not reduced and eliminated by the process: she gains qualities of innocence, refinement and modesty from Joanna, which combine with her innate sexual attractiveness to make her an acceptable wife for Amos Bevan, Boas's friend: 'the daring, ambitious little schemer had become a sweet and modest girl, full of right impulses and deeds' (p. 132). It is true that when he

learns of her past, Bevan, who has proposed to her, repudiates her –
but this is the result of his unworthy prejudices. He is allowed to
experience a change of heart in Australia, and return to woo a
Christine who has added a stronger consciousness of her dignity and
worth to her other qualities: eventually, she consents to marry him
after all. But, before this reconciliation, the bond between the two
women is tried by the intervention of Boas – they suddenly find
themselves rivals for the same man. Boas does not love Christine,
but, after her rejection by Bevan, he is possessed by the idea of
'saving' her by marriage, and he offers to marry her himself. First,
however, he asks Joanna's approval. True to the pattern we have
seen in earlier women's fiction, Joanna is ready to sacrifice her own
love for Boas, for the sake of her 'rival':

> She did not ask his love, she had never looked forward to love's return.
> She only wanted to be free to love him – to hold him in her heart
> without sin. And his marriage to Christine would make her heart empty.
>   But she sat still before him, and while her life died in her she bade him
> marry the girl she had saved from infamy.
>   That sacrifice she did not grudge. To see Christine safe from evil she
> would have cut off every limb from her body. (pp. 121–2)

Christine, of course, in turn refuses Boas, for the sake of Joanna –
'she had been able to sacrifice herself, and to set aside the love of a
good man, for the sake of Joanna, who loved him' (p. 176). The
bond between the two women takes precedence over their bonds to
the man, and survives the challenge of rivalry – though the narrative
rewards them for this self-sacrifice by joining each to the appropriate
man.

While her bond with Christine transforms Joanna in ways that
make her even more 'womanly', it also operates in what seems a
contradictory direction – to make her more independent and self-
assertive. Against the narrative pattern that leads Joanna towards
romance, there works another pattern that leads her towards
independent action. This pattern, however, is carefully contained
within the romance plot – her independence is always dependent on
Boas's inspiration and support, and it increases his admiration for
her. That her independence depends on male support is indicated
from the beginning – she is only able to begin to live her own life
because of a legacy, a house and fortune left to her by a rich uncle.

Interestingly, this gives her independence from her *sisters*, to whose
lives she has sacrificed her youth, and who still exploit her
unselfishness: 'She had stood in the place of parents to them, and for
twenty years had been their slave' (p. 9). This false 'sisterly' bond is
to be replaced by the bond of genuine sisterhood with Christine –
perhaps suggesting that middle-class single women's energies should
not be consumed within the family, but should be turned outwards
to help other less privileged women – though by taking Christine
into her home, Joanna assimilates her into the family. Towards the
end of the novel, however, before Bevan returns to marry Christine,
the two women together are living and working among the poor,
having moved away from Joanna's estate. Careful negotiations are
going on here between the old ideal of women's place in the home,
and a newer ideal of community work. We see these negotiations in
the whole history of Joanna's 'revolt' against her family. Her first
act of insubordination to her sisters, after inheriting her fortune, is a
wish to accept a proposal of marriage from a man she does not love
– 'After all, the despotism of a husband, being natural, must be less
demoralising to a woman than the tyranny of sisters. Why should
she not claim and hold her own advantage?' (p. 8) Her defiance is a
mixture of self-assertion and renewed, higher self-sacrifice. She longs
to be loved: 'Her life was empty and valueless. With love it might be
raised to what heights of noble renunciation and purpose' (pp. 8–9).
The narrative does not allow her this immediate assimilation into
marriage and woman's traditional role: instead, she has to assert her
independence in more radical ways, through the friendship with
Christine, but which still *combine* independent 'purpose' with
'noble renunciation', and involve dependence on a male mentor.

After she has given in to her sisters' veto on her marriage plans, we
learn that 'out of the elements of love and disappointment and
baffled longing she was evolving a germ of self-assertion that would
some day startle herself as much as her little world.' But, as we have
seen, this 'germ' needs Boas's 'man's enthusiam' to make it grow.
Once he has provided her with a purpose in life, however, Joanna
begins to go beyond him: 'The four years had transformed Joanna as
well as Christine. She had become alert, capable, forceful – a
woman of resource; and her name was well known in philanthropic
circles as a power. True, it was a power directed largely by Boas, but
Joanna could act without him now when necessary' (p. 133). Again,
a careful balancing of independence and dependence is being made,

though the rather grandiose conclusion is then drawn – 'She had pitted her will against fate, and the individual had conquered' (p. 133). Here, she seems to participate in New Woman's heroic independence: like other New Woman heroines, the sources of her power are *individualistic*,[6] they do not come from a bond with other women – the bond with Christine gives her love and sexual attractiveness, and provides the purpose for her will to work on, but it is not the source of her power. Christine too develops strength and purpose: 'There was a noble dignity and strength in her appearance that told Bevan the thoughtless child had become a wise and purposeful woman' (p. 181). This new strength is partly due to the suffering his rejection has put her through, and the renewed self-esteem that Boas's proposal gives her: it is not wholly created by the bond with Joanna.

Christine's developed strength is here measured by the impression it makes on her suitor – it makes her more worth winning as a wife. Similarly, Joanna's strength leads to more admiration from Boas: as they search for Christine, Joanna's 'endurance, courage, silence, impressed him. He recognised the strong soul she was' (p. 160). Her strength does not lead her to an independent life – it leads to a closer companionship with Boas, that develops into love, and a reaffirmation of her dependence on him:

> She knew that he had made her life complete, that she owed all that gave it worth and beauty to him. He was the inspiration of the best and highest in her, the power that vitalised every germ of good. . . .
>
> Through the day every action bent towards the light of his approval; every imagination unfolded in the sunshine of his sanction.
>
> She thought, read, wrote nothing that he might not have seen. She did no single act that he could not have owned as his work. (p. 195)

Christine has been married off by now, and it is Joanna's bond with Boas that is now revealed as the mainspring of Joanna's life – sisterhood with Christine is the necessary means to this. Unfortunately, Boas realises that he loves her just too late – nursing her sick and selfish sister, Joanna catches diphtheria and dies. The shock of her death finally brings on his recognition of his love for her. He protests inwardly against the words on her coffin plate, 'Joanna Traill, Spinster' – '"Spinster?" No! Joanna Traill was his wife; but he had not known it till he had seen her name on the coffin plate' (p. 207).

Thus the novel ends not with an affirmation of the worth and strength of spinsterhood, as independence or as sisterhood, but with a more traditional affirmation of Joanna's worth as a wife – Boas's thoughts give her the final accolade. Yet the message is depressingly similar to the ending of *The Story of A Modern Woman*, where independent woman is alone, unhappy and doomed to defeat. Only Boas's admiration and affirmation give strength and meaning to Joanna's life. Her death itself is full of ambiguous meanings – directly, it is caused by an *excess* of self-sacrifice, and by a return to the oppressive family from which she has had to escape – thus, she is unharmed by her excursions among the poor, but destroyed by her return to her Mrs Crane's fashionable world. Fake sisterhood kills her. The 'male' world of action and companionship is valued above the 'female' world of the family and its obligations, though, as we have seen, in order to enter that male world Joanna has to be dependent on a man. But, though Joanna's death is caused by Mrs Crane's false sisterhood, there is also a complicating and more sinister 'cause': the house she has inherited from her uncle has a curse attached – 'a doom had been spoken against the house that no bride should ever go from its threshold' (p. 12). Paradoxically, then, Joanna's death does affirm that she was indeed a 'bride' – only death could prevent a union with Boas. But only death also could make Boas *realise* her true relation to him; and by the curse the dependence of Joanna's strength on her inheritance of male power is shown to be fatal. She can only retain her power if she remains independent (male?); she can only attract a marriage partner by complete self-annihilation. A strange double-bind at the heart of her achievement is revealed: her precarious balance of 'male' independence and dependence on the male is finally impossible to maintain. The friendship with another woman has neither delivered her securely to the traditional destination of marriage, nor given her a different kind of goal. In so far as she is a New Woman, Joanna is, like other New Woman heroines, left in a final loneliness.

The loneliness and isolation of a New Woman in an uncomprehending society is one of the subjects of Olive Schreiner's *The Story of an African Farm*.[7] The heroine, Lyndall, is supposed to have a close friendship with her childhood friend Em, but the need to emphasise Lyndall's isolation and independence, and her difference from a conventional woman like Em, leads to the friendship being underplayed, and indeed undermined by Lyndall's behaviour. Em is the conventional, domestic woman – with the 'low forehead' (I p. 6) of a Marian Erle. She is there to contrast with Lyndall,[8] but it is a measure of Lyndall's emancipation that Em and her qualities have no hold over her, in the way Lucy dominated Maggie's image of desirable female identity in *The Mill on the Floss*. Instead, Em is Lyndall's devoted worshipper, seeing her as a 'princess' (II p. 25), and, with the rest of the characters in the book, testifying to Lyndall's powerful charisma. When Lyndall returns from school, Em is looking forward to showing her her wedding clothes and preparations: 'Lyndall would so like to see it – the little wreath, and the ring, and the white veil' (II p. 23). But Lyndall repels her with her tactless scorn of marriage: ' "I am not in so great a hurry to put my neck beneath any man's foot; and I do not so greatly admire the crying of babies. . . . There are other women glad of such work". ' At this, 'Em felt rebuked and ashamed. How could she take Lyndall and show her the while linen, and the wreath, and the embroidery?' (II p. 29). Lyndall's scorn for the conventional woman's lot drives a wedge between herself and her devoted female admirer.

Lyndall proceeds to take Em's fiancé, Gregory, from her: admittedly, he has fallen in love with Lyndall, but she decides to permit his attentions, and finally agrees to marry him, only because, as we find out later, she is pregnant by another man. When Lyndall starts to encourage Gregory, Em speaks pathetically of her hurt: ' "there are some things you like to have all to yourself, you don't like any one else to have any of them" ' (II p. 117). Later, she generously absolves Lyndall of blame, in the name of their childhood attachment: ' "it made me think about that time when we were little girls and used to play together, when I loved you better than anything else in the world. It isn't any one's fault that they love you; they can't help it. And it isn't your fault; you don't make them love you. I know it" ' (II p. 150). As in earlier Victorian fiction, female friends do not let rivalry for a man come between them: the cynical way Lyndall is planning to make use of Gregory seems a poor way to repay Em's generosity. Lyndall does not in fact marry Gregory – she goes off with her other lover, and dies after giving birth to a dead child. Her only letter to Gregory says ' "You must marry Em" ' (II p. 300). Thus, she does give him back to her friend. But as she despises him, there is something patronising in thus

handing him back; and we find all Em's pleasure in the marriage has
evaporated.

Lyndall does praise Em to Gregory, and reveals true appreciation
of her: Gregory asks,

> '...What is Em like, now?'
> 'The accompaniment of a song. She fills up the gaps in other people's
> lives, and is always number two; but I think she is like many
> accompaniments – a great deal better than the songs she has to
> accompany.'
> 'She is not half so good as you are!' said Gregory, with a burst of
> uncontrollable ardour.
> 'She is so much better than I, that her little finger has more goodness
> in it than my whole body. I hope you may not live to find out the truth
> of that fact.' (II pp. 144–5)

But this appreciation does not connect to the way she behaves to Em
herself. The 'goodness' she speaks of here is not really something she
wants, in the way Maggie wants Lucy's goodness; rather, she seems
to be warning Gregory about the way she plans to treat him. Her
attitude to Em is always patronising, as after their last scene
together, when Em has come to tell Lyndall about a prophetic dream
she has had about her, and Lyndall mutters '"There are some wiser
in their sleeping than in their waking"' (II, p. 151).

Lyndall, as emergent New Woman, must reject and scorn Em's
traditional role; she is engaged in a necessarily solitary quest of her
own – as she says to Waldo, a woman '"must make her way
through life. What she would be she cannot be because she is a
woman; so she looks carefully at herself and the world about her to
see where her path must lie. There is no one to help her; she must
help herself"' (II p. 108). Her essential isolation and independence is
emphasised by her relationship with her own image in the mirror:

> The glass reflected the little brown head with its even parting, and the
> tiny hands on which it rested. Presently she looked up. The large dark
> eyes from the glass looked back at her. She looked deep into them.
> 'We are all alone, you and I,' she whispered; 'no one helps us, no one
> understands us; but we will help ourselves.' The eyes looked back at her.
> There was a world of assurance in their still depths. (II p. 171)[9]

New Woman's heroic self-sufficiency is being celebrated here;

though Lyndall's futile death also symbolises the dangers of her isolated and enclosed position. Neither point could be made as effectively if she was surrounded by a community of like-minded female friends.

Rachel Blau DuPlessis has recently shown how the narrative structure of *Story of an African Farm* is a deliberate attempt to break down conventional narrative patterns.[10] Potential quest, romance and *Bildungs* plots are all aborted. Characters whom we would expect to get involved in each other's lives and plots remain separate and disconnected. The separation of Lyndall and Em, and the failure of their friendship to develop is part of this structure. Em, like Lucy Deane, is left to end the conventional marriage plot with Gregory,[11] but it has become an empty fulfilment for her:

> 'Why is it always so, Waldo, always so,' she said; 'we long for things, and long for them, and pray for them; we would give all we have to come near to them, but we never reach them. Then, at last, too late, just when we don't want them any more, when all the sweetness is taken out of them, then they come. We don't want them then.' (II p. 306)

All the novel's lines of development come to similarly futile conclusions – Em's marriage plot, Waldo's religious quest, and Lyndall's new departure as independent woman. The development of female friendship cannot be part of this structure.

Schreiner's later novel, *From Man to Man*,[12] is more concerned with female solidarity. According to Showalter, it is about 'sisterhood and motherhood';[13] and according to First and Scott, 'It is a novel about the solidarity of sisters.'[14] But it is also about the failure of sisterhood, and the impossibility of solidarity. The novel opens with dedications to two women: Schreiner's sister, and her daughter. What they have in common is that both died as babies: an elegaic note of lost female connection is immediately struck. Though the book celebrates the love between the two chief women characters, the sisters Rebekah and Bertie, they are separated and isolated throughout, each suffering alone and vainly trying to contact the other. This failure of female connectedness is foreshadowed in *The Prelude: The Child's Day*, a sharp evocation of Rebekah's childhood experiences on the day Bertie is born. The *Prelude* ends with an image of the two sisters asleep and inseparably embraced, 'the hands of the sisters so interlocked, and the arm of the elder sister so closely round the younger, that [the nurse] could not remove it without awaking both'. But this picture is ominously darkened: 'the night light shone, casting deep shadows into far corners, especially that in which the two children lay!' (p. 73). And earlier in the *Prelude*, we have seen Rebekah, jealous of her mother and the new baby, discovering another baby lying in the spare room. She gives this baby presents from her toys, and insists ' "It is mine: *I* found it!" ' (p. 41) and ' "*This one* is mine!" ' (p. 42). But it turns out this is Bertie's dead twin, a stillborn baby. Rebekah's futile devotion to the dead baby prefigures her unavailing love for the fallen Bertie, who, from the moment she is seduced by her tutor, is set on a downward path that, in both versions of the unwritten ending, leads to her death. In the *Prelude*, Rebekah then fantasises finding a live female baby of her own, and bringing it up without the restrictions she herself has to suffer as a girl: ' "My baby, I shall *never* call *you* 'a strange child!' You can climb trees and tear your clothes" ' (p. 48); ' "My baby, I'm so glad you're a little girl. I'll make you a pair of thick trousers to climb trees in; these white ones tear so when you slide down, and then the people call you 'Tom Boy!' " ' (P. 56). When she later begs her mother to allow her to sleep with the new baby, she says, ' "I only want to take care of it, and teach it" ' (p. 71). But all these plans of Rebekah's to protect and teach Bertie come to nothing: when we meet Bertie again, as a very young woman, she seems dangerously ignorant and innocent, and Rebekah is about to leave home, abandoning Bertie to the mercies of the male tutor Rebekah has insisted should be appointed to take over her role as her sister's teacher.

The novel proper starts at this point. Rebekah is about to get married and leave home. She asks herself why she is leaving her 'quiet, peaceful life' (p. 85) on the farm, with her parents and Bertie. As with a Brontë heroine, the answer is that 'she was dying of hunger' (p. 86), hunger for some wider experience. The bond between her and Bertie thus implicitly belongs to a world of peace and inaction – again as in Brontë's novels, female friendship is equated with repose: men are needed to create plot. Not only has Rebekah decided to plunge into experience herself, she is also indirectly responsible for the end of Bertie's innocence. As I have said, it is Rebekah who insists that Bertie should have a male tutor, in spite of her prospective husband's warnings about ' "settling [the tutor] and Bertie down every day for three hours with nothing but

the table to divide them and French verbs to unite them! It's a
dangerous thing for any young man, or old either, to have a head of
curls like Bertie's dancing within three feet of him!'" (p. 84).
Rebekah ignores this worldly-wise warning; almost as soon as her
protecting elder sister is gone, Bertie falls victim to the tutor's
seduction. Rebekah's decision to marry somehow involves a
repudiation of the bond with Bertie, and a handing-over of her too
to the depredations of the male.

The evening before Rebekah's wedding, however, there is a little
scene that suggests Rebekah needs Bertie as much as Bertie needs
Rebekah:

> Almost every night when, as a very small child, she had been moved
> into that room, Rebekah had lain by her to sing her to sleep; and when
> she grew older Rebekah had still crept in to lie beside her to talk and
> caress her before she slept. To-night Rebekah put the light down on the
> floor and knelt beside the bed. She put her head down upon Bertie's
> breast, under Bertie's arm, and pressed it there. It was as though, to-
> night, it was she who wanted to be caressed. But Bertie slept on – a deep,
> calm sleep. (p. 91)

This little scene of a failure of communication and support between
the sisters is the forerunner of many others. After she has been
seduced, 'Twice Bertie began a letter to Rebekah; but both times she
tore the letter up, and it was never sent' (p. 101). She never tells
Rebekah the secret of what has happened to her, and so Rebekah is
blocked from all possibility of offering comfort or help. When we
next see the sisters, Rebekah is on a visit to the farm, with her three
children: later we discover that her husband has been repeatedly
unfaithful to her, and she is deeply unhappy, but none of this does
she reveal to Bertie. The two women are in the dark about each
other's most important experiences.

Bertie and her cousin John Ferdinand now begin to fall in love:
Bertie is anxious, and wishes she were 'clever' like Rebekah, but
Rebekah reassures her she will always be loved, which is better than
cleverness. This is followed by another symbolic moment of failed
contact: 'Rebekah made a little caressing movement as though she
would have put out her hand and touched the hand nearest her in
which Bertie held the candle; then she heard the baby crying through
the spare room window and hurried away with her mug' (p. 119).

This prefigures Bertie's stay with Rebekah, when Rebekah is 'generally too busy with her household work and children to have much time to spend with her' (p. 149). Rebekah's marriage and its burdens have taken her away from contact with her sister. She does, however, act the part of protective older sister, and speaks strongly to John Ferdinand about Bertie, warning him not to hurt her or fail her. Her description of Bertie's character brings out the different types of women she and Bertie represent:

> 'Some women with complex, many-sided natures, if love fails them and one half of their nature dies, can still draw a kind of broken life through the other. The world of the impersonal is left them: they can still turn fiercely to it, and through the intellect draw in a kind of life – a poor, broken, half-asphyxiated life, not what it might have been; like the life of a man with one lung eaten out by disease, who has to live through the other alone; – but still life. But Bertie and such as Bertie have only one life possible, the life of the personal relations; if that fails them, all fails.' (p. 121)

We discover later that Rebekah herself is one of the 'complex' women described here. She is the unconventional, intellectual woman, who still has books and ideas to turn to when her marriage fails; Bertie is the more traditional woman, living only through her feelings for others. Later it is stressed that once she is labelled a 'fallen' woman and loses her chances of marriage, all her potential domestic creativity – home-making, sewing, childcare – goes to waste. In her pathetic sexual vulnerability, Bertie is like Marian Erle – she too has a low brow, and masses of hair – while Rebekah is like the more intellectual Aurora. But Rebekah does not need to learn about sexuality or domesticity from Bertie – she is already married, and hopelessly emotionally dependent on her husband, despite his unfaithfulness. There is also no possibility given that Bertie could learn some of Rebekah's strengthening interest in the 'impersonal'. The two types of women diverge, instead of converging. The aim of the book is not to negotiate a compromise which will assimilate the women to society, but to show up the inadequacies of society, and the hopelessness of women's lot: neither of these two opposite types of heroine can find a place in the social order as it is.

Rebekah's warnings to John Ferdinand have no effect, once Bertie has told him about her 'fall': of course, he abandons her. Rebekah cannot be an effective protector, when she does not know the truth.

Bertie now leaves home and goes to stay with Rebekah, again revealing nothing of what is troubling her, despite Rebekah's anxious enquiries. Bertie's secret is betrayed (though not to Rebekah) by two malicious women, Veronica (John Ferdinand's new wife) and Mrs Drummond: Bertie leaves to stay with an aunt, but the new life she builds up there is also shattered when the gossip catches up with her, possibly through Veronica's machinations. Veronica and Mrs Drummond, and the network of female gossip and scandal that they make use of, provide a sinister picture of women's friendship and community. As in *The Mill on the Floss*, female public opinion is unjust and inexorable to women who deviate in any way: as well as destroying Bertie's character, the two women unite in criticising Rebekah and her 'mannish ways' (p. 158). They are also both involved not just in gossip but in specific acts of inter-female betrayal: Mrs Drummond has had an affair with Rebekah's husband Frank, and Veronica betrays Bertie's secret which her husband told her. Veronica's jealousy of Bertie, and determination to destroy her rival, is chillingly conveyed in an earlier scene at the farm, when she finds a daguerreotype of Bertie as a child in John Ferdinand's room, and 'placing her large flat thumb on the face, she pressed; in a moment the photograph had cracked into a hundred fine little splinters of glass radiating from the face, which was indistinguishable' (p. 130). This symbolic annihilation of her rival prefigures the way Veronica later acts to destroy Bertie. The vindictive destruction of the photograph is a secret act of Veronica's: in public, she and Mrs Drummond appear models of the feminine. We find them engaged in traditional domestic tasks as they gossip maliciously about Bertie and Rebekah: 'While Veronica sat upright on a high-backed chair knitting heavy squares for a bed quilt, Mrs Drummond on a low settee, with her head a little on one side, chose carefully the shades of silk for an altar cloth which she was making' (p. 157). Knitting and sewing together, they plot the downfall of other women: conventional women's friendship is seen here as something deeply sinister and malevolent. There is also, however, a sense in which these women are presented as parodies and imposters – Mrs Drummond with her false hair and absent husband, and Veronica with her attempts to imitate Bertie's household ways at the farm. Bertie is the true, traditional, domestic woman, whose sewing is creative as a poem: Mrs Drummond and Veronica, it is implied, are imposters and usurpers. Thus the attack on the female community does not include an attack on traditional 'feminine' values and occupations as such.

Nevertheless, women like Veronica and Mrs Drummond hold the power in the female community at present, and as well as destroying Bertie, they isolate Rebekah. Mrs Drummond remarks that 'women didn't seem to care for Rebekah – she didn't think a woman had called there for over a year; she thought many of them didn't even know she existed, as she never went to church' (p. 157). Rebekah's problem is that other women cannot sympathise with her advanced (to them, eccentric) ideas and behaviour. Mrs Drummond reports that Rebekah 'used to dig her garden with a big spade where people could see her quite well over the gate; she had heard someone say that when she was out at her farm they had seen her climb up a ladder right on to the roof, mending a smoky chimney' (pp. 157–8). Later on, Rebekah tells her children how she has met with a similar incomprehension and ridicule from the coloured women, whom she has tried to befriend:

'... when I go down the Government Avenue, and the coloured girls sitting there laugh because they see I don't wear stays as other women do, it's as if a knife ran into me under my ribs. I know I'm right; that in years to come people will wonder women could be so mad and foolish as to deform themselves. And yet, when these women laugh at me, I am so full of pain I can hardly walk down to the station; and when I come home I feel I want to creep on to the bed and cry. I've tried to like coloured women and do all I can to help them, and then they jeer at me!' (p. 440)

Women of all classes are dominated by conventional prejudices, and Rebekah's attempts to find friends or show solidarity not only fail, but increase her pained sense of difference and isolation. We see her in her little study,[15] thinking out her advanced evolutionary philosophy alone, talking to herself, dreaming of

... what it must be like to be one of a company of men and women in a room together, all sharing somewhat the same outlook on life and therefore thinking somewhat the same thought, and able to understand one another without explanation – a thing she knew was possible somewhere in time and space – which actually did exist – though she might never know it. (p. 174)

Her meeting with Mr Drummond at the end of the book, is her first encounter with such a kindred spirit: but there is no female equivalent, nor is Rebekah especially seeking for one. Her wish for female friendship expresses itself more as a sympathy for suffering, and a pitying desire to help those weaker than herself.[16] Thus she has wanted to 'help' the coloured women, and her suffering over her husband's unfaithfulness leads also to a desire to help other, weaker women: she asks herself,

> 'Are *you* the only creature in the world who has suffered wrong? If life has no value to you, are there not others weaker than yourself to whom you can make it of value? Because in your anguish you are alone and no hand comes to help you, can you put out your hand to none? Are you the only woman in the world who has suffered?' (p. 300)

This leads her to go out and approach the coloured servant with whom her husband Frank has been having an affair – but the girl repels her with rudeness and frightened laughter. Later we do find out that Rebekah has adopted the girl's child by Frank, but no bond has developed between the two women. Similarly, Rebekah's desire to reach and help the suffering Bertie is thwarted. The New Woman is isolated and rejected by the surrounding conforming female community, and cannot reach other suffering and outcast women to form any other kind of bond.[17]

Driven out by the women's gossip, Bertie has left her aunt's with a wealthy Jew who takes her to London: from this point, Rebekah has no knowledge of her whereabouts. Bertie's departure is preceded by two more little scenes of failed female communication. First, she tries to tell her aunt the truth about her seduction, but her aunt stops her, and later says, '"never attempt such confidences as you were desirous of making to me this evening. If a woman has made a mistake there is only one course for her – silence!"' (pp. 329–30). The night before Bertie leaves, she goes into the kitchen and approaches the black servant Dorcas, who is sleeping in front of the fire:

> 'I'm so lonely, Dorcas! Oh, please let me hold your hand!'
> Dorcas snored and turned slightly on her side. Bertie put down her hand under the blanket and took the thick coarse hand of the Kaffir woman and held it tight in her own. 'I'm so lonely, Dorcas!' But Dorcas moved heavily and then lay motionless. Bertie shivered; after a while she

withdrew her hand and rose softly and glided with her naked feet back to her own room. (p. 339)

This echoes the earlier scene, where Bertie was asleep when Rebekah wanted to be caressed. Again, women fail to provide the comfort and sympathy other women need. In London, Bertie is taken to see some scantily-clad dancing girls. She is horrified: ' "Why – don't – their – mothers fetch – them – home?" ' (p. 370) she sobs. A lack of maternal care allows women to be exploited.

Bertie herself is about to be betrayed again by a woman – the Jew's housekeeper, Martha, arranges for her to be caught in a compromising situation with the Jew's cousin. She is thrown out of the house, and later disappears with the cousin. She is last heard of in a brothel in Soho. Like Marian Erle, women have betrayed her into prostitution, and failed to give her motherly protection. But Rebekah does not, like Aurora Leigh, come to save her fallen sister. There *is* a chance meeting in the street – but it is with a woman who only *looks* like Rebekah, and who repudiates Bertie:

> Then [Bertie] looked round and saw, standing close beside her also looking in at the window, two ladies. The elder one was about forty, older than Rebekah and rather taller ... but there was the same full high forehead, the same delicate sharp marked nose dominating the face, a delicate strong rounded little chin and the sensitive strong mouth. She was dressed in a sealskin jacket with a little brown bonnet and skirt, just as Rebekah might have dressed. ...
> Bertie looked at them, and an irresistible impulse came over her; she put out her hand and laid it softly on the sleeve of the sealskin jacket. The woman glanced down quickly, as everyone glances at being touched in London. For an instant she looked at Bertie and took it all in. ... All her face hardened. If she had asked her why she touched her, Bertie would have spoken; but she turned and said to her daughter, 'Dear, we must go now.' (pp. 374–5)

This scene is echoed later, in reverse, when Rebekah thinks she hears Bertie's laugh in a crowd outside a concert-hall:

> ... from the crowd under the veranda there rung out a long, reckless, gurgling laugh. It was unmistakably a woman's. In an instant Rebekah sprang forward and stretched her arm through the window, trying to turn the handle of the door.

'Let me out! – Let me out!' she cried, shaking the door with her left hand as the handle refused to turn. Then the door burst open and she leapt out.

'Rebekah, what are you doing?' Frank stretched out his hand to detain her.

'It's Bertie!' she said hoarsely, evading his hand, and ran across the side walk, now deep in water, towards the veranda, her long train and cloak fluttering out behind her.' (p. 449)

Of course, the woman turns out not to be Bertie, and Rebekah returns dejected. The two parallel scenes of misrecognition and failed attempts at contact typify the sisters' relationship throughout the book.

The novel's narrative structure is highly unconventional and innovative,[18] and one of its innovations is precisely this splitting-apart between the two main characters, so that Bertie's and Rebekah's stories proceed in parallel, without the usual intertwinings and meetings of plot that we would expect. The women are physically apart from Chapter 8 to the end: that is, about three-fifths of the book; and before this they exist in total ignorance of the chief events and problems of each other's lives. The novel is unfinished, but the ending as it stands involves Rebekah's discovery of her male soul-mate and counterpart, Mr Drummond. Paul Foot remarks that 'The ending, I suspect, was exactly as Olive Schreiner intended it,'[19] and it certainly seems more satisfactory than the rather melodramatic reconciliation between Rebekah and the dying Bertie that Olive Schreiner projected.[20] Rebekah is unhappily married to an unfaithful husband, and her meeting with Drummond justifies her persisting idealism about marriage: as she says earlier in a letter of reproach to her husband, '"I know that the loveliest thing that has blossomed on the earth is the binding of man and woman in one body, one fellowship"' (p. 297). Like other New Woman writers, Schreiner here elevates and wishes to purify marriage. Thus the book as it stands works through to a male–female resolution; in the projected endings, Drummond and Rebekah were parted by her marriage, and Bertie died, leaving us with Rebekah in a woman-alone ending, as in The Story of a Modern Woman, or George Egerton's A Psychological Moment.[21] 'There we see the last of Rebekah. As the sun sets, flooding the Karoo flats with radiance and glowing the brilliant mountains as it disappears behind them, Rebekah stands on the summit of the lonely koppie in the soft

effulgence of the evening light. . . .'[22] In none of the possible endings
is it envisaged that Bertie and Rebekah should be happily reunited:
their splitting-apart is absolute and irremediable. Their parallel and
contrasting stories illustrate two different yet similar ways in which
women are oppressed and ill-treated, as 'fallen' women or as
married women. Both, it is implied, become the victims of different
forms of prostitution. Any final rescue of either woman would
lessen the shock value of their fates: the New Woman writer's
stronger awareness of the injustices done to women often caused her
to give a much bleaker picture of women's chances and potential
than earlier women writers had done.[23]

The book thus presents us with an unfulfilled longing for
sympathy and support between women, while showing how present
society makes this longing unfulfillable. Schreiner presents herself as
writing the book for the sake of other women, out of a sense of
solidarity: 'I feel that if only one lonely and struggling woman read
it and found strength and comfort from it one would not feel one
had lived quite in vain.'[24] Here Schreiner is declaring her solidarity
with the female *reader*, and also, implicitly, imagining a friendship
and identification between the reader and the 'lonely and struggling'
women in the book. She herself also felt extreme attachment to
these characters: 'Oh, I love the two women in my book so. I'm
getting to love women more and more. I love men too, so very much
– only they don't *need* me.'[25] As with Rebekah, female friendship is
seen as a matter of helping weaker women: the same applies to
Schreiner's desire to help her 'lonely and struggling' reader. A female
fellowship of help and support is implied between female author,
female reader and female characters – all socially isolated, but
brought together by the medium of the book.[26]

Confidences between women in a moment of friendship are often
central to George Egerton's short stories. Several stories either
consist of or contain one woman confiding her life-story to another
woman, whose own life-choices are changed or explained by the
story. While the female–female interaction between the two women
often takes up the whole story, it is always set within a larger hinted
or implied conventional narrative of male–female relations, as in
Rossetti's poems. In addition, the stories the women confide to each
other always involve their experiences with men: the female–female
interaction provides perspective on these stories, and the possibility

of choice and change, or at least new understanding, through the revelation of other contrasting female roles and experiences. The confidences between the women are presented as the result of a peculiar inter-female intuition and sympathy: the older woman in *The Spell of the White Elf*, through 'some subtle intuitive sympathy', leads the conversation to the subjects that are nearest the younger woman's heart; in masculine company, on the other hand, 'she talked down to the level of the men', which 'of course' they do not realise (p. 77).[27] Women, it is implied, put on an act to talk to men, who are too obtuse to see what is happening; but with other women there is an instinctive penetration to the other's inner truth. Thus the heroine of *A Cross Line* ('Keynotes') says, 'Women talk to me – why, I can't say – but always they come, strip their hearts and souls naked, and let me see the hidden folds of their natures', while 'A woman must beware of speaking the truth to a man; he loves her the less for it' (pp. 28–9). The women in these stories reveal to other women aspects of their inner life which are usually hidden from men.[28]

What is revealed between the women, however, is not as unconventional as one might suppose. In *The White Elf*, it is the career-woman's longing for motherhood; in *Her Share* and *A Psychological Moment*, it is a woman's regret at having let class or religious differences separate her from the man she really loved; in *Gone Under*, it is the fallen woman's utter hopelessness and degradation. As W. T. Stead put it, the 'modern woman' writer's demand for equal rights 'in no way involves or implies any forgetting of her sex, of her destiny, and of her duty as the mother of the race'.[29] Instead, she urges that these traditional female roles should be taken more seriously: Egerton in particular exalts maternity as woman's '*only divine* fibre' ('Discords', p. 100), which raises her *above* man;[30] she also caused some scandal by insisting on the importance of sexual fulfilment for women. While this shocked conventional readers,[31] it also separated her from the movement for women's social and political rights,[32] which one of her characters sees as an expression of 'suppressed sex' ('Discords', p. 194). The character who voices this view is a man, but nothing in the story (*The Regeneration of Two*) belies his opinion: the heroine finds fulfilment in a different kind of female solidarity, that eventually leads to a new kind of male–female bond. That this story does end with a 'free' union rather than a marriage, suggests that Egerton does propose a considerable revision of women's traditional role, and the conventional fictional ending. Similarly, the unconventional household of the career woman in *The White Elf*, in which traditional male and female roles are reversed, and the fallen woman in *A Psychological Moment* who refuses to accept her traditional alternatives of repentance or prostitution, both involve the drastic revision of fictional types. Like the earlier writers I have discussed, Egerton is still involved in a negotiation about female identity, within accepted ideals of womanhood, but she pushes the conventional female ideals of romantic/passionate love and/or motherhood to some more unconventional conclusions. This process of negotiation and revision is best seen at work through her presentation of female friendships.

*The Spell of the White Elf* ('Keynotes') provides a good illustration of this process, and some of its ambiguities. The story is about a significant chance meeting and exchange of confidences between two women, which becomes a turning-point in the life of one of them, the younger woman who narrates the story. As in so much earlier Victorian fiction, this turning-point leads to the woman's marriage: her reluctance to marry is overcome by what she learns about the older woman's life. Within this conventional framework, however, new possibilities for women's lives and new types of female identity are explored.[33] The story is structured as a narrative within a narrative, the younger women's experiences before and after the moment of meeting forming a frame to the older woman's story. The younger woman (neither woman is named) introduces the story as 'momentous' to herself, though it may bore the reader (p. 68). She never directly explains this significance of the story to her own life, but leaves it for us to infer from what she casually reveals about her problems before the meeting and her actions after it. We learn, by the way, that she had a childhood sweetheart, Hans Jörgen, who has gone to America, promising to 'send for' her – 'but of course I laughed at that.' Now he is a great man in Cincinnati, and still 'waits' for her, but she 'told him I thought marriage was a vocation and I hadn't one for it' (p. 69): but Hans Jörgen is still waiting. He is made to seem stolid, reliable and unexciting. Meanwhile, the narrator has 'been alone now for five years, working away' (pp. 69–70). Despite her scorn of marriage, she is becoming discontented with independence: 'Somehow I have not the same gladness in my work of late years.

Working for one's-self seems a poor end even if one puts by money' (p. 70). What the story is going to reveal to her is that even if she does not need a man, she needs a child, and therefore a man just like the responsible Hans Jörgen. The agent of this revelation is, unexpectedly, a highly successful career-woman, who turns out to be a fellow passenger on the boat the narrator is travelling on.

The narrator's Norwegian cousin explains that the other woman is ' "a very learned lady ... she is married. I suppose her husband he stay at home and keep the house!" ' His 'sarcasm' is charitably excused by the narrator, because he 'has just been refused by a young lady dentist, who says she is too comfortably off to change for a small housekeeping business', thus signalling again that the story is centred on the issue of economically independent women, and how and why they should bother with men and marriage. The 'learned lady' is first described as 'A tall woman with very square shoulders, and gold-rimmed spectacles' (p. 72). Other later descriptions pick up the hint of 'masculinity' here:

> She is sitting comfortably with one leg crossed over the other, in the manner called 'shockingly unladylike' of my early lessons in deportment. The flame flickers over the patent leather of her neat low-heeled boot, and strikes a spark from the pin in her tie. There is something man-like about her. I don't know where it lies, but it is there. . . .
> She is kneeling on one knee before the fire, holding her palms to the glow, and with her figure hidden in her loose, fur-lined coat and the light showing up her strong face under the little tweed cap, she seems so much like a clever-faced slight man, that I feel I am conventionally guilty in talking so freely to her. (pp. 74, 76–7)

A new type is being created here, owing something to the conventional man-like spinster, but turning that grim or ridiculous mannishness into something attractive and admirable. She also has some of the charm and freedom of the tomboy, 'shockingly unladylike'. To this is added a grown-up, hero-like strength and courage: as she crosses the gangway onto the boat, the narrator thinks 'she would cross it in just that cool way if she were facing death' (p. 73). To the narrator, she is the intellectual woman as hero, able to beat the men on their own ground – ' "I like to cut them out in their own province" ' (p. 81), she says. But in her conversation with the narrator she is to reveal also the conventionally female qualities of an 'intuitive sympathy' for female

problems, and a longing for motherhood. As we are to find out from
the story she tells, she has found a way of satisfying the aims of both
the 'male' and 'female' parts of her character. She is unable to have
children, but she has satisfied her maternal instinct by adopting a
child – the 'white elf' of the title. To help her combine career,
marriage and child, she has an unusual household – she and her
husband have exchanged roles: '"Positions are reversed, they often
are now-a-days. My husband stays at home and grows good things
to eat, and pretty things to look at, and I go out and win bread and
butter"' (p. 80). In addition, she has the servant Belinda, who
conveniently hates men but loves children – her instincts too can be
satisfied in caring for the white elf. The older woman's descriptions
of the effect the child has on her life are mostly cloyingly
sentimental, but also at times endearingly comic, as she tries to
understand the grammar of baby-talk, or holds the baby '"like a
book of notes at a lecture"' (p. 84). The child educates her in
another set of non-intellectual, 'female' abilities, in which her
husband and Belinda excel her.

This education, however, is only bringing out her own latent
maternal instinct, which is what prompted her to adopt the child in
the first place: '"I was working then on a Finland saga, and I do not
know why it was, but the thought of that little being kept
disturbing my work. . . . I used to fancy something stirred in me, and
the spirits of unborn little ones never to come to life in me troubled
me"' (pp. 81–2). These disturbing thoughts are similar to the
narrator's earlier, undefined discontent with her single life. It is clear
that the story contains a message for the narrator: in the women's
first conversation, the narrator felt that her new friend 'was making
clear to me most of the things that had puzzled me for a long
time. . . . How she knew just the subjects that worked in me I knew
not' (p. 77). The story of the white elf resolves the narrator's own
doubts about marriage, by awakening her maternal instinct: 'Often
since that night I have rounded my arm and bowed down my face
and fancied I had a little human elf cuddled to my breast.' The
narrative breaks off here, and is followed by a short coda. We find
the narrator busy packing; in the bottom of her trunk are some
baby-clothes she could not resist buying in a sale. It transpires that
she has written to Hans Jörgen, and the story ends as she suddenly
sees Hans Jörgen himself 'coming across the street' (p. 90).

What then has made the narrator change her mind? One way to

read the story would be to see the older woman as revealing to her new possibilities of female identity and role, which suggest that she too can combine marriage, maternity and career. She is off to America to re-enact these new female possibilities. But there is also a more conventional way to read the story, that undermines this interpretation. While the older woman is presented as a new kind of female hero, she is also an exceptional, even eccentric anomaly. While her 'man-like' qualities are attractive, they also perpetuate the myth that there *is* something 'unfeminine' about intellectual women: and this impression is reinforced by her barrenness. The adoption of the child, and the unconventional household, can be seen as shifts to make up for an essential lack. They do not offer a model for the heroine to emulate (she, it is implied, will have her *own* child), so much as an extreme instance to prove a point. If even an anomaly like the barren, intellectual woman is drawn by her maternal instinct to find a way of having a child, how much more must a more 'normal' woman like the narrator need one. We do not learn enough about the narrator to judge how 'normal' she is: but the older woman clearly sees her friend's life-possibilities as more conventional, and therefore more desirable:

> 'I like your Mr Hans Jörgen', she said, 'he has a strong nature and knows what he wants; there is reliability in him. They are rarer qualities than one thinks in men, I have found through life that the average man is weaker than we are. It must be a good thing to have a strong nature to lean on. I have never had that.' (p. 78)

Read like this, the story has an unexpected resemblance to some aspects of Dinah Mulock Craik's earlier, more conservative novel, *A Brave Lady* (1870), which is similarly structured as a story told by an admired older woman to a younger friend, who provides a frame for the main narrative. The 'brave lady's' story is one of ill-treatment and betrayal at the hands of a weak-willed husband, which drive her to contemplate leaving him. She only stays on discovering that he has a terminal illness. When she tells the story, she has lost husband and children. Her young confidante is determined not to marry: it is only through the intervention of her older mentor, who discovers that her suitor *is* a strong, reliable man, that she is persuaded to accept him. The older women contrasts her husband and her friend's suitor:

'. . . it would be a comfort to me to give my little girl into safe keeping –
to someone who will take care of her, without tyrannizing over her; who
is a gentle and good man, without being a weak man. Child! if you knew
what it is to have the mere sham of a husband – the mockery of a
protector, against whom one has to protect onself. . .'[34]

The younger woman is married, and bears a daughter whom she
calls 'Josephine', after her older friend. The 'frame' of the younger
woman's story serves to contain the subversive implications of the
older woman's revelations about the shortcomings of marriage: we
see that happy marriages are possible, if men fulfil their traditional
role. The younger woman also brings a vicarious fulfilment to her
friend's blasted life – through her, the female line is carried on, and
the older woman does have a child named after her.

Though the older woman's story in *The White Elf* is one of
success and fulfilment, not failure and disappointment, nevertheless,
in her remarks on Hans Jörgen she reveals an unexpected longing for
a conventional marriage with a 'strong' man. The narrator will go
on to fulfil those conventional longings for her, and to have the
child of her own that the older woman is deprived of. As in *A Brave
Lady*, the older woman's subversive story is contained within a more
conventional frame. In both cases, the central story is made to seem
safely anomalous and exceptional.

The story *Her Share* ('Discords') has a similar structure, in that the
listening woman is about to enact the conventional fulfilment that
the story-telling woman has missed. In this story, the moral of the
central narrative is much simpler and less ambiguous. The listener is
not 'converted' by it, as she is already on her way to married bliss,
but it does show up by contrast the value of what she has chosen. At
the beginning of the story, it is implied that she has just got engaged,
and she goes out into the countryside to enjoy her bliss in solitude.
There she meets another, older woman, with 'a strange quiet
wistfulness in her eyes that made me feel sorry for her' (p. 69). As in
*The White Elf*, sympathy and confidence immediately springs up
between the two women:

. . .she encourages me to talk, and I feel drawn to her. I show her my
ring, and I tell her half shyly of my great happiness, and how I had
wished to get away to realise it quietly – and she smiles in response,
saying:

'Yes, I know that feeling: that is why I came down today.'
 ... when tea is over I follow an impulse and put my hand caressingly on her arm, I ask her if I may go out with her, and she assents with a smile. (p. 70)

Women can immediately identify with each other's experiences.

The older woman then tells her story, of how she, the vicar's niece, fell in love with an Italian craftsman working at the local great house, though they never speak to each other. The night before he is due to leave, he comes and serenades her, plainly declaring his love; but she finds herself unable to speak or act. He leaves her a beautiful wooden box, carved with pictures expressing his love and his loneliness: ' "All the beauty of my life was on the cover, and my life has been as the empty wooden box with a date in it" ' (p. 81). Other imagery confirms this theme of missed sexual and maternal fulfilment: 'she looked like a fruit that has grown to maturity in the shade and withered before it ripened properly' (p. 77). Like the narrator of *The White Elf*, this woman is successful in her career, but feels a lack in her life:

'Now a measure of success has come to me, and comparative comfort, and I thought I would be at peace, and yet.... Vague feelings of disturbance that I used to have in early girlhood – you know them? – that have been hushed to quiescence in the years between, thrill in me now at a sensuous note of music, the coo of a baby.' (p. 73)

But while the narrator of *The White Elf* was lucky to have Hans Jörgen still waiting for her, this woman has missed her one chance of fulfilment, through an inability to act and break through the barriers of class between her and the man.

While the narrator says at the beginning that the story casts a shade on her own happiness, it does confirm the rightness of her own decision. Her new friend is not like the elder sister whom she has come out to avoid, 'whose own unhappy marriage made her a very Cassandra with regard to the fate of others' (p. 68): this woman's story has the opposite implication. The friendship, and what it reveals, can only confirm the younger woman in her own conventional marriage-plot. Egerton's story ends with the older woman's narrative – we do not see any more of the younger woman's reaction – but her contrasting fate is sufficiently implied by her opening comments.

\* \* \*

In *Gone Under* ('Discords') the instinctive sympathy and understanding between the two women is less complete. They are not two versions of the same innate female story, but contrasting types: the sensuous, weak-willed fallen woman, and the brave, inexperienced, independent young girl. Nevertheless, the girl learns to understand and sympathise with Edith, the fallen woman, though ultimately she can do nothing to save her. The girl gains knowledge of the wickedness of men, and is led to question the justice of current social arrangements. Like other New Woman writers, Egerton has two main aims: first, to show the injustices and sufferings of women in the present state of society, and second, to show the utopian possibilities of new roles and structures.[35] Thus in *Gone Under*, we see the hopelessness of the fallen woman's fate, and the inability of another woman to save her, but in *The Regeneration of Two* we are shown a successful experiment in rehabilitating fallen women in an all-women community; and in *A Psychological Moment* we see a woman refusing to accept the conventional fate of the fallen woman, and looking forward to new, undefined possibilities. In *The Regeneration of Two*, the woman 'saviour' has money and power; in *A Psychological Moment*, the 'fallen' woman has toughness and brains.

Neither of these is the case in *Gone Under* – womanly sympathy alone is shown to be inadequate to help a fallen woman, when both women are impoverished, and the fallen woman has no resources of character. In addition, other women fail her: the girl gently rebukes the two maiden ladies who have kept away from her while she befriended Edith:

'She is a lost soul, *I* tried to do what I could for her. You are old, the others were married, you had nothing to lose, and yet you held back. It is good, untempted women like you, whose virtue makes you selfish, who help to keep women like her as they are.' (p. 109)

An overt message about female solidarity is being given: she calls Edith 'sister' at two climactic moments, one when Edith confesses she has had several lovers, and one later when the girl meets Edith in the street as a prostitute. As in *The Story of a Modern Woman*, this message of female solidarity is accompanied by a story that shows its inefficacy, and the powerlessness of women to change their fate.

The two women meet on a transatlantic voyage. Edith is sea-sick and drunk, and ignored by the other passengers: the girl tries to help her. The girl is brave and independent – she has been working in New York for two years, and 'has read much, thought much, worked hard, and lived clean' (p. 83), but she is presented as naive and inexperienced in sexual and emotional matters. She is an observer, who has not come in close contact with other people's complex problems: 'She speculates and weaves stories about the people she meets; they strike her fancy as the characters in a book or picture, and interest her always. She is saved, not knowing them, from finding their limitations' (p. 91). Nevertheless, she has the female sympathetic power to 'draw' another woman's story from her: '"I don't know why I should tell you this – there is something in you draws it out of me"' (p. 97), says Edith, as she tells her story. But what Edith tells her is something beyond her intuition or experience. First, there is the horrific tale of how her lover arranged the murder of her baby. The girl's indignant outburst – '"the brutes! I would have had them up for murder. I would never have rested –"' (pp. 99–100) – is seen by Edith as naive: '"So you think, but I guess you wouldn't. Money can still do everything"'.

The girl can sympathise with Edith's blasted maternal feelings – she has the usual Egertonian belief in motherhood: '"I think the *only divine* fibre in a woman is her maternal instinct"' (p. 100). But Edith's revelations about her unfaithfulness to her first lover with a man she cared nothing for are beyond the girl's understanding: 'The girl is dumb with pained realisation; it is her first actual contact with a problem of such a nature, and so little does she grasp it that she says: "It's dreadful, but you must tell him the truth"' (pp. 103–4). When Edith reveals that she has had yet another lover since then, the girl is about to leave, 'in a confused, horrible dream' (p. 104), but she overcomes her repugnance to return and comfort her 'sister' Edith. Though she cannot understand, she still sympathises and does not judge: '"I have no right to sit in judgement; I have never been tempted. I simply can't understand it"'. The two women then have a very melodramatic Dickensian interchange, in which Edith first asks the girl to kiss her, and then 'the girl bends her head, but the woman drops to the floor with a sharp "No, no", and hides her face in the girl's gown, with the tears streaming down her cheeks' (p. 105). They do finally kiss when they part, but Edith refuses the girl's offers of help and contact: '"Forget me, little sister, good, kind little sister"' (p. 108). When they next meet, Edith is a thoroughly degraded prostitute, who once more melodramatically warns her 'pure' sister away: 'as the eager "Edith, sister!" reaches her, she flings up one arm wildly to hide her face, thrusts out the other to ward the girl off and sobs out, "Oh, oh, no not that!" with a wailing moan' (p. 113). She runs off and disappears.

While Edith is a stereotypical Victorian fallen woman in some ways, she is also a revision of the type.[36] Unlike the redeemable fallen women in *Aurora Leigh* or *Ruth*, she has more than one lover, and unlike the totally lost Esther in *Mary Barton*, or Dickensian prostitutes, it is not need for money that initially drives her to this course, but that '"*one stifles the memory of the first with the excitement of the second*"' (p. 104). She is technically more depraved, but this does not exclude her from the younger woman's sympathy. Her loss of her baby in part excuses her depravity – as the girl says, suppress a woman's maternal instinct '"and it turns to a fibroid, sapping all that is healthful and good in her nature"' (p. 100). But an innate sensuality and weakness is also suggested by her appearance (like the career-woman in *The White Elf*, she is typecast by her physical characteristics): 'the mouth cannot lie – the pout of the wine-red lips, the soft receding chin, and the strange indefinable expression that lurks about them rather fits a priestess of passion' (p. 91). The girl's sympathy for such a woman is beyond the pale of what the earlier Victorian writers would allow; at the same time, this physical typing, as in *The White Elf*, increases the distance, and lessens possible identification between the two women. Edith's effect on the girl is not as a horrible warning of what she could become, nor as an awakener of her own sexuality. Instead, she reveals the hitherto unnoticed injustices of society towards other women: 'The dreadful problem of her fate, and the ultimate fate of all these others would weigh on the soul of the girl; and the question of the justice of the arrangement beat insistently in her tired brain' (p. 110).

This effect is ambiguous: on the one hand, Edith's story reveals injustices, but on the other, it shows the intractability of the problems, and the uselessness of naive solutions. At the end, the girl's 'sympathy with human suffering was no wise blunted, her sense of its inevitability perhaps increased' (p. 110). As in *The Story of a Modern Woman*, female solidarity brings no solutions, and only reveals intractable problems, and there is no conventional marriage ending – the fallen woman probably dies, and the 'New Woman' is left lonely, poor and sad.

In *A Psychological Moment at Three Periods* ('Discords'), the women only meet briefly in childhood, and then have a longer meeting near the end of the story in which they exchange life-stories. Then they separate again and go their own ways, each strengthened by the meeting. The story has a very unconventional structure, focusing on three thematically-linked episodes in the same woman's life. All three episodes emphasise her unconventionality and courage: in the first section, 'The Child', we see her forcing herself to do things she is afraid of, including confessing to her schoolfriends that the stories she has been telling them are all lies. This is where the two women first meet – among the schoolfriends is 'a square-faced girl with steady pale-grey eyes, thin lips, and smooth, foxy hair dragged back from a broad forehead' (p. 4). She has looked sceptical at the stories, but when the girl confesses, she says, '"I think you were a fool to do it"' (p. 8). It is implied that she is less imaginative, more practical and conformist. In the second episode, 'The Girl', we see the adolescence of the main character. She is at a convent school, where the nuns discourage friendships between the girls, but encourage them to fall in love with a favourite sister:

> ... the sisters are favourites and number many 'flames' amongst the crowd of girls filled with sickly sentiment, 'schwämerei', and awakening sexual instinct. They are genuinely in love. ...
> The worst trouble is with the girls from fourteen up; if they fall in love with a 'sister' and become a flame, the matter is simple; she will know how to blow hot and blow cold, and keep them where they are to remain. (pp. 10–11, 12)

The encouragement and manipulation of this kind of sentimental female crush is seen as is a device of the sisters' to control the girls' sexuality: one of them actually says, '"You must postpone your practice in flirtations, meine Fräulein; join the ardent flames instead and burn at the shrine".' Not just flirtations with the opposite sex, but equal friendships between women are inhibited. Our heroine rejects such manipulation: 'This girl will none of it.' She is an odd one out at the convent, 'too sharp-tongued, too keen-eyed, too intolerant of meanness and untruth to be a favourite with her

classmates – too independent a thinker, with too dangerous an
influence over weaker souls to find favour with the nuns' (p. 12).
We see her befriending a peasant girl, and giving her money to go to
the fair, and befriending and protecting Katrine, a mentally-retarded
pupil. These are not, of course, equal friendships: the girl's sense of
justice and her protection of the weak are being emphasised here.
This kind of effective help for other, deprived women, contrasts
with the useless and unreal sentimentality of the other pupils'
crushes on the nuns, and the nuns' cynical exploitation of their
feelings. At the fair, to which the school party is going, she helps
Katrine to ride on the roundabout, and then has a horrific vision of
the suffering and injustice 'behind the scenes' of society, as she sees
that the hurdygurdy is operated by an idiot boy, strapped to a pole,
with a whip nearby. In the final section, 'The Woman', both the
scene in the playground, and the meaningless music of the
fairground will recur in her memory, as she herself experiences
suffering and injustice, and faces it with her characteristic honesty
and courage.

In 'The Woman', a man blackmails her into becoming his
mistress. We are not told the contents of the letters he possesses, but
we infer she is protecting someone else. What seems to pain her most
about her 'fall' is that it has cut her off from 'them' at home, 'the
beings who are more to her than all the world beside' (p. 36). We
never learn who they are – the only one of them described is another
woman, Molly, 'with her clear true eyes, odd tender face, and
pathetic droop of mouth' (p. 35). At the end of the story, the only
service the heroine asks of her childhood friend is to get in touch
with (presumably) this woman:

'. . . I would like to do something for you.'
'Would you?'
'Ah then I would!'
The girl rises and takes a leather photograph case out of her bag. She
points to one.
'If I give you her address, will you go to her and tell her of me? Say I
will write in some weeks' time.'
'I will.' (p. 66)

Thus the heroine's 'fall' is presented as severing some essential
female–female tie in her life, which can perhaps be repaired by the
intervention of this other woman who befriends her. Nevertheless,

this continuing female bond in the heroine's life is very much in the background of the story, only hinted at; as in Egerton's other stories, the female friendship that we do see in detail is a brief encounter, a short, transforming interchange of experiences.

The heroine's reaction to her 'fall' is in many ways unconventional. She refuses to be contaminated by it, or almost to be involved in it at all. She shames the man by her cold, correct compliance:

> She accepted everything with the same irritating indifference. It stung him into efforts to impress her, with the disconcerting result that she made him feel underbred. She left him no fault to find, the things that irritated him most in her were rather praiseworthy than otherwise. She might have filled the position of a legitimate duchess, but as a mistress she was not amusing. (p. 33)

Finally, he grows tired of her, and attempts to pay her off. She refuses his money, and only makes sure he gives her the incriminating letters. Once she is free, she feels shame only because she did not love him:

> . . .She feels so bruised, so shamed, and yet she asks herself. Why shame? Is not that, too, a false conception based on custom? No, not in her case. Her soul-soiling is not because she lived with him, but because she lived with him for a reason other than love – because it involved a wrong to another woman. (p. 50)

Here we find her redefining and questioning her role as 'fallen woman'. The affair was 'a wrong to another woman' because the man is married: at this very moment, 'There is a knock on the door' (p. 50), and the other woman enters – not, in fact, his wife, but a representative married woman. She is to reveal the sham of married life, the prison she finds herself in; her suffering has led her to idealise the fallen woman and what she has done. The fallen woman in turn disillusions her, describing her own even greater suffering: the two become illustrations of two different ways women can be exploited and abused. Nevertheless, they each gain strength from telling and sharing their experiences, and we find they have each worked out a position of strength and endurance in which to survive and perhaps progress in what seemed at first hopeless situations. Their encounter enables them to understand and define their lives, and gives them both courage to continue. In addition, it serves especially to confirm and develop the fallen woman's redefinition of her role, and her refusal to accept her traditional fate. The discontented, admiring married woman confirms the readers' view of her friend as a courageous innovator, not a pitiable outcast. Their meeting is totally unlike any previous literary encounter between 'pure' and 'fallen' women, though the heroine has also had some conventional reactions from other 'pure' women, and is at first suspicious of her visitor:

'I wanted to see you for myself' ...
'Under existing circumstances I am at a loss to know why. There can be but one reason – a kind intention on your part to persuade me to repentance. The day before yesterday I got this letter ... from Mary O'Mahoney, you know, the Queen's counsel's wife. She enclosed a medal and an introduction to a convent where they receive Magdalens of a better class, with means enough, in fact, to indulge in genteel contrition. They find them occupation, and, I presume' – with bitterness – 'white sheets to stand in. No doubt she meant it kindly; but I fail to see why she or any other woman should stand in judgement over me.' (p. 53)

But the other woman has come with no such judgemental intentions. All these years, she has remembered the scene in the playground: '"I have never forgotten you; you were younger than I was, but you influenced me –".' Though she was trained to conform, secretly she admired the other's unconventionality and courage: '"I told you you were a fool, do you remember? That was the outcome of home training; in my heart I envied you your courage".' Similarly, now she envies her 'fallen' friend: '"I envy you the self-reliance that gave you courage to do it – and courage to face life again having done it – alone, as you mean to do".' In contrast, her own conventional married life is 'a lie': '"I haven't a spark of your courage. I am a coward, just a soft thing beside you. I would give all I ever dreamt of to have it or your truth. I am a living lie, acting a lie daily, and even if I could, I wouldn't change it; I am afraid of public opinion"' (p. 54). She now tells her life-story: she has allowed pressure from her Catholic family to separate her from the Protestant man she really loved. Like the older woman in *Her Share*, she has lacked the courage to defy convention and marry her soul-mate. Instead, she lets her parents marry her to a man she detests. So far she has presented herself as a cowardly victim: but next she reveals some strength and resourcefulness:

> 'Two years ago my aunt left me her money. There is a great power in money to a woman, and I knew more than before – I knew how to use it. . . . I made it understood that no penny of mine would go out of my keeping. I refused to share in any dealings. I am a good business woman now. My babies died, and at my death neither family nor husband nor church'll benefit; every penny of it will go to him or his [meaning her lover]. That's my satisfaction.' (p. 57)

This development from a hopeless position of exploitation and weakness to one of some independence and self-assertion is to be paralleled in the fallen woman's account of her situation.

The younger woman, listening to the story, now realises why her friend wanted to see her: '"I think you came to me because you thought that I too loved as you do, and that I had courage to put all aside for it"' (p. 58). The older woman has thought her friend represented a contrast, the choice she herself could not make: but in fact their predicaments are surprisingly similar. Both have been forced into sexual relationships with men they do not love. The 'fallen' woman claims to suffer most, however, and she tells her story so that '"it may help you to forget your own fate to realise another's harder one"' (p. 59). A competition in female suffering seems to be going on: but as she speaks, the younger woman talks herself into a new courage and hope. She describes the two 'roads' set out by society before the fallen woman, repentance or prostitution: '"If she is of the kind to rebel at the dreary road Christian charity indicates to her, she is free to seek the broad road to destruction as a pleasanter alternative"' (pp. 60–1). She states her determination to take neither road, but to '"stand by my own action"' (p. 61), and to make her own living. She remembers sources of joy in art and nature that no one can deprive her of, and ends with hope, which she conveys to her friend: 'The latter is looking at her with eager eyes and parted lips, and when the girl, roused from her thoughts, smiles at her, she draws her down and holds the throbbing head to her heart' (p. 64). There is another embrace between the two women as they part: 'She nestles with tears in her smiling eyes into the big woman's arms, kisses her back, and pushes her gently out of the room' (p. 66).

But why does she push her out? Why not continue this newfound friendship and sympathy into the uncertain future? The contradiction here between embracing and pushing away runs through the whole scene: it both affirms and denies the value of women's friendship. To begin with, in her long speeches the younger woman has been working out her own thoughts and plans, oblivious to the other woman: 'She has been clothing the thoughts of months into words and she has completely forgotten her audience of one' (p. 64). At the end, the final comment on the encounter is, 'The meeting has touched her, helped her to formulate her vague ideas, given her, as it were, a friendly set-off on her way' (p. 66), nothing more. In addition, the essence of the philosophy of life she has been working out is independence and self-sufficiency. She rejects all help: '"I seek pity, help, friendship from no one.... I shall apologise to no man, court no woman's friendship"' (p. 61); she offers no help to her friend: '"I can't help you. You must find yourself ... *always you must come back to yourself.* That is your problem, and one which you must solve alone. You've got to get a purchase on your own soul. Stand on your own feet"' (p. 64). What she hopes from the meeting is that more women will be taught this doctrine of self-help: '"Go, big woman, and if you find other women weaker, teach them to be sufficient to themselves – give of your largesse, but hold your own soul in the hollow of your hand and give no man a mortgage on it"' (p. 65).

In order to revise the role of the fallen woman, Egerton has grafted onto it the spirit of the independent entrepreneur: '"There is no power strong enough to crush a man or woman determined to get on"' (p. 62), asserts the heroine.[37] The message of individualism undercuts the power of the friendship, and also draws attention to the way Egerton always limits and contains the female–female encounters in her stories. In *The White Elf* and *Gone Under*, the encounters take place in the necessarily temporary environment of a sea voyage: at the end, the two women must part and go their separate ways, though in *Gone Under* this is reinforced by an explicit warning away by Edith. In *Her Share*, the women meet while both on a temporary visit to the country. In *A Psychological Moment*, they are in a hotel in Paris – both again have lives elsewhere. In all cases, the meeting resolves or clarifies issues of female identity and role, and then sends the two women away on separate journeys to deal independently with their problems. It is only in *A Psychological*

*Moment* that explicit attention is drawn to this device, and it is linked to an ideology of individualism.

The story ends with the heroine alone, facing an unknown future. As in *The Story of a Modern Woman*, we end with a picture of New Woman alone and embattled – but here there is hope instead of despair: 'One great star blinks down at her like a bright glad eye, and hers shine steadily back with the sombre light of an undaunted spirit waiting quietly for the dawn to break, to take the first step of her new life's journey' (p. 66). The strength and independence of the New Woman is seen as a more important value than her solidarity and community with other women.

*The Regeneration of Two* ('Discords') is unusual in that continuing friendships between women, rather than brief encounters, are part of the story. The central, life-changing encounter is in fact between a woman and a man: a bored, fashionable woman meets a poet, who tells her of his disillusionment with women. She is prompted by the encounter to discard her artificial life-style, and to set up a community of 'fallen' women, who maintain themselves by spinning and weaving. She is presented as motivated by a sense of female solidarity: 'she espoused the cause of all women, without reference to character or exhortations to repentance' (p. 205); 'It has cost her pains and anxiety to set her scheme for helping wretched sisters out of the mire' (p. 212). Nevertheless, we learn hardly anything about the women as individuals: they are a generalised background to her transformation. She is very much queen and patroness of the community: 'Her heart warms as she looks round her big kitchen, filled with people all dependent on her in some way' (p. 215). The community is the means of her personal transformation, which will reunite her as a fit mate with the poet. The chair in her room is always turned to look down the road, as if she is waiting for him: eventually, he reappears, injured and needing to be rescued by her in a snow-storm. He is struck by her transformation – now she has become his ideal woman, and she offers herself to him in a free union, which he accepts.

As in the earlier fiction I have discussed, her contact with other women, and specifically fallen women, has made her more womanly, more sexually attractive, and readier for a male–female consummation. Her attractiveness, however, is described entirely as *power*, not as a discovery of vulnerability: her lover sees her as 'a silver witch', a powerful female rescuer who overawes him. In the community, she has her own female power-base which gives her the strength to take the risk of free love with a man. Her strength, nevertheless, is based on a very traditional notion of womanhood – as is suggested by the traditional female activities of spinning and weaving that support her community. She has discarded 'artificial' clothes and manners, and become a more 'natural' woman – the kind the poet was looking for: '"I thought to find her nature's best product, of all things closest in touch with our common mother. I hoped to find rest on her great mother heart; to return home to her for strength and wise counsel; for it is the primitive, the generic, that makes her sacred, mystic, to the best men"' (p. 197). The woman's return to more 'natural' and traditional ways has also given her a traditional mythic power, as 'witch' or 'Snow Queen'. The community as a whole appeals to the poet's mythologising imagination: 'This description of the colony of women managed by a woman, going their own way to hold a place in the world in the face of opinion, has fired his fancy – a wonderful song is singing in him' (p. 232).

Though the poet has been the main agent of the woman's transformation, another woman has also played a minor role: her servant, Aagot. In her initial discontented, artificial phase, it is Aagot who tries to help her and with whom she discusses her problems. They do not have a conventional mistress–servant relationship: Aagot 'speaks respectfully, yet there is the note in her voice that one uses to a child or an invalid; indeed she is on terms of companionship with her mistress' (p. 165). Aagot first humours her mistress, then she offers female sympathy and advice: '"At times – at night I do feel as if I could just cry without knowing why. I suspect all women do – it's part of our nature. Fruen ought to do something"' (pp. 165–6). In the conversation that follows, 'Fruen' rejects with scorn the traditional female charitable occupations, *and* the modern women's rights movement:

'... they go in for suffrage, social reformation, politics, all sorts of fatiguing things. I thought of doing something of that kind myself, of having a mission; but it would last just as long as it was a new sensation. Besides, I didn't care much for any of the advanced women I met, they were so desperately in earnest, they took it out of me so. I am too selfish, I am afraid, Aagot! ... I *want something for myself!*' (p. 167)

So we must see the women's community she founds as something different from the conventional women's 'charity' for fallen women and also as distinct from any feminist political movement. It represents a third possibility, based on a return to what are assumed to be women's traditional roles and powers. In her confrontation with the disapproving pastor, the woman defends her championship of the fallen women in the name of woman's traditional role as mother, which has always made her *superior* to man:

> 'Her maternity lifts her above him every time. Man hasn't kept the race going, the burden of the centuries has lain on the women. He has fought, and drunk, and rioted, lusted, and satisfied himself, whilst she has rocked the cradle and ruled the world, borne the sacred burden of her motherhood, carried in trust the future of the races.' (p. 207)

The community is an attempt to embody this 'new standard of woman's worth' (p. 241), based on a revaluing of her traditional roles. It is also, as the woman's words to Aagot suggest, '"*something for myself*"', not just selfless charity or political activism. The community gives her her own sense of power and value, in addition to giving her protégées a sense of self-worth. The community is part of her own self-development, confirming both her unconventional morality, and her traditional womanhood, as well as her power as a leader and organiser. All these qualities make her a match for the poet – the community functions to get her the man she wants.

In her earlier conversation with Aagot, after she rejects charity and politics, she also rejects men. Her husband has just died, and what she has experienced of conventional marriage has made her rejoice in her new freedom. At this point, Aagot confides to her a story about her own life, which foreshadows developments in the rest of the story. Her mistress asks, '"Were *you* ever in love, Aagot?"' (p. 168), and Aagot tells her of a romance that happened to her in Spain, when she was a girl. She encounters her soul-mate, but two days after he has declared his love, he is taken ill and dies. Now, much later, she is planning to marry a crippled cousin, for the sake of his children – '"I don't want a husband – I should hate it. The one I wanted lies out there under the olive-trees in the Catholic churchyard. I just want the children"' (p. 1707). In this, she is a bit like the career-woman's servant, Belinda, in *The White Elf*, who also wants children and no husband. Her solution of marrying the cousin, like the career-woman's adoption of the white elf, suggests different, unconventional possibilities for women's lives, by which they can satisfy their maternal instinct. Later, we find the cousin has died, so Aagot gets the children at no cost.

The relevance of Aagot's story to her mistress's plight is not at first clear. But her affirmation of true love stands against her mistress's disillusion with men; and it is Aagot who now sends her mistress out, on the expedition that leads to her meeting her own soul-mate. In addition, the unconventional household that Aagot proposes for herself, prefigures the even more unconventional community her mistress eventually sets up – both are unusual ways of fulfilling 'womanly' powers and instincts. Aagot's resolution to act to get what she wants prefigures her mistress's similar decision: her story suggests new possibilities of love and fulfilment. When the community is set up, Aagot is of course her mistress's right-hand woman in the organisation: the cooperation between mistress and servant is similar to that between the career-woman and Belinda in *The White Elf*. These mistress-servant relationships can be read as examples of cooperation between women of different classes: but we may also think how very convenient it is that there are such servants of limited ambition to enable the 'top' women to fulfill themselves in all possible ways. Though it is Aagot's story that points to the fulfilment her mistress finds with the poet, there are some signs later that Aagot resents his intrusion into the all-female idyll she has helped her mistress to create – 'Aagot wishes him away, that is sure' (p. 246). But this feeling is not really investigated or taken seriously – the story proceeds inevitably to its revised-conventional conclusion, with the union of New Woman and New Man. The New Woman's identity as a blend of progressive, unconventional, independent organiser and powerful archetypal natural woman has been largely created through her leadership of an unconventional yet traditional community of women.

# Notes

## INTRODUCTION

1. (1929) (Granada, London, Toronto, Sydney, New York, 1977, pp. 78-9).
2. *Archetypal Patterns in Women's Fiction* (Indiana University Press, Bloomington, 1981). p. 85.
3. (Columbia University Press, New York, 1980).
4. Pauline Nestor's recent book, *Female Friendships and Communities: Charlotte Brontë, George Eliot, Elizabeth Gaskell* (Clarendon Press, Oxford, 1985) seems to be a discussion of ideas about female friendship, using material from journalism, biography and literature, rather than a literary analysis: Janice M. Bowman Swanson's interesting PhD thesis, 'Speaking in a Mother Tongue: Female Friendship in the British Novel', ranges from Jane Austen to Virginia Woolf, but includes a stimulating study of Charlotte Brontë's *Shirley*, focusing on the way the friends come to share a special language (University of California at Santa Barbara, 1981).
5. '(E)Merging Identities: The Dynamics of Female Friendship in Contemporary Fiction by Women', *Signs* 6, no. 3 (Spring 1981), pp. 414, footnote, 415.
6. Jean Kennard, in *Victims of Convention* (Archon Books, Hamden, Conn., 1978), comments on 'a serious problem in current feminist criticism generally: the tendency to treat literature, particularly the novel, as mimetic in the simplest way, as the documentation, more or less accurate, of certain human experiences' (p. 10). More recently, Toril Moi has made similar criticisms, in *Sexual/Textual Politics: Feminist Literary Theory* (Methuen, London and New York 1985), Introduction and Part I, esp. pp. 2-8, 45-6.
7. *Writing Beyond the Ending: Narrative Strategies of Twentieth-Century Women Writers* (Indiana University Press, Bloomington 1985), pp. 2, 3. DuPlessis derives her concept of ideology as 'a system of representations by which we imagine the world as it is' from Althusser (*For Marx*, trans. Ben Brewster, New Left Books, London [1977], p. 233, quoted by DuPlessis, p. 3; see also her note 9, p. 198). The way she connects literary and social convention is also influenced by Raymond Williams, *Marxism and Literature*

(Oxford University Press, Oxford, 1977). Another good short explication of the Althusserian concept of ideology and its feminist application is to be found in Penny Boumelha's *Thomas Hardy and Women: Sexual Ideology and Narrative Form* (Harvester Press, Brighton, 1982), pp. 4–6.

8. For some interesting ideas on absent mothers in nineteenth-century women's literature, see *The Lost Tradition: Mothers and Daughters in Literature*, eds Cathy N. Davidson and E. M. Broner (Frederic Ungar, New York, 1980), Pt. II, 'Daughters of the Patriarchy', pp. 56–109, esp. Susan Peck Macdonald, 'Jane Austen and the Tradition of the Absent Mother', pp. 58–69.

9. I am not using the words 'woman writer' in any essentialist sense: rather, they refer to a position constructed by Victorian sexual ideologies. It is not part of my project in this book to provide a sustained and detailed comparison between 'male' and 'female' texts – obviously many of the conventions used by women writers were also used by men, but I would argue that the particular kind of negotiation I am interested in is not found in 'male' texts. Meredith's *Diana of the Crossways* (1884) is the nearest a 'male' text comes to the kind of patterns I find in 'female' texts, but interestingly a male 'messenger' intervenes to act between the women friends, and he and the more conventional friend operate in collusion to prevent the heroine's more unconventional excesses, and eventually to assimilate her to marriage with him.

10. See Martha Vicinus, *Independent Women: Work and Community for the Single Woman, 1850–1920* (Virago, London, 1985); also note 15 below.

11. (Croom Helm, London and Canberra, 1982), p. 115.

12. p. 188.

13. *The Daughters of England: Their Social Duties, and Domestic Habits* (Charles Griffin, London, 1845), p. 281.

14. Shirley Foster remarks on Victorian women writers' dual position:

> ... certain criteria were laid down for female novelists, neglect of which led to charges of unwomanliness; an acute conflict of roles was almost inevitable for the woman writer, who, by the very act of entering the male world of letters, was challenging the traditional female spheres of private endeavour and economic dependence. (*Victorian Women's Fiction: Marriage, Freedom and the Individual* [Croom Helm, London, 1985], p. 12.)

15. Judith Lowder Newton comments on

> ... the current debate over the degree to which the ideology of women's sphere 'deplored the treatment of women as sexual objects or domestic drudges, advocated improvement in women's education, upheld models of women as responsible mothers of citizens'. By stressing a difference between women and men, the ideology 'got around the question of inferiority and superiority'. It laid a basis upon which to claim a role in civil and public life for middle-class women, and it provided the basis of a 'subculture among women that formed a source of strength and identity and afforded supportive sisterly relations', a view which implies that 'the ideology's tenacity owed as much to women's motives as to the imposition of man's or society's wishes'. The ideology of women's sphere, in short, has been seen as articulating 'a social power based on women's special female qualities rather than on general human rights. For women who previously held no

particular avenue of power of their own ... this represented an advance' (*Women, Power, and Subversion: Social Strategies in British Fiction, 1778–1860* [University of Georgia Press, Athens, and Methuen, London, 1981], pp. 161–2).

The quotations are from Nancy F. Cott, *The Bonds of Womanhood: 'Woman's Sphere' in New England, 1780–1835* (Yale University Press, New Haven, 1977), pp. 206, 203, 205, 197, 200.

16. George Eliot, *Middlemarch* (1872), 'Prelude'.

17. Todd comments on this maternal quality of fictional female friendships, pp. 2–3, as does Swanson, p. 3.

18. Just how impossible it is to superimpose modern and Victorian concepts is suggested by Vicinus, when she describes how Sara Burstall, writing in 1907, 'defined homerotic friendships in terms of women's traditional sphere, as an encouragement to marriage' (*Independent Women* p. 189) – even the 'homoerotic' element here is assimilated into the heterosexual.

19. Some of Mrs Gaskell's short stories do have women-together endings, as opposed to marriage endings: but these always occur when the women's heterosexual possibilities have been blighted in some way, by death or disgrace: interestingly, the death of children seems to be necessary to such an ending – the women are consoling each other for their losses, not reaching a triumphant consummation (see 'Libbie Marsh's Three Eras' and 'Lizzie Leigh' [both 1855] in *Lizzie Leigh and Other Tales* [Oxford University Press, Oxford, 1913]). Similarly, the women-together ending of George Eliot's *Romola* (1863) is presented as 'not so much a genuine and fulfilling alternative as a last resort' (Nestor, p. 177).

20. The friends do share fantasies about female sexuality (see pp. 122–7 above), but these are first introduced in the context of 'Nunnwood' and the ruined nunnery there: the ideological polarity seems to be between a chaste, undisturbed female sexuality, and the disturbing desires introduced by the male.

21. See Adrienne Rich, 'Compulsory Heterosexuality and Lesbian Existence', *Signs* 5, no. 4 (Summer 1980), pp. 640–9. For a discussion of these problems of definition in lesbian criticism, see Bonnie Zimmerman, 'What Has Never Been: An Overview of Lesbian Feminist Criticism', in Elaine Showalter (ed.), *The New Feminist Criticism* (Virago, London, 1986), pp. 200–24.

22. p. 113.

23. *Daughters*, p. 281.

24. E.g. David Copperfield and Steerforth, Dr Jekyll and Mr Hyde, Bradley Headstone and Rogue Riderhood, Bulstrode and Raffles. In Jane Eyre and Bertha Mason of course we have an example of a destructive *female* double who has to be eliminated – but the book also contains examples of transforming female friendship.

25. *The Reproduction of Mothering: Psychoanalysis and the Sociology of Gender*, (University of California Press, Berkeley LA and London, 1978).

26. See esp. Abel, '(E)Merging Identities', and Judith Kegan Gardiner, 'On Female Identity and Writing by Women', *Writing and Sexual Difference*, ed. Elizabeth Abel (University of Chicago Press, Chicago, 1982). pp. 177–91. Gardiner also provides a survey of critics using Chodorow's and related theories, in 'Mind

Mother: Psychoanalysis and Feminism', *Making A Difference: Feminist Literary Criticism*, ed. Gayle Greene and Coppélia Kahn (Methuen, London and New York, 1985), pp. 134–8. See also Marianne Hirsch, 'Mothers and Daughters: Review Essay', *Signs* 7, no. 1 (Fall 1981), pp. 200–22.

27. pp. 200–1.
28. There are counter-arguments to the 'essentialist' objection. Chodorow is not originally a psychologist, she is a sociologist: and she stresses that the psychological patterns she is tracing are the result of social structures – i.e. the family and work structures that mean women do primary parenting – though of course her theories show why these structures are self-perpetuating. She does, however, want to make room for *change* – the point of her book is to suggest that we should change parenting roles, and that men should take on more primary parenting, and so alter all the patterns. There are arguments between her and her critics as to whether, on her model, any such change is possible. For critiques of Chodorow, see Judith Lorber, Rose Laub Coser, Alice S. Rossi and Nancy Chodorow, 'On *The Reproduction of Mothering*: A Methodological Debate', *Signs* 6, no. 3 (Spring 1981), pp. 482–514; Judy Housman, 'Mothering, the Unconscious, and Feminism', *Radical America* 16 (Nov./Dec. 1982), pp. 47–62.
29. pp. 113, 115.
30. 'The Female World of Love and Ritual', in *Women's America: Refocussing the Past*, eds Linda K. Kerber and Jane De Hart Matthews, (Oxford University Press, Oxford, 1982), pp. 156–79. A similar point is made by Lillian Faderman's *Surpassing the Love of Men: Romantic Friendship and Love between Women from the Renaissance to the Present* (William Morrow, New York, 1981), though Faderman does not sufficiently distinguish between literary and other kinds of evidence, and she reads all her friendships, ahistorically, as examples of potential or frustrated lesbian consciousness.
31. There are also many examples of other, more particular discrepancies between 'life' and 'art' – for instance, Swanson comments that 'While Charlotte Brontë is more apt [than Jane Austen] to give her female characters the joy of each other's company, there is a restraint in the expression of their affection which her own letters to a close friend, Ellen Nussey, do not show' (p. 27), and Nestor notices in particular that in a letter 'Charlotte Brontë addresses to her girlhood friend, Ellen Nussey, the words Jane Eyre later speaks of Rochester' (p. 5). In fiction, heterosexual romance takes precedence: as Foster remarks, Victorian women writers, 'in apparent contravention of their own experience, . . . focus centrally on courtship and marriage in their books' (p. 14). Goreham actually sees 'life' and 'art' in *inverse* relationship as far as the female community is concerned:

> A girls' relationship to the female members of her family – mothers, sisters, aunts, – was depicted as one of close, supportive companionship, of an intimacy based on the fulfilment of a shared role. Perhaps because, in real life, such relationships figured much more prominently in female experience than did relations with males, they tended to figure less in idealisations. (p. 48)

32. p. 7.

33. An important exception here is the fiction of Mrs Gaskell – see pp. 89–9 above.
34. Elizabeth Barrett Browning, *Aurora Leigh*, I 40.
35. See Vicinus, *Independent Women*.


## CHAPTER 1

1. See Dolores Rosenblum, 'Christina Rossetti: The Inward Pose', pp. 93–5, in *Shakespeare's Sisters*, eds Sandra Gilbert and Susan Gubar (Indiana University Press, Bloomington, 1979), for a similar interpretation of this poem. Rosenblum explicitly takes the younger sister as a 'stand-in' for the authoritative mother. Rosenblum misses the point about 'what the golden sister is embroidering' (p. 93). See also Winston Weathers, 'Christina Rossetti: The Sisterhood of Self', *Victorian Poetry* 3 (Spring 1965), pp. 81–9.
2. *Essays of George Eliot*, ed. Thomas Pinney (Routledge and Kegan Paul, London, 1963), p. 311.
3. All quotations from *The Mill on the Floss* are from the Penguin edition (Harmondsworth, 1979).
4. See Ellen Moers, *Literary Women* (W. H. Allen, London, 1977). Ch. 9, 'Performing Heroinism: The Myth of Corinne', pp. 173–210, esp. pp. 174–5 where *Corinne* is related to *Mill on the Floss*.
5. A similar point about this passage is made by Shirley Foster, p. 205.
6. pp. 59, 68.
7. See Mary Jacobus, 'The Question of Language: Men of Maxims and *The Mill on the Floss*', pp. 49, 51; and Margaret Homans, 'Eliot, Wordsworth, and the Scenes of the Sisters' Instruction', pp. 57–8, both in Abel (ed.), *Writing and Sexual Difference*.
8. All quotations from *Villette* are from the Penguin edition (Harmondsworth, 1979).
9. Linda C. Hunt dismisses Lucy's friendship with Paulina, saying that Lucy cannot identify with Paulina because Lucy's 'experiences have simply been too different' ('Sustenance and Balm: The Question of Female Friendship in *Shirley* and *Villette*', *Tulsa Studies in Women's Literature*, 1 [Spring 1982], pp. 62–3). But it is Lucy's attraction to potentialities that are *not* expressed in her own life that makes her bond with Paulina so close.
10. See Sandra Gilbert and Susan Gubar, *The Madwoman in the Attic*. (Yale University Press, London, 1979), p. 404, where they conclude that 'Polly acts out all those impulses already repressed by Lucy, so that the two girls represent the two sides of Lucy's divided self'. Terry Eagleton remarks that 'Lucy's tight-lipped treatment of [Polly] signifies the erection of a blandly rational barrier against her own coldly unacknowledged impulses. Lucy projects herself into Polly and then coolly dissociates herself from that self-image' (*Myths of Power: A Marxist Study of the Brontës* [Macmillan, London 1975], pp. 63–4).
11. Gilbert and Gubar suggest that Paulina 'is, in fact, Lucy Snowe born under a lucky star' (*Madwoman*, p.427).
12. See Gilbert and Gubar, *Madwoman*, pp. 426, 428.

## CHAPTER 2

1. See Nina Auerbach, *Woman and the Demon: The Life of a Victorian Myth*, (Harvard University Press, London 1982), Ch. V, 'The Rise of the Fallen Woman', pp. 150–84, and p. 67 above.
2. Ibid.
3. This pattern is reversed in Annie Holdsworth's *Joanna Traill, Spinster* (1894); see pp. 142–50 above.
4. *Sexual Politics* (Rupert Hart-Davis, London, 1971), p. 38.
5. Vicinus, *Independent Women*, p. 78. See also pp. 74–80.
6. See Eric Trudgill, *Madonnas and Magdalens: The Origins and Development of Victorian Sexual Attitudes* (Holmes and Meier, New York, 1976), pp. 289–90, 306; Cora Kaplan, Introduction to Elizabeth Barrett Browning, *Aurora Leigh* (Women's Press, London, 1978), pp. 24–5; and Auerbach, op. cit., pp. 150–84.
7. Dots in square brackets – [. . .] – signify that I have ommitted some of Barrett Browning's text. Dots without brackets are part of the text. This applies to all my quotations from *Aurora Leigh*.
8. See Kaplan, Introduction, p. 16.
9. See Virginia Steinmetz, 'Images of "Mother Want" in Elizabeth Barrett Browning's *Aurora Leigh*', *Victorian Poetry*, 21, no. 4 (Winter 1983), pp. 351–67. According to Steinmetz, lines 285–7 of Book Six 'allude[s] to the unconscious mother-searching of all the characters' (p. 359). Dolores Rosenblum sees Aurora's meeting with Marian as symbolising Aurora's crucial recovery of her mother, but she does not interpret it from Marian's side ('Face to Face: Elizabeth Barrett Browning's *Aurora Leigh* and Victorian Poetry', *Victorian Studies*, 26 no. 3 [Spring 1983], pp. 321–38).
10. Steinmetz notes how Aurora follows Marian 'as a small child, in total dependence and identification' here, but does not mention the first appearance of the 'plank' metaphor, where Marian follows Aurora (Steinmetz, p. 360). Intent on decoding the symbolic significance of the relationship for Aurora, most critics have not noticed the important *reciprocity* of the friendship.
11. 'Women's Writing: Jane Eyre, Shirley, Villette, Aurora Leigh', *Ideology and Consciousness*, no. 3 (Spring 1978), p. 46
12. Rosenblum interprets Marian's 'imperfect' and 'changeful' face as part of Barrett Browning's strategy to humanize or give expression to 'the silent, iconic female face' that haunts Victorian male art (pp. 331, 322, 325). I would read the descriptions of Marian's face, however, as signifying vulnerability, lack of identity, dependence, and oppression. While Rosenblum's interpretation depends on the idea of Aurora finally discovering Marian as a mother's face that looks back at her, that responds, there is nowhere a description of Marian's face doing this to Aurora – we always see it as an image of pathos, looked at by Aurora.
13. See Elisabeth G. Gitter, 'The Power of Women's Hair in the Victorian Imagination', *PMLA*, 99, no. 5 (October 1984), pp. 936–54, esp. pp. 936, 938, 941.
14. See ibid., p. 950 for other examples.
15. See Kaplan, Introduction, p. 20, and Gilbert and Gubar, *Madwoman*, pp.

18–19. Barbara Charlesworth Gelpi remarks that the portrait 'mirrors [Aurora's] ambivalence toward femininity itself' ('*Aurora Leigh*: the Vocation of the Women Poet', *Victorian Poetry*, 19, no. 1 [Spring 1981], p. 40).

16. Steinmetz sees the two women as projections of Aurora's ambivalent feelings towards her mother, 'her splitting of pre-oedipal impulses toward mother into the desire to possess Marian Erle and the desire to destroy Lady Waldemar' (pp. 353–4).

17. p. 25.

18. Gelpi identifies Lady Waldemar as Aurora's Jungian 'shadow', whose 'attitudes and reactions are uncomfortably and unadmittedly close to Aurora's own' (p. 40).

19. Gelpi sees Aurora's identification with Marian as signifying her reconciliation with her own 'womanhood' (p. 45); Gilbert and Gubar see it as her acceptance of a role of 'sympathy and service' to Romney (*Madwoman*, p. 577). Rosenblum rejects Gilbert and Gubar's interpretation of this as a 'compromise', and sees Marian as 'a symbol for the birth of self' ('Face to Face', p. 333), allowing Aurora 'to go on to fulfill her own womanly nature' (p. 327). Only Steinmetz points out the importance to Aurora of both identifying with *and* rejecting the sort of femininity that Marian represents (pp. 357, 365). None of these critics notes that Marian too changes, through her relationship with Aurora, at the end of the poem.

20. The reconciliation of the 'man' and the 'woman' in Aurora is the central theme of Gelpi's article (pp. 38–48).

21. p. 175.

22. George Eliot, *Adam Bede* (1859) (Penguin, Harmondsworth, 1980), p. 204; quoted by Auerbach, p. 175.

23. p. 175. Persistent references to the unprecedented colouring of Dinah's face as a sign of her growing love for Adam, can be found in *Adam Bede*, pp. 521, 522, 528, 535 and 550.

24. p. 175.

25. *Madwoman*, p. 566. Dorothy Mermin also sees Laura as 'in effect a fallen woman', and links Lizzie's rescue of her with Christina Rossetti's work in a 'Home for Fallen Women' ('Heroic Sisterhood in *Goblin Market*', *Victorian Poetry* 21, no. 2 [Summer 1983], p. 111).

26. Cora Kaplan emphasises that 'Lizzie goes out determined to cure, not absolve, her, by getting her sister more of what she wants' ('The Indefinite Disclosed: Christina Rossetti and Emily Dickinson', in *Women Writing and Writing about Women*, ed. Mary Jacobus [Croom Helm, London] 1979, p. 67).

27. Jerome J. McGann points out that 'Although the lines describe the evening rest of the sisters *after* Laura's encounter with the goblins, the passage does not draw any moral distinctions between Laura and Lizzie. In the perspective of Christina Rossetti's poem, Laura remains fundamentally uncorrupted' ('Christina Rossetti's Poems: A New Edition and a Revaluation', *Victorian Studies* 23, no. 2 [Winter 1980] p. 253).

28. Gilbert and Gubar call the sisters' world 'effectively matrilineal and matriarchal' (*Madwoman*, p. 567). Mermin comments, 'The children are apparently all girls and are exhorted to keep the female circle complete. This is a world in which men serve only the purpose of impregnation' (p. 114).

29. See p. 87 above.
30. For the 'barrenness' imagery and its implications, see Mermin, p. 108.
31. See pp. 111–37 above.
32. *Shirley* (1849) (Penguin, Harmondsworth, 1974), p. 189.
33. See Gitter, p. 143.
34. When Robert Moore says he has been assuming from her behaviour that she is in love with him, she interprets him scornfully: '"That is to say, that I am a traitor to all my sisters: that I have acted as no woman can act, without degrading herself and her sex"' (p. 500).
35. See Mermin, pp. 108–9; Gilbert and Gubar, *Madwoman*, p. 574.
36. Charlotte Brontë, *Jane Eyre* (1847) (Penguin, Harmondsworth, 1966), pp. 104, 363.
37. McGann emphasises this ideal of female independence in the poem: 'the goblins' power over the women comes ultimately from the women's (erroneous) belief that the goblins have something which the women need, that the women are incomplete.... Lizzie's heroic adventure on her sister's behalf dramatizes her integrity, her freedom from dependency on the goblins' (p. 250).
38. See pp. 111–37 above.
39. Gilbert and Gubar point out that the sisters' 'effectively matrilineal and matriarchal world' turns out to be 'a heaven of domesticity', and both women become 'angels in the house' (*Madwoman*, p. 567).
40. Mermin, p. 108.
41. *Daughters of England*, p. 281.
42. McGann also notes the importance of Rossetti's conservatism here: 'her conservative posture once again proved an asset to her work, for in accepting the traditional view of "a woman's place", she uncovered a (secret) position from which to cast a clear eye on the ways of her world' (p. 254).
43. p. 115.

## CHAPTER 3

1. For the influence of George Eliot on the writing of *Sir George Tressady*, see Peter Collister, 'Portraits of "Audacious Youth": George Eliot and Mrs. Humphry Ward', *ES* 64, no. 4 (1983), pp. 296–317.
2. See W. A. Craik, *Elizabeth Gaskell and the English Provincial Novel* (Methuen, London, 1975), pp. 212, 250.
3. Craik calls her 'a most unusual heroine' (p. 245).
4. All quotations from *Wives and Daughters* (1866) are from the Penguin edition (Harmondsworth, 1969).
5. Craik compares Molly and Cynthia to Maggie and Lucy: 'Maggie, the subdued heroine, contrasts with her brilliant and beloved cousin Lucy, as Molly does with her brilliant step-sister, though their roles are reversed in that Stephen Guest, Lucy's lover, defects to Maggie, while Roger Hamley only comes to Molly after Cynthia has cast him off' (p. 204). I would suggest their roles are reversed and confused more pervasively than this: in so far as Molly is

'subdued', she is more like *Lucy* than Maggie; and Cynthia's sexually attractive 'brilliance' makes her more like *Maggie* than Lucy. To call Maggie 'subdued' and Lucy 'brilliant' is to falsify their roles in *Mill on the Floss*, in order to make them more closely approximate Molly and Cynthia respectively.

6. For the significance of this mother/child relationship as part of the book's pattern of mother/daughter relations, see Jacqueline Berke and Laura Berke, 'Mothers and Daughters in *Wives and Daughters*: A Study of Elizabeth Gaskell's Last Novel', Davidson and Broner, p. 100.

7. It is fear of Molly's awakening sexuality that precipitates Mr Gibson into his disastrous marriage with Cynthia's mother, with the intention of providing female supervision and protection for Molly. Jacqueline and Laura Berke remark, 'so Mr Gibson views the situation, and so we may infer Gaskell herself viewed it: that at certain stages of a young woman's development she must be in close touch with the female principle' (p. 105). It is not, however, Mrs Gibson but Cynthia who embodies 'the female principle' that Molly becomes 'in close touch with' – it is notable that her principal confidant changes from being her father, to being Cynthia, with a brief transition via Roger in his 'brotherly' role.

8. It is, however, Mrs Gibson who has the ridiculous and pretentious idea of a *formal* 'coming out' for the girls (p. 274).

9. *Wives and Daughters* is of course unfinished, but everything points in the direction of a marriage between Molly and Roger. Molly, in accordance with feminine modesty, reacts with horror to Cynthia's implication that Roger can switch his affections so easily from Cynthia to her. But it is clearly what both of them want – like Edmund in *Mansfield Park*, Roger only needs a decent interval in which to discover his true feelings. Craik notes the similarities of the plots of *Wives and Daughters* and *Mansfield Park* (pp. 203, 246, 252), especially Cynthia's resemblance to Mary Crawford, and Molly's to Fanny Price. This makes their friendship all the more remarkable: we cannot conceive of Fanny and Mary as genuine friends.

10. p. 95.

11. Patricia Spacks comments on how Molly has 'a number of different models available to her' while she is 'learning how to be a woman' (*The Female Imagination* [Allen and Unwin, London, 1976], p. 89 – quoted by J. and L. Berke, p. 105).

12. Elaine Showalter points out the way Mrs Gaskell saw no problem in reconciling her 'womanly' role as wife and mother, with her career as a writer (*A Literature of their Own* [Virago, London, 1978], pp. 69–72).

13. All quotations from *Middlemarch* are from the Penguin edition (1965).

14. *Madwoman*, pp. 514–19.

15. *Daughters of England*, pp. 301, 305–6.

16. Ibid., p. 302.

17. (1876) (Penguin, 1967), p. 150.

18. (Harmony Books, New York, 1980), pp. 8–9.

19. See K. A. McKenzie, *Edith Simcox and George Eliot* (Oxford University Press, Oxford, 1961), p. 97.

20. *Daughters of England*, p. 303.

21. Though it is Rosamond who is supposed to be the 'actress', Dorothea's entrance here is explicitly presented in terms of stage performance ('if she had entered before a still audience as Imogene or Cato's daughter'). Ellen Moers calls the passage 'one of Dorothea's typical Corinne-like entrances'; in her rather harsh judgement, 'Dorothea Brooke in *Middlemarch* is the worst kind of product of the myth of Corinne ... for she is good for nothing *but* to be admired' (pp. 194–5). This is rather sweeping, but it is true that Eliot cannot do without admiration for her heroine, and her imagination continually presents Dorothea as spectacle to a (usually male) audience. Dorothea is allowed to get away with this because, unlike Rosamond or Gwendolen, she is sublimely unaware of the audience and her effect on them.

22. This is also true of Daniel's 'saving' effect on Gwendolen in *Daniel Deronda*.

23. *The Women of England: Their Social Duties, and Domestic Habits* (Fisher and Sons, third edition, London, 1839), p. 224.

24. *Madwoman*, p. 518.

25. Gilbert and Gubar claim that 'While Rosamond's confession to Dorothea is "a reflex of [Dorothea's] own energy".... Rosamond acts independently later to inform Will that Dorothea knows the truth about his love' (ibid., pp. 518–19). But this action is also motivated by her resentment at Will's reproaches, the motive that undermines the value of her action here. '"You will have nothing to reproach me with now"', she writes in her note to Will (p. 862).

26. Collister comments that 'The evidence of George Eliot's influence on Mary Ward during the writing of this novel is unquestionable' (p. 311), and in particular the scene between Letty and Marcella 'has its source in the celebrated conversation between Dorothea and Rosamond Lydgate' (p. 313). He sees 'conscious imitation' in this scene (p. 317).

27. *Sir George Tressady* (Smith, Elder, London, 1896). All quotations are from this edition.

28. For Mrs Ward's attitudes to feminism, and in particular her anti-suffragist stance, see Enid Huws Jones, *Mrs. Humphrey Ward* (Heinemann, London, 1973), pp. 136–40.

29. *The Singular Anomaly: Women Novelists of the Nineteenth Century*, (University of London Press, London, 1970), p. 122. The quotation from Sir George Tressady is in a note to this page, on p. 169.

30. *Literature of Their Own*, p. 229.

31. This is true in *Sir George Tressady*; but Showalter also points out that 'Ward shared with the suffragettes, and particularly with Mrs. Pankhurst, a sense that women were united by the terrible and holy suffering of childbirth' (*Literature of Their Own*, p. 229). This sense is expressed in her novel *Robert Elsmere* (1888), in the feelings of Catherine Elsmere after her painful experience of childbirth (Showalter, *Literature of Their Own*, pp. 230–1).

32. *Sir George Tressady* is the sequel to *Marcella* (1894), in which the plot reached the usual conclusion with the heroine's marriage: the later novel is 'further adventures' of Marcella.

## CHAPTER 4

1. G. H. Lewes criticised the novel for its inability to settle on a subject:

   The authoress never seems distinctly to have made up her mind as to what she was to do; whether to describe the habits and manners of Yorkshire and its social aspects in the days of King Lud, or to paint character, or to tell a love story. All are by turns attempted and abandoned ... ('Currer Bell's *Shirley*', *Edinburgh Review*, 91 [January 1850] p. 159)

   More recently, Terry Eagleton has described it as 'a fragmentary sequence of portraits, vignettes, dramatic interludes' (p. 81). Though it is possible to see a thematic connection between the different subjects or fragments, on first reading the text does present itself as a series of digressions, one of which is centred on the female friendship between Caroline and Shirley.

2. Robert Bernard Martin describes it as 'curiously huddled and cramped' (*The Accents of Persuasion*, Faber and Faber, London, 1966, p. 139).

3. Hunt, p. 60.

4. *Madwoman*, p. 397. Helene Moglen in *Charlotte Brontë: The Self Conceived* (Norton, New York, 1976, p. 186) writes of 'the almost parodic comic ending'.

5. Gilbert and Gubar see in *Shirley* a 'tension' between Brontë's 'personal allegiances and the dictates of literary convention' (*Madwoman*, p. 395).

6. All quotations from *Shirley* (1849) are from the Penguin edition (Harmondsworth, 1974).

7. Janice Swanson notes that the friends' mutual 'creation of resonant yet distinctive selves', is, 'like Shirley Keeldar's vision', 'never fully "possess[ed]"' (p. 78).

8. p. 77.

9. Swanson remarks that 'Charlotte Brontë warmed to this friendship more than was necessary in order to delay the inevitable marriages' (p. 77). Eagleton sees Caroline's friendship with Shirley entirely as a 'surrogate' for her relationship with Robert: 'Shirley provides Caroline with a kind of sexual surrogate for Robert: she is introduced into the novel when Caroline is in the throes of frustrated passion, in order to sublimate and displace the sexual feelings which Moore fails to reciprocate' (p. 58). He implies that the relationship with Robert is the 'real thing', and the relationship with Shirley is only important as a displacement of feelings more appropriately given to a man. He ignores the possibility that Brontë is suggesting 'that female friendship could be a preferable alternative to romantic attachments to men' (Hunt, p. 55). Pauline Nestor also sees Shirley as a substitute for Robert: 'Shirley is the figure through whom Caroline's love is in time transferred to Robert' (p. 119); she ignores the fact that Caroline is already desperately in love with Robert *before* she meets Shirley.

10. p. 59.

11. Ibid.

12. Hunt argues that the female friendship in *Shirley* is also curtailed because of 'economic realities' that dictate the heroines' marriages: the marriages show what is possible in 'the actual world', as opposed to the wishful fantasy of a

self-supporting female friendship. But this is patently inapplicable to either woman: Shirley is independently wealthy, and Caroline is supported by her uncle; and it is the marriage-ending that is presented by the self-conscious, ironical narrator as a fantasy (Hunt, pp. 55, 59).

13. p. 94.
14. See Martin, pp. 130–1; and Asa Briggs, 'Private and Social Themes in *Shirley*: *Brontë Society Transactions*', 13 (1958), p. 203.
15. pp. 129–32; see also p. 129 and note 31 below.
16. Swanson stresses the similarity between the friends, as opposed to the contrast usually seen by critics (p. 77).
17. *Madwoman*, pp. 382–3.
18. For this view, see e.g. W.A. Craik, *The Brontë Novels* (Methuen, London, 1968), pp. 138, 142.
19. p. 67.
20. Hunt notes the way proper young ladies always appear in 'sets' in the book, and behave in unison (p. 57).
21. There is also no question that Miss Mann and Miss Ainley should get together to support and sustain each other, as Nina Auerbach notes, contrasting the integration of Miss Matty's life into the community of the *Cranford* ladies with 'the layers of bleakness in the lives of Miss Mann and Miss Ainley, the grimly spotless spinsters in Charlotte Brontë's *Shirley*, who performed innumerable and unyielding good works but seem never to approach each other' *Communities of Women: An Idea in Fiction* (Harvard University Press, Cambridge, Mass., and London, 1978, p. 85). On the other hand, Miss Ainley has been defined as happy and content with her isolated life; and we later hear of Miss Mann being taken to a spa by Hortsense, another of the book's spinsters.
22. As Pauline Nestor puts it, 'the result of Caroline's association with Miss Ainley and Miss Mann is, in effect, to undertake an apprenticeship in the very self-denial she has rejected' (p. 122).
23. As Martin says, the conflict in the novel is not so much between masters and men, as 'between the feminine viewpoint and the essentially masculine outlook of the world of commerce and politics' (p. 138). Moglen also sees in *Shirley* Brontë's realisation 'that in the female subculture values have been developed in relative isolation. Because they are different from those of the 'official' society, they offer a critical perspective of accepted structures and attitudes' (p. 158).
24. Swanson shows how the antagonism between the men in the book is embodied in their language (p. 82). Moglen also comments on the conflicting interests among the male leaders (p. 161).
25. p. 57.
26. Gilbert and Gubar comment on how the women's relationship has 'a fine, subtle sexuality, absent from their manipulative heterosexual relationships' (*Madwoman*, p. 382).
27. p. 105.
28. See Moglen, p. 163.
29. p. 58.
30. Swanson explores the idea of the two women sharing a private female language (pp. 12, 78, 99).

31. See Martin, pp. 129–32. This misinterpretation means Martin must dissociate Caroline from many of her other opinions – e.g. he remarks that though Caroline opposes Joe Scott at the end of this chapter, the misogynistic views Joe expresses 'are really her own opinions'; and her later outburst on the fate of single women he attributes to authorial intrusion.

32. See Hunt, p. 58.

33. *Madwoman*, p. 383.

34. p. 143. Moglen too criticises Shirley here, and sees 'sexual competition and social differences' as 'divisive' forces to which the friendship succumbs (pp. 181–2).

35. *Madwoman*, p. 396.

36. Ibid., p. 393.


## CHAPTER 5

1. (Heinemann, London, 1894). All quotations are from this edition.

2. W. T. Stead, 'The Novel of the Modern Woman', *Review of Reviews*, 10 (1894), 71.

3. It is true that Dixon presents Mary as a transitional type:

> Born too late for the simple days of the fifties, when all it behoved a young girl to do was to mind her account book, read her Tennyson, show a proper enthusiasm for fancy-work stitches, and finally, with many blushes, accept the hand of the first young man who desired to pay taxes and to fulfil the duties of a loyal British subject.... Mary was yet too soon for the time when parents begin to take their responsibilities seriously, and when the girl is sometimes as carefully prepared, as thoroughly equipped, as her brother for the fight of life. (p. 14).

But there is no sign in the book of how this more modern parental attitude could have saved her. She could have been more efficient as a career-woman, but her isolation would not have been alleviated.

4. (Heinemann, London, 1894). See Auerbach, *Woman and the Demon*, p. 130, for an interesting short interpretation of this novel.

5. p. 71.

6. See pp. 152, 178 above.

7. (Chapman and Hall, London, 1883), 2 vols (facsimile published by Garnett, New York and London, 1975). All references are to this edition.

8. Vineta Colby comments on Em as 'a sad, stolid figure who represents normalcy, one who patiently loves, suffers, and waits on the sidelines as the others throw themselves into life's battles' (p. 67). Patricia Stubbs also contrasts Lyndall and Em: 'She is quite different from the submissive Em, who philosophically accepts what seems to her to be her fate – the unending, numbing routine of farm life. Em is the 'little woman' who stays at home while Lyndall ... goes off to broaden her education at a town boarding school' (*Women and Fiction: Feminism and the Novel 1880–1920*, Harvester Press, Brighton, 1979, p. 113).

9. Ruth First and Ann Scott, in their biography of Schreiner, comment on how

this passage 'suggests the very aloneness, the imperative to self-reliance that haunts her to the end of her life' (*Olive Schreiner*, André Deutsch, London, 1980, p. 103).

10.  pp. 21–30.

11.  Showalter notes this similarity to *Mill on the Floss*, (*Literature of Their Own* p. 201).

12.  *or Perhaps Only* (Virago, London 1982). All references are to this edition. *From Man to Man* was unfinished, and was not published until 1926, after Schreiner's death. It was, however, begun in 1873, and after about 1893 Schreiner was only engaged in revising it, so I have treated it as a late nineteenth-century novel (see 'A Note on the Genesis of the Book', by S. C. Cronwright-Schreiner, *From Man to Man*, pp. 483–93).

13.  *Literature of Their Own*, p. 201.

14.  p. 175.

15.  Showalter comments on the isolation and claustrophobia of Rebekah's 'private room' (*Literature of Their Own*, pp. 202–3).

16.  The same is true of Schreiner herself:

> Her response to the suffrage movement was characteristically a defense of the weak and persecuted:
>
> > My heart feels so tender over a baby girl because of all the anguish which may be before it. I always think of it when I touch and hold in my arms the dear little female bodies; which no love can shield from the anguish which may be waiting for them. I have done all I can to help free women, but oh it is so little ... I don't think you can understand how I love those suffragettes in London ... (Colby, p. 91)

17.  Gail Cunningham remarks on how none of the New Woman writers 'allow[s] their heroines to feel themselves part of a wider movement; the New Woman fiction as a whole gives the impression that large numbers of women are struggling in determined solitude to achieve an end which, because they are alone against society, is pre-ordained to be unattainable' (*The New Woman and the Victorian Novel* [Macmillan, London 1978], p. 77). See also note 37, below.

18.  Blau DuPlessis comments that '*From Man to Man*, then, reconciles novelistic narrative with imbedded discourse, diaries, letters and meditations, and thus is an early, though unfinished, example of the apologue form that is used later in the century by Doris Lessing in *The Four-Gated City* and Virginia Woolf in *The Pargiters*' (pp. 28–9).

19.  *From Man to Man*, Introduction, p. xiii.

20.  See First and Scott, p. 174, for the two reported versions of the ending.

21.  See p. 179 above.

22.  S. C. Cronwright-Schreiner's account of what Olive Schreiner told him about how the novel was to end, *From Man to Man*, p. 506.

23.  Cunningham comments on the 'relentless catalogue of catastrophe' in New Woman fiction: 'These novelists were trying to do two things at once: firstly, to argue the moral and social case for a high degee of emancipation, and secondly to show how firmly entrenched were the creeds and conventions which opposed women. In the first instance they were putting forward high-

# Notes to pages 162 to 163

minded principles, in the second describing the stark reality of practice. Since the system is pernicious, the odds so heavily weighted, it would be absurdly utopian, the argument goes, to portray a New Woman succeeding in her aims' (p. 49).

24. 'A Note on the Genesis of the Book', p. 493.
25. Ibid., p. 489.
26. Judith Kegan Gardiner has used Chodorow's theories to explain this special closeness and identification between female author, character and reader in women's novels, positing that '"the hero is her author's daughter"':

> The maternal metaphor of female authorship clarifies the woman writer's distinctive engagement with her characters and indicates an analogous relationship between woman reader and character....
> ... Through the relationship between the narrator and the reader, such fictions re-create the ambivalent experiences of ego violation and mutual identification that occur between mother and daughter. The woman writer allies herself intimately with her female reader through this identification. ('On Female Identity', pp. 179, 88)

Gardiner is writing about twentieth-century women writers here: in applying her ideas to Schreiner, I would like to stress that this pattern of identifications is part of a particular political strategy adopted by women writers of her time, not just a manifestation of unconscious psychological tendencies (see Showalter, *Literature of Their Own*, pp. 182–3 for the 'Feminist Novelists'' programme of solidarity with women readers, characters, and other writers).

27. 'Keynotes', in *Keynotes and Discords* (Virago, London, 1983). All references to Egerton's stories are to this edition. 'Keynotes' and 'Discords' are numbered separately in this edition: I will indicate after the title of each story that I quote from which collection it belongs to.
28. This sort of revelation was Egerton's main aim in writing the stories: 'I realised that in literature, everything has been better done by man than woman could hope to emulate. There was only one plot left to tell, the *terra incognita* of herself, as she knew herself to be, not as man liked to imagine her' ('A Keynote to *Keynotes, Ten Contemporaries*, ed. John Gawsworth [Ernest Benn, London 1932], p. 60).
29. p. 65.
30. For the 'Feminist Novelists'' exaltation of motherhood, see Showalter, *Literature of Their Own*, p. 188. Showalter also comments on how these writers took over and took seriously the 'Ruskinian' theory of women's influence – 'the feminists merely transposed it into an activist key, making the ideal of true womanhood the basis of the politics of the female subculture.... They took the idea of female influence seriously, and they intended to make it a genuine source of power' (ibid., pp. 184–5).
31. Stead, for one, was shocked, finding 'passages in "Keynotes" that suggest anything rather than an English matron', and judging 'the spectacle the reverse of edifying' (ibid., pp. 68–9). For more shocked contemporary reactions, see Stubbs, pp. 110–11. Stubbs herself sees Egerton as 'an important figure in the struggle to force sexuality back into fiction' (ibid., p. 110).
32. Martha Vicinus, in her Introduction to the Virago edition of *Keynotes and*

*Discords*, notes how Egerton 'differed from her contemporaries in her portrayal of solutions to these situations [the injustices suffered by women]; she advocated not restraint and meaningful work, but sexual fulfilment and power' (p. ix).

33. Vicinus points out that several women writers at this time 'experimented with remaking the traditional realistic novel. . . . Within the conventional tale of courtship and marriage we have an effort to explain and analyse other, more inchoate desires and hopes of women' (ibid., pp. xvi–xvii).

34. (Hurst and Blackett, London, n.d.), pp. 341–2.

35. As Vicinus puts it, Egerton, like other 'New Women', 'confronted the very limited range of alternatives available to women with an honesty and anger that shocked and fascinated readers', and 'was fearless in presenting the evil consequences of the continued ignorance and victimisation of women', but also 'her works celebrate the potential in women', and 'Under the guise of the realistic, Egerton wrote utopian fiction, a fiction that tries on different models of behaviour for different women' (Introduction to *Keynotes and Discords*, pp. viii, xix, ix, xvii). Stubbs makes a similar point: 'She could always sympathise with and understand what women had often been reduced to, and she was able to see an ideal future in which sexual discrimination no longer existed, when women were free' (p. 111). For some reason, Showalter gives an extremely partial and depressing reading of Egerton's stories, focusing on the negative and omitting the celebratory and utopian aspects of her work *Literature of Their Own*, pp. 213–14). Her only comment on the relations between women in the stories is 'the heroines make other women the subjects of their hatred and refuse to confront men' (ibid., p. 213), ignoring the sympathetic and supportive relationships between women in so many of the stories.

36. According to Vicinus, Egerton's 'portrayals of fallen women, injured wives and victimised women are more conventional, more predictably nineteenth century' than the new 'utopian' female roles and identities she creates (ibid., p. xix); but, as Cunningham points out, 'no novelist of the mid-Victorian period who wished to arouse sympathy for a fallen woman would risk portraying her as remotely sensual' (p. 29), which Edith clearly is in this story.

37. Stubbs comments interestingly on the equation of independence with isolation in New Woman fiction, and its connection with liberalism: 'the emphasis on isolation as a condition of freedom, and the inability to see a collective solution to women's problems is only to be expected in an age of individualism. Nineteenth-century feminist thinking was rooted in liberalism; its whole emphasis was on the problem of individual self-development and fulfilment, and it focused on the question of individual rights. If politically minded feminists saw women's problems in this light, then it is hardly surprising that novelists followed suit, and continued to assume that a woman could only 'find' herself through a solitary progress towards self-knowledge, which could only go on outside normal social relations' (pp. 125–6).

# Bibliography

Abel, Elizabeth, '(E)Merging Identities: The Dynamics of Female Friendship in Contemporary Fiction by Women', *Signs* 6, no. 3 (Spring 1981), pp. 413–35.

————(ed.) *Writing and Sexual Difference* (University of Chicago Press, Chicago/Harvester Press, Brighton, 1982).

Aguilar, Grace, *Woman's Friendship: A Story of Domestic Life* (Groombridge and Sons, London, 1850).

Auerbach, Nina, *Communities of Women: An Idea in Fiction* (Harvard University Press, Cambridge, Mass. and London, 1978).

————, *Woman and the Demon: The Life of a Victorian Myth* (Harvard University Press, London, 1982).

Berke, Jacqueline and Berke, Laura, 'Mothers and Daughters in *Wives and Daughters*: A Study of Elizabeth Gaskell's Last Novel', Davidson and Broner, pp. 95–109.

Bernikow, Louise, *Among Women* (Harmony Books, New York, 1980).

Boumelha, Penny, *Thomas Hardy and Women: Sexual Ideology and Narrative Form* (Harvester Press, Brighton, 1982).

Briggs, Asa, 'Private and Social Themes in *Shirley*', *Brontë Society Transactions*, 13 (1958), p. 203.

Brontë, Charlotte, *Shirley* (1849) (Penguin, Harmondsworth, 1974).

————, *Villette* (1853) (Penguin, Harmondsworth, 1979).

Browning, Elizabeth Barrett, *Aurora Leigh* (1857) (Women's Press, London, 1978).

Chodorow, Nancy, *The Reproduction of Mothering: Psychoanalysis and the Sociology of Gender* (University of California Press, Berkeley and London, 1978).

Colby, Vineta, *The Singular Anomaly: Women Novelists of the Nineteenth Century* (University of London Press, London, 1970).

199

Collister, Peter, 'Portraits of "Audacious Youth": George Eliot and Mrs. Humphrey Ward', *ES* 64, no. 4 (1983), pp. 296–317.

Cott, Nancy F., *The Bonds of Womanhood: 'Woman's Sphere' in New England, 1780–1835* (Yale University Press, New Haven, Conn., 1977).

Craik, Dinah Mulock, *A Brave Lady* (1870) (Hurst and Blackett, London, n.d.).

——, *A Woman's Thoughts About Women* (Hurst and Blackett, London, 1858).

Craik, W. A., *The Brontë Novels* (Methuen, London, 1968).

——, *Elizabeth Gaskell and the English Provincial Novel* (Methuen, London, 1975).

Cronwright-Schreiner, S. C., 'A Note on the Genesis of the Book', Schreiner, *From Man to Man*, pp. 483–93.

Cunningham, Gail, *The New Woman and the Victorian Novel* (Macmillan, London, 1978).

Davidson, Cathy N. and Broner, E. M. (eds), *The Lost Tradition: Mothers and Daughters in Literature* (Frederic Ungar, New York, 1980).

Dixon, Ella Hepworth, *The Story of A Modern Woman* (Heinemann, London, 1894).

DuPlessis, Rachel Blau, *Writing Beyond the Ending: Narrative Strategies of Twentieth-Century Women Writers* (Indiana University Press, Bloomington, 1985).

Eagleton, Terry, *Myths of Power: A Marxist Study of the Brontës* (Macmillan, London, 1975).

Egerton, George, 'Keynotes' (1893) and 'Discords' (1894), in *Keynotes and Discords* (Virago, London, 1983).

Eliot, George, *Adam Bede* (1859) (Penguin, Harmondsworth, 1980).

——, *Daniel Deronda* (1876), (Penguin, Harmondsworth, 1967).

——, *Middlemarch* (1872) (Penguin, Harmondsworth, 1965).

——, *The Mill on the Floss* (1860) (Penguin, Harmondsworth, 1979).

Ellis, Sarah, *The Daughters of England: Their Social Duties, and Domestic Habits*, (Charles Griffin, London, 1845).

——, *The Women of England: Their Social Duties, and Domestic Habits* (Fisher and Sons, third edition, London, 1839).

Faderman, Lillian, *Surpassing the Love of Men: Romantic Friendship and Love between Women from the Renaissance to the Present* (William Morrow, New York, 1981).

First, Ruth and Scott, Ann, *Olive Schreiner* (André Deutsch, London, 1980).

Foot, Paul, New Introduction, Schreiner, *From Man to Man*, pp. ix–vxii.

Foster, Shirley, *Victorian Women's Fiction: Marriage, Freedom and the Individual* (Croom Helm, London, 1985).

Gardiner, Judith Kegan, 'Mind Mother: Psychoanalysis and Feminism', Greene, Gayle and Kahn, Coppélia (eds), *Making A Difference: Feminist*

*Literary Criticism* (Methuen, London and New York, 1985), pp. 113–45.

———, 'On Female Identity and Writing by Women', Abel (ed.), *Writing and Sexual Difference*, pp. 177–91.

Gaskell, Elizabeth, *Lizzie Leigh, and Other Tales* (1855) (Oxford University Press, Oxford, 1913).

———, *Wives and Daughters* (1866) (Penguin, Harmondsworth, 1969).

Gawsworth, John (ed.), *Ten Contemporaries* (Ernest Benn, London, 1932).

Gelpi, Barbara Charlesworth, '*Aurora Leigh*: the Vocation of the Woman Poet', *Victorian Poetry*, 19, no. 1 (Spring 1981), pp. 35–48.

Gilbert, Sandra and Gubar, Susan, *The Madwoman in the Attic* (Yale University Press, New Haven and London, 1979).

——— (eds), *Shakespeare's Sisters* (Indiana University Press, Bloomington, 1979).

Gitter, Elisabeth G., 'The Power of Women's Hair in the Victorian Imagination', *PMLA*, 99, No. 5 (October, 1984), pp. 936–54.

Goreham, Deborah, *The Victorian Girl and the Feminine Ideal* (Croom Helm, London and Canberra, 1982).

Gorsky, Susan R., 'Old Maids and New Women: Alternatives to Marriage in Englishwomen's Novels, 1847–1915', *Journal of Popular Culture* 7 (1973): pp. 68–85.

Hirsch, Marianne, 'Mothers and Daughters: Review Essay', *Signs* 7, no. 1 (Fall 1981), pp. 200–22.

Holdsworth, Annie, *Joanna Traill, Spinster* (Heinemann, London, 1894).

Homans, Margaret, 'Eliot, Wordsworth, and the Scenes of the Sisters' Instruction', Abel (ed.) *Writing and Sexual Difference*, pp. 57–71.

Housman, Judy, 'Mothering, the Unconscious, and Feminism', *Radical America* 16, (Nov./Dec. 1982), pp. 47–62.

Hunt, Linda C., 'Sustenance and Balm: The Question of Female Friendship in *Shirley* and *Villette*', *Tulsa Studies in Women's Literature*, 1 (Spring 1982), pp. 55–66.

Jacobus, Mary, 'The Question of Language: Men of Maxims and *The Mill on the Floss*', Abel (ed.), *Writing and Sexual Difference*, pp. 37–52.

Jones, Enid Huws, *Mrs. Humphry Ward* (Heinemann, London, 1973).

Kaplan, Cora, 'The Indefinite Disclosed: Christina Rossetti and Emily Dickinson', in Jacobus, Mary (ed.), *Women Writing and Writing about Women* (Croom Helm, London, 1979). pp. 61–79.

———, Introduction, Browning, *Aurora Leigh*.

Kennard, Jean, *Victims of Convention* (Archon Books, Hamden, Conn., 1978).

Leighton, Angela, *Elizabeth Barrett Browning* (Harvester Press, Brighton, 1986).

Lewes, C. H., 'Currer Bell's *Shirley*', *Edinburgh Review*, 91 (January 1850), pp. 153–73.

Linton, Eliza Lynn, *The Girl of the Period and Other Social Essays*, 2 vols (Richard Bentley and Sons, 1883).

——, *The Rebel of The Family* (Chatto and Windus, London, 1880).

Lorber, Judith *et al.*, 'On *The Reproduction of Mothering*: A Methodological Debate', *Signs* 6, no. 3 (Spring 1981), pp. 482–514.

Macdonald, Susan Peck, 'Jane Austen and the Tradition of the Absent Mother', Davidson and Broner, pp. 58–69.

Martin, Robert Bernard, *The Accents of Persuasion* (Faber and Faber, London, 1966).

Marxist-Feminist Literature Collective, 'Women's Writing: Jane Eyre, Shirley, Villette, Aurora Leigh', *Ideology and Consciousness*, no. 3 (Spring 1978), pp. 27–48.

McGann, Jerome J., 'Christina Rossetti's Poems: A New Edition and a Revaluation', *Victorian Studies* 23, no. 2 (Winter 1980), pp. 237–54.

McKenzie, K. A., *Edith Simcox and George Eliot* (Oxford University Press, Oxford, 1961).

Meredith, George, *Diana of the Crossways* (1884) (Virago, London, 1980).

Mermin, Dorothy, 'Heroic Sisterhood in *Goblin Market*', *Victorian Poetry* 21, no. 2. (Summer 1983), pp. 277–81.

Millett, Kate, *Sexual Politics* (Rupert Hart-Davis, London, 1971).

Mitchell, Sally, *The Fallen Angel: Chastity, Class, and Women's Reading: 1835–1880* (Bowling Green University Popular Press, Bowling Green, Ohio, 1981).

Moers, Ellen, *Literary Women* (W. H. Allen, London, 1977).

Moglen, Helene, *Charlotte Brontë: The Self Conceived* (Norton, New York, 1976).

Moi, Toril, *Sexual/Textual Politics: Feminist Literary Theory* (Methuen, London and New York, 1985).

Nestor, Pauline, *Female Friendships and Communities: Charlotte Brontë, George Eliot, Elizabeth Gaskell* (Clarendon Press, Oxford, 1985).

Newton, Judith Lowder, *Women, Power, and Subversion: Social Strategies in British Fiction, 1778–1860* (University of Georgia Press, Athens and Methuen, London, 1981).

Pinney, Thomas (ed.), *Essays of George Eliot* (Routledge and Kegan Paul, London, 1963).

Pratt, Annis, *Archetypal Patterns in Women's Fiction* (Indiana University Press, Bloomington/Harvester Press, Brighton, 1981).

Pullan, Matilda, *Maternal Counsels*, (Darton and Co., London, 1855).

Rich, Adrienne, 'Compulsory Heterosexuality and Lesbian Existence', *Signs* 5, no. 4 (Summer 1980), pp. 640–9.

Rosenblum, Dolores, 'Christina Rossetti: The Inward Pose', Gilbert and Gubar, (eds), *Shakespeare's Sisters*, pp. 82–98.

——, 'Face to Face: Elizabeth Barrett Browning's *Aurora Leigh* and

Victorian Poetry', *Victorian Studies*, 26, no. 3 (Spring 1983), pp. 321–38.

Rossetti, Christina, *Poetical Works* (Macmillan, London, 1904).

Schreiner, Olive, *From Man To Man, or Perhaps Only* (1873–c. 1893, 1st published 1926) (Virago, London 1982).

———, *The Story of An African Farm* (Chapman and Hall, London 1883), 2 vols (facsimile, Garnett, New York and London, 1975).

Showalter, Elaine, *A Literature of Their Own* (Virago, London, 1978).

Slater, Michael, *Dickens and Women* (Dent, London, and Stanford University Press, CA, 1983).

Smith-Rosenberg, Carroll, 'The Female World of Love and Ritual', Kerber, Linda K. and Matthews, Jane De Hart (eds) in *Women's America: Refocussing the Past* (Oxford University Press, Oxford, 1982), pp. 156–79.

Spacks, Patricia, *The Female Imagination* (Allen and Unwin, London, 1976).

Stead, W. T., 'The Novel of the Modern Woman', *Review of Reviews*, 10 (1894), pp. 64–76.

Steinmetz, Virginia, 'Images of "Mother Want" in Elizabeth Barrett Browning's *Aurora Leigh*', *Victorian Poetry*, 21, no. 4 (Winter 1983), pp. 351–67.

Swanson, Janice M. Bowman, 'Speaking in a Mother Tongue: Female Friendship in the British Novel' (PhD. Thesis, University of California at Santa Barbara, 1981).

Stubbs, Patricia, *Women and Fiction: Feminism and the Novel 1880–1920*, (Havester Press, Brighton, 1979).

Todd, Janet, *Women's Friendship in Literature* (Columbia University Press, New York, 1980).

Trudgill, Eric, *Madonnas and Magdalens: The Origins and Development of Victorian Sexual Attitudes* (Holmes and Meier, New York, 1976).

Vicinus, Martha, *Independent Women: Work and Community for the Single Woman, 1850–1920* (Virago, London, 1985).

———, Introduction, Egerton, *Keynotes and Discords*.

Ward, Mrs Humphry, *Delia Blanchflower* (Ward, Lock and Co., London, Melbourne and Toronto, 1915).

———, *Marcella* (1894) (Virago, London, 1984).

———, *Robert Elsmere* (1888) (Oxford University Press, Oxford, 1987).

———, *Sir George Tressady* (Smith, Elder, London, 1896).

Watt, George, *The Fallen Woman in the Nineteenth-Century English Novel* (Croom Helm, London, 1984).

Weathers, Winston, 'Christina Rossetti: The Sisterhood of Self', *Victorian Poetry* 3, no. 1 (Spring 1965), pp. 81–9.

Williams, Raymond, *Marxism and Literature* (Oxford University Press, Oxford, 1977).

Woolf, Virginia, *A Room of One's Own* (1929) (Granada, London, Toronto, Sydney, New York, 1977).

Yonge, Charlotte, *Womankind* (Mozley and Smith, London, 1876).

Zimmerman, Bonnie, 'What Has Never Been: An Overview of Lesbian Feminist Criticism', Showalter, Elaine (ed.), *The New Feminist Criticism* (Virago, London, 1986), pp. 200–24.

# Index

Moglen, Helene, *Charlotte Brontë*
193–5
Moi, Toril, *Sexual/Textual Politics*
183
monitory image 43, 115, 119, 172
monster, woman as 4, 16, 114
moon 18, 132, 136
mother 63, 83, 98–9, 130, 135, 184,
187–8
mother-child relationship 8–10, 50,
60–1, 66, 83, 154, 165–7, 191
mother-daughter relationship 2, 7–10,
19, 29, 33, 72, 78, 109, 153,
168, 191, 197
motherhood 139, 153, 163–7, 171–2,
181, 197
mothering 56, 72, 81, 83, 87–8, 94,
106, 119, 135
motherlessness 2, 7, 12, 56–7
mother-substitutes 12, 33, 83, 87–8,
118, 144
myth 20, 73, 95, 114, 127–8, 130,
167, 180

narrative 3, 9, 13–14, 50, 56, 113–14,
147–8, 162, 166–9
devices, 2, 4, 77
progression towards marriage 1, 20,
23, 35, 69, 89
structure 9, 13, 22, 81, 111, 113,
116, 138–9, 144, 153, 161, 164,
168, 173
turning-points 3, 16, 67, 109, 164
types of 22, 112 (see also plot)
Nature 11, 19–20, 54–5, 61, 63, 79,
95, 100, 102, 111–12, 119, 122–
4, 128–30, 132–3, 136, 146,
177, 180, 182
negotiation 4, 6–8, 12–14, 16, 49–50,
111, 139, 148, 156, 164, 184
Nestor, Pauline, *Female Friendships
and Communities* 183, 185–6,
193–4
New Man 182
New Woman 6, 144, 149–50, 152,
159, 173, 179, 182, 198
fiction 6, 11, 13–14, 138–9, 198
writers 6, 138–9, 161–2, 170, 196

Newton, Judith Lowder, *Women,
Power, and Subversion* 184–5

parenting 9, 186
Paris 56, 64
past world 20, 112, 122–3, 126
patriarchy 13, 75, 128–9, 138
physical contact 7, 12, 72, 82, 94,
109, 135
plot (see also narrative) 53, 82, 84, 90,
113–14, 125, 140
climax 109
resolution 3, 12, 23, 29, 37, 51, 67,
84, 102, 106
romantic 17, 22, 26, 33, 35, 51, 77,
112–13, 143, 147
types of 12, 153
Pratt, Annis, *Archetypal Patterns in
Women's Fiction* 1
prostitutes 51, 146, 170, 172
prostitution 160, 162, 164, 177
psychological theory 8–10, 186

rape 56–8, 61, 64, 72
reciprocity 52, 58–9, 76–8, 83, 87, 98,
101, 107, 109, 131, 141, 188
reconcilation between women 23–4,
36, 161
reformation 56, 86, 177
religion 144
repose, friendship as 114, 116, 123,
125, 132, 135, 154
repression 39, 49, 70, 73–4, 76, 136
rescue 21, 52, 58, 67–9, 72, 76, 82–4,
94, 96–8, 101, 106, 109, 131,
141, 145, 147, 180
revisionism 117, 128, 130, 140, 164,
172, 175–6, 182
Rich, Adrienne, 'Compulsory
Heterosexuality and Lesbian
Existence' 185
rivalry between women 1, 3, 9, 11–12,
16, 27, 37, 51, 77, 82, 88, 94,
98–9, 117, 131, 147, 151, 157
Romantic Nature poetry 13, 114
Rosenblum, Dolores
'Christina Rossetti' 187
'Face to Face' 188–9